# Crohn's
# &
# Other Shit

---

## Tales of me and IBD


By


## J.F.LENITY

For the Current Mrs Lenity

Despite all my sangfroid, one spectre creeps forward from some dim crevice of my mind. If it is cancer, and I do die, she's bound to seek solace with him. The thought is a twisting dagger to my innards. I've long known that my wife had another man; his name is John Lewis and middle-class women fall at his feet.

# Contents

# A is for...
## About This Book

I have Crohn's colitis.

Given the title of the book this will come as no surprise to you. There is every possibility that you, or someone close to you, is in a similar position, hence your interest. If you are new to the club then allow me to offer my commiserations, you have a miserable time ahead.

Crohn's disease does not go away, there is no cure and treatments can be a bit hit and miss. It would help if we knew what causes it, but we don't, at least not with absolute confidence.

However, a diagnosis of inflammatory bowel disease (IBD) is not the end of the world. Far from it. Chances are it won't kill you[1]; it will not take your sight; you will retain the use of your limbs; your memory will be unaffected; no vegetative state will ensue; your winkle (if you have one) will not shrivel and drop off. In short, it could be a lot worse. If I was in the business of doling out advice (and I must stress that I am not!) I would recommend that you keep that perspective in your locker for use as and when needed.

I should provide a word of explanation about the term *Crohn's colitis.* What I mean by this is Crohn's disease which is centred on (though not exclusive to) my large intestine. I do not have

---

[1] This was not the case in the past where the strictures, ulceration and chronic diarrhoea associated with the disease could certainly get the job done. The disease can, however, lead to the development of bowel cancers with obvious implications.

Crohn's *and* colitis (I am not that unlucky[2]) and although I have seen the term used by others in a different context, in my case it was born of clerical pedantry on the side of the then DHSS[3]; more of which later. I generally refer to myself as having Crohn's and the reason I have used the double-barrelled form in the title of this book is because, firstly, I am partial to a bit of alliteration and, secondly, because much of the content is applicable to both diseases. We are all IBDers after all.

I was diagnosed with Crohn's in 1985 and there have been times when it has taken over my life completely. Conversely, there have been times when I did not know I had it. This waxing and waning, the peaks and troughs of activity are very much in the nature of the beast. Nevertheless, it remains a constant companion.

How then should we accommodate this consort? I wish I could offer up an answer, but I doubt that a *one size fits all* formula exists. For example, there is a sentiment that is often applied to illness[4], in fact it strikes me that it is a bit of a mantra. It goes something along the lines of:

*...blah de blah de blah...but I steadfastly refuse to let this thing define me!*

This is not a maxim that sits well with me. I understand where it comes from, and I'm all for a bit of spunk now and again but that sort of stuff is, well, just not my bag. It's always struck me as a superfluous thing to lose sleep over anyway. Frankly, if you have IBD and want something to worry about, there are better

---

[2] You may read that it is impossible the same person to get both Crohn's and colitis. This is a fallacy; it is rare but not unheard of.

[3] Department of Health and Social Security.

[4] And to misfortunes in general

candidates available. That said, if it helps you in any way then who am I to criticise. More power to your elbow matey.

It all boils down to individuality; we all have our own way of dealing with things. Mine, I suspect, is quite a boring, *muddle through* approach. I do not personify my illness; it is not an enemy to be defeated or beast to be slain or anything creative like that. It is just a series of symptoms that I am required to accommodate in some way. Clearly, I have a limited imagination.

Also, whilst we are on the subject of personal preferences, I am happier when things are out in the open[5]. Again, this is not everyone's cup of tea. I have never shirked from discussing my Crohn's and everyone I know is fully aware that I have it. No doubt I am, at times, referred to in the...*oh I have a friend with that...* context. I am perfectly happy to be viewed in that way. If I am defined by it, then fine; I don't see what the big deal is anyway. I have Crohn's disease, and this is a book about it.

Well, mostly.

One of the inspirations for this book came from a reflection on personal pain. Specifically, the question: *what was the worst physical pain I had experienced?* From there I set to thinking about all the things that have gone wrong with my body over the years and how they were dealt with. From that grew a list of anecdotes which, with a bit of jiggery-pokery, became arranged in (more or less) chronological order.

Not surprisingly it is dominated by inflammatory bowel disease as all my other maladies have been relatively tame in comparison, yet they have all contributed to the canon of

---

[5] Excluding browser histories, obviously.

experience in their own way. Just because you have IBD does not mean you are immune to all the other available afflictions; if anything, it makes you more of a candidate. In fact, it was not until I started writing this that I began to wonder about the potential links between my different maladies.

There may be people who look upon this work as something of a conceit:

"How dare he?" they might say, "the cheeky sod's not even dying!"

To which, were I a smart-arse, I would reply that, philosophically speaking, we are all dying from the moment we are conceived. I might even quote Samuel Becket: *They give birth astride a grave, the light gleams an instant, then it's night once more.*[6] However, I do take the point. If you are looking for heroics coupled with a poignant and a tearful ending, then you would be better served by *Lassie Come Home* than by this. This is not a book about battling against unassailable odds or prejudice. No miraculous cures are involved. No legal battles against giant corporations take place. I have no radical theories regarding causes or cures. In fact, there is not a lot of technical talk at all; I prefer to leave that sort of thing to those qualified to deliver it.[7] And, despite my culinary credentials, I offer no diet plans or recipe advice.

It is a history of my health, and my experience of British health care; take from it what you will.

---

[6] Waiting for Godot
[7] You may note that I have not included any technical references; this is because no one bothers to read them

## Acne
See Dermo Stuff

## Adolf
I am delivered into the world on April 20, 1966 at the maternity unit of the Northern General Hospital in Sheffield in what is then the West Riding of Yorkshire. The same day, seventy-seven years earlier in Braunau am Inn, then part of Austro Hungary, Klara, third wife of customs official Alois Hitler, is going through similar rigours to those my dear mother faces. Klara prevails and is also rewarded with a son. She names him Adolf.

Yes, I share a birthday with Hitler, which is one of the reasons I never bother reading horoscopes[8] and why I dispensed with *My Struggle* as a working title for this book. I am sure my mother was unaware of the significance of April 20, I only found out myself when I was in my teens. If she had known, I like to think she would have made the effort to hang on a bit; crossed her legs or something.

In truth it has never presented me with any problems and when I've mentioned it to people it generally represents a source of amusement. The exception to this being a German student I once shared a flat with, the conversation going something along the lines of:

"I have the same birthday as Hitler."

"What, April 20?"

Which makes you wonder, does it not, why anyone would know that?

I've never felt Hitler and I have much in common. I have

---

[8] That and because they are complete, nonsensical mumbo-jumbo.

nothing against Jews (see "Circumcision"), I don't mind being mistaken for one, which happens occasionally, and I even took a Barbra Streisand lookalike for a wife. I'm not a vegetarian, and I couldn't grow a toothbrush moustache to save my life on account of having something of a barren philtrum. Zapata, Fu Man Chu, the leather-clad one from The Village People I could achieve with aplomb but when it comes to Hitler and Chaplin I fall flat.[9] Aside from the aforementioned birthday, our only common traits, as far as I can see, are a love of dogs, rampant flatulence[10] and a spectacular holiday retreat high in the Bavarian Alps[11].

Which brings me around to the point I am trying to make which is this. Finding out that a famous person shares your affliction creates a weird sense of validation. Even if that person is one of history's most infamous. I would go further, I'd say it enhances it; Adolf Hitler might represent the epitome of evil to most people, but you can't deny, as gut-troubled celebrities go, he is definitely an A lister.

Following this thread, I decide to look for other famous tummy sufferers. The roll call includes:

Shinzo Abe, Prince Albert, Alfred the Great, Anastacia, Linda

---

[9] I may be talking out of turn here but I suspect Chaplin was sporting a falsy!

[10] There is so much written about Hitler and his health (syphilis, Parkinson's, Huntington's, borderline personality disorder, narcissism, a missing bollock) that it is difficult to sift fact from fiction here; not helped by the Furher's apparent hypochondria. However, there does seem to be evidence that Hitler suffered from bowel problems for most of his life and it has been speculated that he may have had irritable bowel syndrome.

[11] I joke of course, we are very much a Filey family

Carter, Kurt Cobain, Dynamo the magician, Eisenhower, Darren Fletcher, J.F Kennedy, Stewart Lee, Louis XIII, Beth Orton, Steve Redgrave, Jerry Sadowitz, Cybill Shepherd, Ken Stott, William Wilberforce, Ray Wilkins.

That is by no means an exhaustive list, just the ones that I have heard of.

I wish I had known in 1985 that I had something in common with Wonder Woman but prior to my diagnosis I knew absolutely nothing about IBD or irritable bowel syndrome (IBS). I don't think many people did. As for Crohn's disease? Not a chance. Had I been down to my last six tiles at Scrabble I might have tried to make a case for SNORCH or even SCHORN, but CROHNS would not have entered my head.[12] At the time my diagnosis felt like something of a novelty.

Not the case now, though. Gut trouble, it seems, has been on the rise for some time and what was once considered a blight on western societies is now a global condition. Which is disappointing for anyone who revels in the novelty of their ailment but nice in that it spurs on the Great and the Good to get involved. For anyone newly burdened with a diagnosis a celebrity endorsement is a timely bit of empathy. All right, some of them took their time about going public (I'm looking at you Alfred the Great) but better late than never, eh.

The other aspect of all this closet-exiting is that it helps to combat the anatomical stigma associated with bowel problems, which is a subject I shall address in the next section, the irreverently titled...

---

[12] Yes, you're right, it wouldn't be allowed anyway. Remember, no one likes a Scrabble pedant.

## Arse

Well, this is the crux of the matter, isn't it? Private parts. The problem is not so much that the bowel is afflicted, nobody talks in hushed tones about a swollen appendix, do they? No. The issue here is what is emitted and from where it appears; to wit: shit, farts and arseholes. Anything associated with that crowd we are taught to regard as dirty.

This was not always the case, in years gone by we pretty much lived in our own filth and what wasn't chucked out of the window into the street was spread on our vegetables[13]. This *Golden Age of Filth* did not last for ever, the introduction of sanitation did for it; we went crazy for sewerage, disinfectant, public health. Poo became something to be feared because it caused disease. It was dirty and, by association, shameful. The sooner it was flushed away (in the privacy of a little room dedicated for the purpose) the better for everyone.

We now take for granted that pooing is a solitary activity. Most people I know would baulk at the prospect of a communal dump; it is not something that happens in the normal, day to day, *private* way of doing things. Just the thought of public conveniences is enough to terrify many. My teenage daughters would rather die than use the school toilets. I was the same at their age; I don't think I ever managed a school poo until sixth form. Though in all fairness my school's toilets were not very welcoming; all the doors had been kicked in and they were invariably booby trapped with bits of shit strategically smeared on handles and the like. They were no place for the unwary.

Even now, despite the anonymity afforded by a private cubical, and all my years of scatological travails, I still hesitate before

---

[13] In a fertilizer rather than gravy sense.

letting rip in a public loo. It is as if I were involved in something incompatible with the facility; waiting for someone to cry out: "my God you won't believe what he's doing in there!" Which is crazy because we all know what public toilets are for.[14]

This is one of the first things you really need to get your head around with IBD, there is little scope to remain demure. So be warned! At the very least you will mess up the odd toilet. You will have to rush off in the middle of polite conversations and there may be times when you shit your kecks (to use the local parlance) in the process. You will make nasty smells. Strange noises will emit from your body. You will be required to make embarrassing explanations. Social events will fill you with nervous tension. Your back passage may be so raw that you can hardly walk but you avoid talking about it because a sore arse is not a proper ailment. You may sweat profusely such that your bed and body stink from it, but you are forced to abide because you are too knackered to do anything else.

And all that is without the medicos being involved. There is a whole host of ignominious medical procedures to look forward to there. Including the insertion into your anus of (and this is in no particular order): fingers, liquid, gels, foams, medications and cameras. You will be pumped full of air or flushed through with dense slurry, both of which will eventually make their exit via the standard route. And, strange though it may sound, there will be laxatives; pints of them, which are just as unpleasant going in as coming out[15]. You will be required to poo in a pot and you will hand it over to someone knowing they will soon be poking around in it. You may be cut

---

[14] Not necessarily, see Prostate for alternative motives.

[15] Personally, I think more so.

open. You may even have to do your business into a plastic bag attached to a fleshy spout poking from your belly, occasionally adjusting the seal to let out the fart gas that would otherwise send it ballooning around the room. And so I say to you, if you can suffer just a subset of all that and still blush at the mention of the word fart, "then you're a better man than I am Gunga Din."[16]

## Arthralgia
See "Joints"

## Arthritis
See "Joints"

## ASMR
(See "Tingly Brain")

## All-Bran Anyone?
Even in childhood I have my share of bowel problems though nothing that appears, on the surface, to be a precursor to the Crohn's disease that is to follow in my late teens. I suffer from constipation as a youngster. I cannot say for certain when this begins but my late uncle often recounted the tale of Toddler Lenity producing a "huge cannonball" on Bridlington beach[17] and I suspect that some degree of retention problem existed back then in my nappy era[18].

---

[16] In the interests of completeness, I should point out that it may also bugger up your joints, eyes, skin and possibly hair; increase your risk of gallstones, kidney stones and deep vein thrombosis.

[17] It was given a shallow grave and left for the tide to deal with, which was a perfectly acceptable turd disposal practice in the late sixties.

[18] I should say *first* nappy era.

By the age of seven I am only emptying my bowels once a fortnight and it is always quite an effort; crimson-faced, eye-bulgingly so. Annoyingly, my fortnightly urges often come when I am out and about (perhaps the action of walking spurs it on) which is inconvenient to say the least. I therefore develop a trick of sitting down on the street and encouraging the escapee to return whence he came. I don't think this helps with my condition.

Whether I have some predisposition to constipation I cannot say but I suspect much of my irregularity is down to diet. I am a finnicky eater and exist on Mother's Pride jam butties and tinned peas. These days, the first advice to the constipated is to drink more water. As a child I never drink water (I don't like the taste[19]) and take only milk or pop[20], but mainly milk, so perhaps there is a dairy aspect to it too.

As usual I finish up at some or other clinic being prodded and poked; I am sent away with a large brown glass jar full of some sort of granules. They look like instant coffee but have a vague smell of chocolate to them. They taste disgusting and, needless to say, I don't bother with them after the first mouthful.

Another remedy offered me is the suppository. These come in two varieties: a fat, greasy, streamlined type that looks like an art deco slug and a smaller, white variety which you would swear was a peppermint unless you knew better. I have pleasant memories of neither and I don't suppose my mother (who had the onerous task of administering them) looked back on them with any fondness either.

At one point I am presented with an enema. A polythene bag of

---

[19] I'm still not mad on it

[20] That's *soda pop* in American English

soapy looking fluid out of which is sprouting a long and menacing tube. I come very close to experiencing this; the protective cap has been removed and I have assumed position when a rush of fear arrives and does the job for me.

Eventually some decent sort of frequency develops, and I put these particular rectal tortures behind me. I wonder now whether the improvement coincided with me becoming a prodigious consumer of tea, thus keeping my bowel properly hydrated. Or perhaps it is the general improvement in my diet that does the trick? Interestingly, until this point it is rare for me to break wind, extremely rare. No matter how much my pinky finger is pulled nothing comes out. Whilst much is made of gut bacteria these days and its importance to health, in the 1970s it appears that this is more in the realms of alternative medicine and, as far as my experience of mainstream medicine was concerned, largely ignored. I assume that the introduction of fibre to my diet creates the right conditions for bugs to thrive and that the change in my intestinal flora is the reason that I, henceforth, become something of a one-man methane factory.

## Audi Coupe

At around the age of sixteen I experience a brief bout of insanity. At least this is my interpretation at the time.

The family have been watching some-or-other late-night film at the conclusion of which I decide to go to bed. I take myself upstairs and then, after shedding my clothes, proceed to put my feet and legs through the arms of an old grey sweater in the manner of stepping into pyjama bottoms. Obviously, this is not terribly successful, my toes barely make it to the elbows and I am left thrashing about bare-arsed on the floor trying to force the issue. An audience (little brother and mother) gather and, not to put too fine a point on it, piss themselves laughing. My response is to shout obscenities at them and kick at the sleeves even harder. At some point I abandon the task and slip into bed.

I awake the next morning feeling quite troubled. I can remember everything that has happened, including how it had felt; it is this that worries me. You see, during its performance, my contortionist floor show had seemed to me to be the most normal thing in the world; a regular bedtime routine. It is not pleasant to open your eyes in a morning, remember your previous night's manoeuvres and conclude that sanity has abandoned you. A troubled and difficult day follows, with the spectre of madness never far from my thoughts.

In actual fact, it is soon explained to me, I am not mentally ill, at least not in that respect, what I had experienced was somnambulism or sleepwalking to give it its more common moniker. My pyjama antics become a funny (if a little bit embarrassing) incident and I think nothing more of it.

A year or so later it rears its head again, this time I am on a family holiday. In the middle of the night I get out of bed, step into the kitchen area, grab a box of matches and begin, one by one, striking and dropping them around the caravan. All of this I am aware of, yet I cannot prevent myself from performing this dangerously nonsensical act. This is one of the problems with sleepwalking, the same skewed logic that features in dreams still applies during their physical manifestation. Which is bad because, as you know, dreams can be as weird as shit.

A science field trip, autumn 1983, and I have gone to bed in a shared dormitory at Malvern Youth Hostel. For whatever reason, and I cannot offer any explanation of this, I have an overwhelming urge to climb on top of an Audi Coupe. You may recall that that particular model, circa 83, has an attractively styled, sloping tailgate. I am so drawn to this aspect of the design that I choose to stand upright on it. To my great disappointment and surprise (so much for the durability of German engineering!) my feet go straight through and I thud down and into the boot.[21]

Of course, the car is just a delusion. What has happened is that I've climbed down from my bunk, crossed the dormitory, opened the window and stepped out onto the roof of an aging conservatory. I wake in a daze, walking around, pondering the sticky sensation under my bare feet.

Obviously, a guest jumping from a first-floor[22] window, passing through a glass conservatory, chopping through two heavily-laden wooden shelves in the process, before coming to rest on top of a fridge does not go unnoticed. There is no way I can slip back upstairs and plead ignorance on this one. Apart from the wreckage there is also the little matter of all the blood. It is everywhere; walls, floor, fridge, me! My trance-like plodding prior to waking up has done a fine job of spreading it around.

The alarm is raised, and people begin appearing. One of our party, Martin W... is immediately sick which, if anything, only adds to the mess. Another, I never knew his name, announces that he has no sympathy for young lads who go out drinking. I haven't been drinking[23] and, even if I had, the self-righteous old twat has no need to voice his opinions at that moment. I could

---

[21] That's the trunk in American
[22] That's second floor in American
[23] Well not much; four pints at most.

have died; would that have been sufficient to earn his sympathy?

The ambulance arrives and takes me to Worcester Royal Infirmary. I am wrapped in one of those red, ambulance blankets which serves to keep me warm and to cover up the embarrassment of my underpants which are getting on a bit.[24] This is my first trip in an ambulance and I tell the ambulanceman as much, but he doesn't seem interested in conversation and we never really develop the theme.

The nurse charged with fixing me up is similarly taciturn and is equally disinterested in learning that this is also my first experience of stitches. From my position the damage doesn't seem too bad, all things considered. There is a four-inch cut down my shin which requires the needle and thread, and a piece missing from my right heel which would have been sewn up had there been any skin there to work with. The majority of the repairs centre on my back which, of course, is not visible to me so I have little idea of the true scale of the job. She works on it for some time. There are, it transpires, several significant lacerations, pre-eminent of which is a cut running down the inside of my left shoulder blade which must have been eight or nine inches. I don't know if any sort of numbing is used or whether the nurse has an exceptionally light touch but the whole procedure is remarkably painless.

Crucially I remember the most important aspect to having stiches and that is being able to enumerate them. Everyone knows this. No one ever refers to just "stiches"; no one says: "I

---

[24] Marks and Spencer Y-fronts. In an orange, ribbed fabric (they might have even been thermals); they were still in good condition but not terribly cool.

jumped through a glass roof, and needed stiches", that's only half a story. Your interlocutor will almost certainly counter with: "how many?". If you can't put a figure on them, your stiches aren't worth a damn. I ask my angel of mercy. She steps back slightly, gives her handywork a slantindicular look and says:

"A lot."

A bit unprofessional in my opinion.

Back at the youth hostel I manage to get a couple of hours sleep with a view to getting a bit more during the day when everyone else is out yomping around Elgar country hammering at rocks.[25] Fat chance! Apparently, it is against hostel rules for members to stay in the buildings during the day even if they have been sliced up the night before. I think it's down to insurance issues which, considering their conservatory is now a blood-spattered wreck, seems very much in the realms of shutting the stable door after Dobbin has legged it.

There is no prospect of me walking anywhere much, the hole in my heel precludes it. Luckily, a lovely man (I wish I could remember his name) offers to drive me around, following the rock bashers in a similar way to one of those support cars you see in the Tour de France. Not only do I get to see several interesting Precambrian exposures, but I also hear the merits of the Leyland Princess 1800. It certainly is a roomy and comfortable ride[26], perfect for someone recovering from a recent conservatory accident.

---

[25] It was a geology field trip in case you were wondering.

[26] Due (respectively) to the transverse mounting of the 1798cc B series pushrod straight four engine and the presence of British Leyland's Hydragas suspension.

Returning to the subject of blood-spattered wrecks, for some reason (I cannot explain why) I keep hold of my jumping pants even though they are sodden with blood. Initially (and this demonstrates how ignorant seventeen-year old boys are of clothes washing) I assume they will be pressed back into service. Obviously, they aren't, instead they somehow find their way to a little-used cupboard and almost thirty years later I come across them. They are like a larger version of those beef jerky dog treats.

Incidentally, pictures of Malvern Youth Hostel (including the rebuilt conservatory) can be found via a brief search of the internet. Similarly, the Audi Coupe and Leyland Princess 1800. The last episode of midnight wanderings of any significance occurs in the early nineties when I am living in a flat in the former Great Western Hotel close to Bournemouth railway station. Once again it involves me trying to get out of a window. However, the window in this instance is on the fourth floor[27] and, had I succeeded, it would almost certainly have resulted in my sorry carcass being splattered on the pavement below. Thankfully, I fail to open the window due to a sticky mechanism.

These days I make a point, when staying in hotels and the like, of tying up windows before going to bed. It is a little embarrassing when anyone not in the know sees it (hotel staff and so on) but not as embarrassing as being a mysterious collection of broken bones, viscera and the torn remnants of a Wee Willy Winky nightshirt.[28]

---

[27] Fifth floor in American
[28] My boudoir attire of choice.

## Autism

Our son, D.... is officially placed on the autistic spectrum in 2013, he is ten years old. In truth we have tagged him as *a funny bugger* from a very early stage, but like many parents we just keep an eye on his *peculiarities* and hope they go away. They don't. He has Asperger's Syndrome although it strikes me that the term is not used as readily as it once was, the broader "on the spectrum" epithet is preferred. It is less restrictive, and it cuts out the ...erga/erja pronunciation debate.

Not surprisingly, we do our fair share of reading-up on the subject which is good in that we gain a deeper understanding of the condition but bad in that it gives CM (Current Mrs) Lenity a new hobby. In the space of a few months she diagnoses more people than your average clinician could manage in a professional lifetime. One of her earlier diagnoses is me.

I made the mistake of telling her that as a young child I could not stand my nails to be cut; it was the sensation in my finger-ends immediately after the event that drove me mad. I would resist all attempts at trimming to such a degree that my hands began to resemble those of Ming the Merciless, only smaller and without the rings. My mother's solution was to cut them whilst I slept. This admission was more than enough to pique CM's interest.

She cites other examples including: requiring oxygen at birth (whatever difference that makes), my rarely leaving the house, being scared of the pedal bin, a memory for historical facts and failing to enjoy the toneless singing of a women who cannot even be bothered to find out the correct lyrics to her favourite pop songs. She makes me a list. CM makes a lot of lists. She really likes lists. I mean *really* likes lists! See what I am getting at? Pot-kettle-grimy arse anyone?

I wonder sometimes whether we are not all on the spectrum to some degree. Which is fine because suddenly, and it does strike me as such, there has been a sea change in attitudes to autism. When we first suspected D... was *not quite right* it didn't seem like something to relish, but these days (and we are only talking a difference of a few years) you cannot shift for parents telling you their kids are high-functioning[29] autistic. Autism is the new rock and roll.

Sadly, as far as CM's diagnosing is concerned, autism is just the start of it. After reading Jon Ronson's book, *The Psychopath Test*, she is now an expert at spotting potential axe murderers too. There is a new list. As far as I know I am not on it.

# B is for...

## Back Passage

Late 1984 and I am having a troublesome poo. It hurts. But not in the manner that I am accustomed to, that is to say, *the pain of the strain.* I am familiar with torture of trying to push an immovable object, I suffered years of constipation as a child, (see All-Bran Anyone?) this is sharper, more stabbing. In addition, it is sort of asymmetrical, if that makes sense, to one side more than the other. I have a quick look in the bowl to see if I have inadvertently consumed something scratchy[30] and reel at the sight. There is an old fashion maxim that runs:

"Blue and green should never be seen."

Well to that you can add:

---

[29] The high-functioning bit is important, it says *okay, he might be a little tosser at the moment but twenty years from now and you're looking at the next Alan Turing.*

[30] I don't know what, pine cone or hedgehog, something like that.

"Brown and red, almost dropped dead!"

It seems to me to be perfectly natural to experience shock when you suddenly see your own claret spilling out. Apart from in matters of family planning (i.e. finding out she's not up the duff) the presence of blood is generally regarded as bad thing. I take a moment to regain my composure then I wipe my bum. It hurts more, and when I check the paper it too is bright red. I have an inkling of what is going on here. I suspect I have haemorrhoids or to give them their street name, piles.[31]

I consult parents on this matter. One of them must know a thing or two about the subject as I have often seen the tubes of bum cream kicking around the house. It turns out that both of them are seasoned Chalfonters[32]. Based (I must stress) on description alone, they confirm the diagnosis. In Anusol terms we are now a three tube household.

I don't get a lot of joy from Anusol, likewise Germolene. Although the blood is intermittent the pain is constant. Post poo it is really biting and leaves me hobbling for hours. Clearly my nobbies need something a bit more robust, and in pursuit of this I take a trip to the doctors.

I have no recollection of receiving a digital examination (i.e. taking a finger up) and that kind of memory tends to stay with you. In fact, I don't think the doc even makes a visual reccy. But that is often the way of it then, if a patient says he has farmers

---

[31] I have no idea why piles are called piles, but it was good news for rhyming slang enthusiasts. Spare a thought for Emma Freud.

[32] I once spent New Year in Chalfont St Giles. At the time it was the poshest place I had ever been. I remember meeting a beautiful young woman in a pub whose only desire was to listen to my accent. These days even the family dog ignores me.

he probably has farmers and you medicate him accordingly.

The name of the medication I am given escapes me but it resembles Vaseline and comes in a tube with a long nozzle. The idea being that the nozz goes up the catflap and the contents of the tube are squeezed through it and into the theatre of operations. I don't know who designed it, but they clearly haven't tested it in the ambient temperature of South Yorkshire. The stuff is too stiff to travel up the pipe. It is a waste of time. The tube splits before anything emerges from the nozzle. I resort to finger application and manage to coax some grease past the rim but in terms of relief it barely registers.

My next prescription is a real step up. Again, I don't know what it is though I suspect it is a either a local anaesthetic or some form of anti-inflammatory. It comes in a small aerosol and looks a bit like shaving foam. Supplied with its own applicator syringe it comes with a warning never to fire the foam directly from the tin into the anus. I have no intention of ever firing aerosols up my arse, but I recognise that some fellas are attracted to that sort of behaviour and the advice is noted.

The shaving foam seems to do the trick, the symptoms disappeared after a week or so and I go back to normal. However, the bleeding soon returns, but with a difference. Whereas before there would be lots of pain and some blood, now there is barely any pain and lots of blood. I am referred to a specialist at the Hallamshire Hospital.

It seems to be standard procedure, in NHS hospitals at least, to sit a patient in a little room for a period before being seen by a consultant. Better still, make sure the room contains a medical trolley loaded with apparatus but cover it with a sheet so only the amorphous shapes of the torture instruments can be seen. Then let imagination do the rest.

My first digital examination and it is not nearly as bad as I am anticipating[33]. It is performed whilst I lie on my left side, knees to chin because it's all about angles and bringing the elbow in to play; like when you stuff a chicken. Presumably left-handed doctors get you to lie on your right side.

Next comes the hardware, I don't get a good look at it, but I assume this is an anoscope, a rigid tube that is shoved up the jacksie allowing a clearer view of what's going on inside. It feels not dissimilar to the digital exam, though a bit colder and with less wiggling about.

"You have fissures." The doctor announces, without looking up.

"Fishes?" Up my bum?

Then:

"Have you had sexual activity recently?"

What does he mean? Is he asking me if I've been bummed? Does he think I am a homosexual? Do I come across as a homosexual?

I tell him *no* in the most masculine voice I can manage considering my prone position. I don't know if he believes me or not.

There is nothing to be done for my fishes I am told. As long as you treat them nicely (keep your stools soft, avoid straining, rein in the buggery, that sort of thing) they tend to heal of their own accord. He is quite correct, they do.

There is one particular piece of advice I take from the consultation which serves me well during my subsequent adventures and which I offer up here to anyone with the

---

[33] It is no doubt a significant improvement on the old-time analogue version.

misfortune to present crimson:

"Remember, a little bit of blood goes a long way."

## Bacon
See Dark Arts

## Bandaging
(see also "Under the Knife" re. clingfilm)

Back passages again, this time in the architectural sense. I am raised in a terraced council house and the only access to our back yard and garden is the passageway we share with our immediate neighbours. The passage is nicely straight and tarmacked but deceptively sloping and with a bit of a camber to it, so it is well designed for first tempting, then tripping four-year-old boys. I frequently come a cropper whilst running into the house for something or other; never anything urgent of course, you run everywhere at that age.

If you are wondering why a four-year-old was running about on the street unsupervised then you are not familiar with council estates in the 1970s. That is just the way it is; we run wild, it is like Lord of the Flies with Raleigh Choppers.[34]

I digress. Returning to my back passage, on one occasion I really go for it, landing on my knees and taking two big chunks out of them in the process. Sobbing away (I am quite an accomplished sobber) I hobble into the house for help. I am cleaned up, Dettolled (always Dettol) and Savloned (usually

---

[34] It sounds unbelievable now but at the time that was the done thing. There were loads of us charging around with sticks, dodging cars and paedophiles. There were always a few dogs too. I can't remember the last time I saw a dog chase a car; that age, it seems, has passed. Dogs today are too sophisticated, they're all inside on their PlayStations

Savlon, occasionally Zam-Buk) and I am bandaged and sent out to play on the street. It doesn't occur to me that my dressings are in anyway over-engineered; I just accept that a mile and half of bandaging is the done-thing for passage-tripping injuries. Besides, I have other fish to fry, I have street dogs to cavort with and sticks to wield. It isn't until I wander onto the far end of the road and am accosted by a much older boy (I guess about age six) that it dawns on me that anyone else but my mother would have just slapped on a couple of sticking plasters. I look ridiculous; short trousers, with a pair of skinny white legs hanging down from them, each divided at the knee by a bulbous linen binding. Add to that the restrictions that this places on my running and you can understand why I draw the attention of this youth. He stops yards from me, points at my knees and laughs theatrically. Every time I see Nelson from the Simpsons I am reminded of it.

My mother is particularly keen on the bandaging sub-set known as crepe. Our house is always well stocked with crepe bandages and you can usually pick out the residual scent of Sloan's liniment in the air. (See "Embrocation")

It wouldn't be the last accident I have in a passage. I still have a scar on the palm of my right hand dating from around seventy one; that was a proper cut and allowed my mother carte blanche with her bandaging. My arm looked like a large cotton bud.

I managed to repeat my knee bashing feat forty-odd years later, due this time to an absence of lighting, and not me tearing about. It shakes me to the core! What is it about falling down as an adult that makes it so much worse than when you are a child? I don't cry on this occasion, but I want to; I really want to. It is weeks before I feel up to wielding sticks or running with street dogs again.

## Black Fingernail
(See "Physics A Level")

## Bloody Flux
See "Back Passage and Growing (Further) Up"

## Boils
See "Dermo Stuff" and "Cysts"

## Bone Spurs
See "Bunions"

## Bovine TB
In early 1985 I begin to get the feeling that something isn't quite right with me. It's nothing specific, just a sense that I'm not firing on all cylinders. What my mother terms "...feeling off the hooks" though I have no idea where that phrase originates from.

It starts with a couple of doses of the sniffles, general lethargy, that sort of thing. Then I begin, on occasion, to get a bit loose; not diarrhoea as I know the term, that is to say thin brown liquid, more of a porridge consistency.[35] At the time this isn't such a bad thing as I am still having problems with haemorrhoids and fishes[36]. This continues through spring and into early summer, just before I am due to retake my A levels.

Whether there is a stress-related element to it I cannot say but things ramp up a gear or two at this time. I am getting a lot of abdominal pain, of both the stabbing and cramping variety. My bowel movements increase in frequency and are often just liquid; it seems that everything I eat just shoots through. In

---

[35] Type 5 as opposed to 7 on the Bristol Stool Scale
[36] Fissures

response, I restrict my diet; better, I reason, to eat nothing than suffer the flux. After a while you can get so used to a restricted diet that food begins to lose its appeal; the appetite fades away. Within weeks all I am living on is lemon flavour French set yoghurts and Bourneville chocolate.[37] Weight falls off me, I become weak, which doesn't help with the fatigue one bit. (see "Lethargy")

I sit two of my exams in pain, tired out and wanting to fart and shit constantly. Luckily, I have a week's grace before the next round which, I reason, should give me a chance to recover a little. My optimism is misplaced, I worsen. In the end our GP, Dr D... makes a home visit and the next thing I know I am in the back of an ambulance on my way to Lodge Moor Isolation Hospital suspected of having TB.

Lodge Moor is a fascinating place[38], it was built in the late nineteenth century as an isolation hospital, primarily to treat smallpox. As a child my mother spent months shut away there having contracted Diptheria. Whilst she was away World War Two started, but I don't believe the two events were connected. As you might expect for an isolation hospital it is located on the very outskirts of the city, at the edge of the moor. It is bleak and exposed, but the views are very impressive. It has gone now, replaced with housing, although some of the buildings (including the clocktower) have been retained.

During my association it houses a spinal unit and, as I sit in the

---

[37] Set yoghurts were a new thing to us then; it was like Sheffield had stepped into the Jet Age.

[38] Another interesting fact about Lodge Moor; an American jet fighter crashed into it in 1955 killing a patient (Elsie Murdock) and injuring seven others.

back of the wagon, the ambulanceman tells me, incredulous of tone, about the profusion of speed bumps on an approach used for delivering patients with broken backs. I get the feeling that he expresses these views to all his passengers, with the possible exception of those that actually have broken backs.

I am wheeled in and on to my ward. It's miles away! The corridors at Lodge Moor Hospital go on forever. They are so long that senior nurses are equipped with Segways[39] to get them from A to B as swiftly as possible. It is a strange sight; the corridors are glazed and other, parallel corridors can be seen in the distance.  From time to time, a straight-backed and ostensibly motionless matron will traverse at speed across your line of vision. It is all very Flash Gordon.

I am given a high-backed leatherette chair to sit in and a nurse comes and takes some details, eventually giving me a dinky little plastic bracelet with my name on it. Next, I am sent for blood tests. This may sound strange, but although I am nineteen I have not had blood taken before; I am quite apprehensive. When it's all over and I haven't blubbed I feel mighty proud of myself.

I am to get a private room, one of the perks of having TB; about the only one I suspect. There are private rooms either side of me, all served by the same corridor, a bit like old-fashioned railway carriages. The walls of the rooms are glazed, with full length curtains for privacy. I take a look through the glass to see who my neighbours are. Left is empty, to my right a very elderly man is lying motionless in bed. He looks dead though I

---

[39] The Segway did not arrive until 2001 so this is clearly a misnomer. In truth I do not know what they were but they were Segway-esque in form so I am sticking with it.

assure myself that if he had expired someone would have noticed and done something about it.

From what I can tell most of the ward is occupied by geriatric patients, women one half, men the other. Not that I get out much. I am to be kept in isolation and anyone who comes in contact with me, including visitors, have to dress in a large white smock and mob cap.

It also means that everything I need to do must be accomplished within the confines of my Hannibal Lecter style glass cage. This I struggle with. Peeing in a bottle is no problem but shitting on a commode fills me with dread. The commodes in operation are really just wheelchairs with a hole in the seat and a little shelf underneath where the bed pan sits, poised to catch the goods. After spending my life pooping in a small, private, home vestibule to be asked to do it on a chair in the middle of a large room seems unnatural. I feel really exposed. And the process itself is alien too. The thing has arms on it, and it's on wheels (it takes me a while to realise it has a brake) and there is no reassuring drop and splosh, it just builds up below me, the moist heat rising and condensing on my buttocks. It's like sitting on a bowl of Scotch broth.

If all this is not bad enough, I then have to shout for a nurse to come and take it away. This is generally left to one of the trainees who then have the onerous task of examining the specimen and concocting an accurate description. Before long my chart has a list of entries all reading: *offensive smelling semi-formed.* I assume this relates to stools and not the patient. Offensive smelling does not do it justice; *satanic* would be closer to the mark. This is another problem with shitting in a dish, there's nothing to keep the stench in. The hospital relies on a really powerful air freshener and I get through pints of it;

the memory of its strong chemically-lemon odour is still with me to this day.

Because the commode business is so unpalatable to me, I make every effort to limit my visits by holding the crap in for as long as I can. The tactic proves to have unwelcome consequences, particularly for the junior doctor charged with performing a sigmoidoscopy on me. Having assumed my foetal position his first words on inserting the scope are:

"I can't see much, there's quite a lot of stuff up here!"

At this point the seepage begins and, to the nurse:

"Pass me a kidney dish would you?" Then:

"Better have another."

Eventually culminating in:

"More dishes! For the love of God more dishes!" As it gushes out. I shall never forget the panic in his voice; I think I fill four in total though the last one isn't quite to the brim. I don't see that particular doctor again.

The consultant charged with working out what is going on is called Dr MacK... and he looks every inch the red-bearded, claymore wielding, scourge of the glens until he opens his mouth at which point he suddenly becomes very English. His second in command, at least as far as my treatment is concerned, is a young woman whose name I have forgotten. What I do remember is that she has a penchant for brightly coloured tights (red or green usually) which I find to be both exotic and alluring. I am also attracted to her sturdy ankles which I cannot account for. I will say though, in my defence, I am only nineteen, and what young man doesn't go through a sturdy ankle phase at some stage in his life?

Between them they outline how they are going to investigate me; much of it sounds quite unappealing. First up will be a chest X-ray, then ultrasound scan. After that comes a barium enema, then a barium meal. I am also to expect a visit from a dietician. This occurs the next day and in contrast to everything else going on, is most pleasant.

The dietician is a lovely, dark-haired little woman with a kind and softly spoken voice. I had never made the connection before writing this book but she has the soothing quality about her that I now associate with ASMR (see "Tingly Head"). Yes, granted, there are moments when I picture my Hoffman to her Bancroft[40], but they are in the minority, for the most part I just enjoy listening to her voice.

She is quite shocked when I tell her about my Bourneville and French set yoghurt diet[41]. Making a quick calculation (serene pencilling action by the way) as to what my daily calorie count is confirms her fears. I can't remember the exact figure but it is sufficiently meagre for her to start pushing protein my way. That day a portion of boiled fish arrives, and fish really isn't my thing. I could probably manage it battered on a bed of chips, perhaps smothered with mushy peas. I have even been known to consume an occasional boil-in-the-bag cod in butter sauce, but this? Not in a million years will I be eating this. It's just a huge slab of white flesh swimming in a puddle of grey water. And so fishy; in-your-face levels of fishy. Even from under its cloche it stinks the room out; a room from which I cannot escape. It's half an hour before a domestic rescues me.

I haven't any sort of appetite to start with, my diet lady will have to do something a bit better than boiled fish to entice me.

---

[40] The Graduate. *Are you trying to seduce me Mrs Robinson?*

[41] Though not at all phased by the concept of a yoghurt that is *set* so clearly she was quite the sophisticate.

Luckily, she has also specified what I believe these days is termed elemental nutrition (EN); a nutrient-rich drink formulated to be easily digested. It comes in a little carton to which a straw is glued. I think its name is Nutrinel, but I am not absolutely sure. The point is, it is benign sustenance, I can stomach it and so, at last, I am getting some calories into me. Strangely enough, years later, following surgery, I am offered a similar product and the stuff makes me gag; strange how our tastes change.

I discover something about the "undead" neighbour to my right; he has dementia. I know this because he spends all night (every night!) shouting out numbers at the top of his voice. "SIX,...TWENTY NINE,...FORTY THREE,..."

There doesn't seem to be any pattern to them, at least not an obvious one. Though, truth be told, I am not following it in any detail; I am far too irritated. It is hard enough to sleep anyway, especially since I'm prone to sweats and when you are lying on a rubberised mattress the juice doesn't really have anywhere to go.

"SIXTY ONE,...EIGHTY EIGHT,..."

I speculate that he might have been a bingo caller in his younger days. If he was then I don't reckon much to his technique; where are the little ducks and the fat ladies? Perhaps he was once an American football player; they have a thing about shouting out seemingly random numbers[42]. It's hard to reconcile this wizened little man with sixteen stone of gridiron beefcake.

A busy day, I am X-rayed until I am blue in the face this morning with an ultrasound scan scheduled for the afternoon.

---

[42] Why do they do that?

I am told the ultrasound is nothing to worry about; the worst part is the cold jelly they smear you in. Actually, that's the best part; it's a therapy in its own right.

Laxative time! Tomorrow's barium enema requires of me a clean bowel and that means flushing out with laxative. I don't mind popping a couple of Senokot for them if it helps; there can't be too much to flush out, I don't eat.

A poor assumption on my part. My laxative arrives in a jug; two litres of it. It is flavoured with some or other fruity concoction but still tastes foul. It takes me two hours to down it at which point the next one arrives. A little later it starts to work, and I spend about another hour on the commode. There's more in the night:

"TWENTY FIVE,...SEVENTEEN,...NUMBER TWO,...NUMBER TWO,...NUMBER TWO."

Next morning breakfast arrives. It's another jug of laxative.

Early afternoon and I am handed a weird smock thing to put on and warned that it ties at the back and not at the front. A lot of patients get this wrong apparently. It shows the trust that people have in medical staff that they would, in good faith, put on such a garment without wondering: *just a minute, why are my cock and balls hanging out for no obvious reason?*

I am wheeled to X-ray and helped onto a large stainless-steel table and asked to assume the foetal position. I feel the slap of the Vaseline on my tradesman's and a quick digital is performed. After that, what looks like a sex toy[43] is inserted into me and secured by means of tape across my hairy buttocks so there is some future unpleasantness to look forward to there.

---

[43] Pink and ribbed. Presumably the ribbing is to stop it falling out; hope that is the case.

The sex toy is attached to a tube which runs to a bag of milky white fluid below the table. No doubt that is the barium. Someone somewhere must have pressed the start button because the bag starts to rise and as it passes my level I have a sensation of being "filled up".

Next, everyone bar me runs behind a screen and I am warned to take a grip of the two handles sticking up from the table. The table starts to tilt; left, right, forward, back; at one point I am almost completely upside down. It's like a fairground attraction, only rather slow and boring. You wouldn't pay to ride it, even with the sex toy.

I hold my breath as snapshots are taken of me in a variety of poses...

*Yeah Baby, work it, work it!, the camera luvs ya!*

...after which the mechanised bag descends to below table level and all the milk drains out of me. It looks a little streaky now; I hope there are no plans to reuse it.

Not *all* the milk drains from me. After I am unplugged, and in the process, depilated, I am shown to a toilet and I get rid of the dregs. It is so dense that it just sits on the bottom of the pan refusing to be flushed.

The following day I am scheduled for a barium meal which I am hoping will be more palatable than the laxative though there is every chance that it is worse. I have studied geology and am familiar with barium sulphate in its mineral form (baryte) and it never struck me as particularly toothsome. I don't get to find out. When I reach X-ray I am informed that a barium meal will not cut it as far as my investigation is concerned. They want to look at my small intestine and the problem with drinking the solution is that the stomach lets it out in dribs and drabs which leads to a patchy coverage. The solution? Bypass the stomach!

Put a tube through my nose, down my throat, past my stomach and into my duodenum.

It is not a pleasant experience, although the tube is mercifully narrow (see gastroscopy). The extraction of the tube on completion is quite amusing though. Rather like removing a sticking plaster, a rapid removal of the tube is regarded as favourite and it's an odd sight watching it cross-eyed as it streams out of your face, wads of snot flying off in all directions.

After a week the novelty of friends and family dressing up in silly clothes has worn off and I am struggling to find things to occupy myself with. Everyone here is up and about so early in the morning which is a pain in the arse when you are nineteen and spending every night at the mercy of the wailing number man. I make up for the night-time's shortfall by sleeping in the day and it is questionable as to how much of this is driven by illness and how much by boredom. I try to do a bit of reading (a Blandings compendium), I listen to hospital radio, I have a couple of those word search books, but these are not enough. I shave every day, not because I have an affinity to grooming but because it kills a few minutes of the morning. I am missing my dogs and my telly.

It seems I have overdone it on the grooming; I have attracted a couple of admirers. Both young nurses. Sounds good? Actually, not so good. One of them is a bit on the large side for me and she has a quite prominent moustache. She keeps offering to give me a bath despite my insistence that even if I needed one, I am perfectly capable of washing myself.

What can I say? I was a callow youth, I was tethered to popular perceptions of feminine beauty; add to that my blazing optimism as to my own worth and she was obviously heading down a road to disappointment. As far as I was concerned if a woman was going to help out with my ablutions she would look like Kelly LeBrock[44] and not Frank Canon.[45]

Now, grizzled and sagacious that I am, I know never to look a gift horse in the mouth, even if it is a bit bristly. I could have had no end of fun with her had I been a little more mature. Such is life. As a learned academic once said: "you know shit at nineteen..." or something along those lines anyway.

The other nurse to have fallen for my charms is even less appealing, he's a man. He keeps slinking in and sitting on my bed and telling me, in his patently effeminate voice, about how many birds he has hit with his car that morning.[46] I laugh along nervously, not wanting to tell him that it all sounds a bit of a shame for the birds; he seems to relish the carnage. I don't think I would want to get involved with someone who enjoys mowing down wildlife in a Ford Escort. And there is, of course, that little matter of him being a bloke. I may be jumping to conclusions here, after all I am the only other male of a similar age in the vicinity and it is perfectly natural that he should gravitate towards me, but something tells me he has a different agenda going on. Wait till he draws the short straw with my

---

[44] From the film "Weird Science". Although I never saw this until later it is just too good an example to ignore. Two nerdy boys create the perfect woman (LeBrock) on their computer. She comes to life and at one point joins them in the shower.

[45] Roly-poly, nineteen seventies, LA detective with a moustache. Look him up. If you make allowances for the age and the bald head it is a striking resemblance.

[46] I couldn't drive at that time and took him at face value. Now a licence holder of some twenty-five years I've only ever hit one bird and I drive a bloody big pick-up so I suspect he was spinning a yarn there.

bedpan, see if he's so keen to sit on my bed after a couple of encounters with *semi-formed, offensive smelling.*

I get a visit from a doctor; he has news for me. I have Crohn's disease. He writes the name on a piece of paper. It's quite unusual it seems[47]. I am not surprised. I don't know why but I always suspected I was special. Having been given this news I perhaps should have next asked: "how long have I got Doc?" or something along those lines but I don't recall saying anything at all.

I am started on medication that very day. Suphasalazine[48], which are large, round, yellowy-orange tablets. They are quite dusty which makes them a little unpalatable. In addition, I am to take steroids. Will this mean I turn into Sylvester Stallone? I already have a passing facial resemblance. Despite all the talk about steroids in the news I have no real idea of what they are. I am to have a corticosteroid (Prednisolone) rather than an anabolic steroid which are the ones body builders and athletes use. They are small, white and insignificant in appearance which totally belies their subsequent effect which is both rapid and profound. Within a day or two I can run a mile. I should qualify that, I *feel like* I can run a mile; which is quite different. There is no muscle on my legs so I obviously can't. Anyway, I had never run a mile before I was ill so it seems unlikely now. I am also hungry. Ravenous, and I set about shovelling food into

---

[47] Hard to believe since we hear so much about it now.

[48] Street name Salazopyrin

my face at an alarming rate.[49]

## Bunions

The top of my feet are home to bone spurs which I have had since my early teens. They are quite painful in the early days due to shoe rubbing but then if you have bone spurs and run around in tight trainers all the time what do you expect? It's asking for trouble. They're not quite bunions but they are the closest I've got.

## Burns

Nothing worth mentioning here either. See "Callouses" for the effect of flour on burns.

## Breast Feeding

I was a bottle-fed baby. Why that came about I cannot say, I suspect that it was down to obstreperousness on my part; I was a finnicky eater as a child. It occurred to me recently that this may have had an impact on the development of my gut flora and, by extension may have paved the way for IBD. Who knows? Some studies have shown a tentative link between the two but they are few in number and relatively limited in scale so the jury is out on this one.

## Broken Bones

Though not for want of trying (see "Audi Coupe") I have only ever had one broken bone. It occurred one Friday night back in the summer of 1984 when, after stopping for a post-pub pee in

---

[49] I did enjoy the food at Lodge Moor, particularly the fried breakfasts, they were superb. Things have changed in hospitals since then, they don't believe in edible food anymore, it's too much of an incentive for people to stay.

a secluded corner of Wadsley Bridge I am jumped upon by an assailant. He comes at me from behind, but I slip my head out of his armlock[50] and deliver a few amateurish punches to his face. I suppose they are uppercuts, but I wouldn't like to offer them up for technical scrutiny. All this time, I would like to add, my brave companions whom I was expecting to dive into the fray at any moment, have carried on walking. By the time my attacker cries "uncle" and runs off they are half a mile up the Halifax Road, and I am alone nursing a painful fist. The first knuckle is obviously distorted, pushed back into my hand. My forefinger is difficult to move, and my hand has already starting to swell.

The upshot is that I spend the night in A&E with my father who is none too happy about it as we are due to go on a family holiday the next morning. I tell the nurse some far-fetched tale about tripping up and banging my hand; as if the good folk there have never seen a fist-fighting injury on a Friday night in Sheffield! There is very little left to tell other than to say the X-ray confirms the fracture, and to describe the cast I am given which extends all the way up to my elbow. It seems a bit excessive. Indeed, I have seen broken knuckles since, and they have all been much less extensive, consisting of just splint and hand bandaging, but I am sure there was good reason for it. Maybe I have one of those faces that invites excessive bandaging? (see "Bandaging"). Perhaps the staff were having a bit of a laugh; that kind of thing used to go on back then. During a spell in hospital with a collapsed lung, my well-

---

[50] The advantage of having a curiously small head (See Head Size)

endowed friend Hamish came out of anaesthetic to find a nurse had tied a red ribbon to his cock; a rather neat bow apparently. It would never happen today...which is a shame in some respects.

# C is for
## Callouses and Cracks

The early nineties and I am squiring[51] a woman from Enfield in Middlesex (what man doesn't at some stage?) who is enamoured with the softness of my hands. It is one of only three things going for me as far as she is concerned.[52] Soft hands had never struck me as a feature before this point but I suppose it made sense from her perspective.

Fast forward a few years to the time when I have a food business and the change could not be starker. I have thick callouses on my right hand from handling a chef's knife, with complimentary callouses on my left knuckles through guiding a blade during hours of dicing. In addition, because of the constant hand washing, my skin dries out and begins to crack, and because I am making, for the most part, pies, flour gets into the cracks and prevents them from healing. No amount of moisturising helps, and it gets to the stage where my hands bleed. This is compounded when I catch the back of my hand on the underside of the grill; weeping burn/self-raising is another bad combination. I have the hands of a leper and if it wasn't for the gloves I wear on the market stall I do not think I

---

[51] I don't like the term *dating,* it always makes me think of archaeology.

[52] The other two being my sexual prowess (obviously) and a perceived resemblance to former Specials front man Terry Hall

would shift a single pie.

Industrial injuries are not limited to my *dannies*, other extremities get in on the act; namely my feet. I never knew this, but wearing backless shoes makes the skin on your heels crack, and I am spending long hours every day standing in kitchen clogs. My feet look like the East African Rift viewed from space; I can barely walk on them. It takes a different shoe and a couple of tubes of patent heel gel to put me back to normal.

I say normal, my feet are getting progressively tougher on the soles. I think it is an aging thing, a combination of drying skin and years of wear and tear. There are points in life when you cannot help but wonder: *have the last vestiges of my youth finally left me?* Receiving a scraping tool and a tube of Dr Scholl foot softening cream from your wife at Christmas is one of those moments. That is not to say it isn't a bloody useful gift, it is. I use it regularly. In fact, were it not for my foot rasping regime, I would be sporting a pair of hooves by now and, bearing in mind that I look a little like Nosferatu the vampire these days, you will understand why I don't want to go any further down the satanic route.

## Circumcision

I cannot tell you exactly when this occurred other than to say I was very young; pre-school age, but older than two as I remember the house we were living in at the time. I think I am experiencing some stinging whilst having a wee and no doubt (because this always happens) I am whisked off to the doctor's immediately and presumably referred to the Children's Hospital thereafter.

All I remember of the process is being on my back in a starkly lit room whilst men in rubber gloves get on with cutting whatever they are cutting somewhere down below. I also remember the stinging pain of urination in the aftermath; it made me cry but at that age so did the fire engine scene in Trumpton.[53] The pain of piddling eventually went, and I thought nothing more of it.

Years later and we sit, as a family, watching television. I cannot say what the program is but reference is made to circumcision. Not having reached the age at which you learn to look thinks up in a book rather than ask your parents I pose the question: "What's circumcision?"

"It's what you had; when you were little." Comes the answer.

Fair enough, it took them long enough to put a name to it but now I know. It isn't until I have my first taste of hardcore pornography[54] that I discover (and I apologise for the pun) that my circumcision is a load of old cock. I have a foreskin, I still do, as a matter of fact. It remains attached, and apart from the occasional complaint due to overuse, we remain very happy together.

It seems my pseudo-circumcision is not a one off; I recently saw an interview with Patrick Stewart, aka Jean-Luc Picard of the Starship Enterprise, where he confessed to being given the same duff info. The difference being that I was a teenager when I had my epiphany, he had to be told by his wife! Even then he had to have it confirmed by a doctor. And he has the cheek to deliver man-to-man talks to Acting-Ensign Wesley Crusher!

Stewart hails from Huddersfield so perhaps our examples say something about the quality of sex education in God's Own

---

[53] If you are similarly afeared I recommend hiding behind the settee until it passes. Alternatively stick to Camberwick Green.

[54] The viewing, not making of.

County.

I am being unfair; I would lay odds on Yorkshire's shortcomings being replicated across the nation. The problem lay, I believe, not with the schools but with the so-called moral guardians of the nation who seemed to have had an enormous influence on what could be taught. Sex education was delivered diagrammatically, often in cross section. Heaven forbid that we should see a photograph that showed anything more detailed than a hairy triangle.

Sex was taught from a scientific, rather than a social angle which, frankly, left it rather lacking. It was scant preparation for real life and when I did finally come face to face with a genuine vagina it was something of a shock. All that moisture! Combined with all the spare meat! It left me in mind of a poorly wrung-out window leather. Ah, the romance of youth.

## Clinodactyly

This sounds more exotic than it is. I have bent fingers. My little fingers to be precise; they bend in towards their next-door neighbours. They don't hurt and don't cause any physical impairment. I have had them all my life and similar bends (though not as pronounced) were seen on my father's hands and are present on those of my son and eldest daughter which seems to imply a genetic element to the thing.

I did a bit of looking-up on the subject, which is where I found the posh name, and it does appear to be a genetic trait; either as an isolated anomaly or as a symptom in a list of syndromes, all bar one of which I have never heard of. Worryingly, and I say this only because it fuels CM's diagnosing mania, a link with autism has been mooted.

On the plus side, some folk regard it as the sign of a creative or artistic temperament and I once read that, historically, a bent little finger was considered a sign of royal lineage.[55] A number of renaissance paintings (including works by Botticelli and Da Vinci) show subjects sporting bent 'uns suggesting the trait was fashionable in the period. Or perhaps we clinodactylians are just natural posers?

## Concussion
See "Knocked out"

## Constipation
See "All-Bran Anyone?"

## Cramp
Not, as you might suspect, the cramp associated with Crohn's, so called stomach cramps, but the sort that you see footballers rolling around with when the match has gone into extra time. These are skeletal muscle cramps and, I have just discovered, are sometimes called a *Charlie Horse* or a *corky.* I shall be using both of these colloquialisms in the future.

I first experience cramp at around the age of thirteen. Resting on the settee having spent the afternoon at football training, out of nowhere, the muscle in my right thigh contorts into a knot and sends me into a blind panic. I have never experienced anything like this before and have no idea what to do. Plus, it is really bloody painful! I fall off the settee and roll about the floor clutching my leg; probably hyperventilating and certainly moaning, no doubt in the high-pitched voice of a little girl on helium. Thankfully, it passes relatively quickly leaving me relieved but with an achy leg for a few days. *You can stuff your*

---

[55] I always knew I was special.

*football training if that's what it does to you,* I thought, and consequently didn't bother with anything strenuous for several years after.

These days a game of squash is enough to Charlie Horse me and this invariably happens without warning in the middle of the night. Although I now have some idea about stretching and massaging out the knot of muscle in my thigh. This still involves me dancing around (in a nightie) making a lot of silly noises. I think we just have to accept that this is the way of things with me and Charlie Horse.

Other popular areas for cramp are my feet and sometimes my hands. On rare occasions I can develop a cramp from yawning. This is perfectly true. When it first happened, I was a teenager and it scared the shit out of me. I thought my face had broken. There I was walking along Halifax Road, presumably a little bored because I yawn which sends something popping out from below my chin completely locking my jaw up. Close to tears I do the natural thing one does with a sudden injury and that is to grab it. In itself this is no help at all but as I gently massage the contorted guider upwards it moves back into its original slot leaving me with residual pain but greatly relieved. I told loads of people about this at the time and everyone looked at me like I was mental and so I gave up on looking for empathy. It is only now, with the benefit of age, that I feel confident enough to reveal it.

Interestingly it is thought that quinine can help relieve cramp and so if you are ever looking for an excuse for a G&T, there you go.

## Cricked Neck

We all get a crick in the neck from time to time, don't we? It's not a big deal, a tad uncomfortable but it goes away in a day or so. Not something you would want to dedicate a section of a book to. I agree. However, there have been a couple of occasions when cricks have left me virtually unable to function. By rights they should come under trapped nerves, thus affording them the gravitas they deserve but I prefer the term cricked neck; it has a more homespun feel to it.

1988 and I am a student in Newcastle; I have just celebrated the completion of an exam paper culminating in a journey to somebody's house in Jesmond for a bit of a party thing. I don't know Jesmond (it's where the posh students lived) rarely do I venture out of Fenham. If I'd had any money and/or sense I would have taken a taxi home. Instead I set off to walk across Newcastle which is my undoing.

To cut a long story short, within half a mile I am in the back of a panda car, arrested on suspicion of burglary. Apparently, I have broken into a pub and purloined a load of cigarettes; I don't even smoke which should be obvious from a search of my pockets, but you know how it is with police and evidence.

I'm not trying to say all police are idiots and/or dishonest and/or plain bastards; of course, they aren't. But, and it's a big but, some of them are! These two were prime examples. One of them has a beard which tells you something, because the only people with beards in the nineteen eighties are Peter Sutcliffe and members of the Mujahedin.

The initial questioning is disturbing and ever so slightly entertaining:

"Why don't you just admit it son, you tried the job and couldn't pull it off?"

Guess who got a Sweeney video for his birthday? And is it necessary to twist my arm up my back as I am escorted into the station? I don't offer any resistance, that would be the stupid thing to do; they are after an excuse to give me a kicking. I have some idea that I can refuse to speak until I've seen "my brief" but since I don't actually have a "brief" I have to settle for a telephone conversation with a duty solicitor. He is a complete waste of space and quite obviously resents being woken up.

I am required to remove the laces from my shoes in case I am tempted to hang myself with them. How that is likely to happen since it is obvious that even combined, they are no longer than three inches is anyone's guess. They are in a very tatty state and if removed will almost certainly not go back into the shoes. Rather than risk hours of licking, squinting and threading when I eventually do get out of here, I opt to surrender by shoes instead. After this I am shoved into a cold cell for a few hours, at the end of which I make and sign a statement. I am chucked out onto the street as the sun is rising. I have no idea where I am.

You are probably wondering where all this vented spleen is leading, I shall tell you. The following day I have the mother of all cricked necks. I can hardly get out of bed. My head is permanently fixed to my shoulder and the pain when I move shoots across my scapula and down my arm. I don't know precisely what brought this on, perhaps sitting against a cold brick wall for hours? Maybe having my arm twisted up my back contributed? I cannot say for certain that Northumbria Police caused my cricked neck but the evidence for it stacked up better than the burglary rap they were trying to pin on me.

In great pain I hobbled to the University health practice.

"I don't like the look of that," the doctor said as I took of my shirt.

"What d'ya mean?"

"These spots. Hmm."

My back is still, at this time, decorated with the remains of tiny pimples caused by (I suspect) my medication, Azathioprine.

"I think they are from my Crohn's drugs," I suggest, but he doesn't seem to be listening.

"They look like shingles to me."

"Oh... Well you know best I suppose."

"I think we'll have you in and keep an eye on it."

With which I am admitted to some sort of residential clinic thing which I had no idea even existed. The cricked neck loosened off within a day or two but medical opinion was still holding onto shingles, so I was there for the best part of a week. I even sit a couple of my second-year exams in there; palaeontology and structural geology if I remember correctly. Of course, I don't have shingles, that pleasure is yet to come, and I go away wrapped in the same pimply skin I arrived in.

I suppose the doctor was just being cautious, which was ok; I am all for that kind of thing. It wasn't an unpleasant place to stay, a bit dull, but you can't expect dancing girls can you? And all that peace and quiet provided me with ample opportunity to plan my next pub heist.[56]

Late nineties and after years of failing to produce an heir to the Lenity millions my wife and I have applied to adopt (see "Test Tube Babies"). Quite correctly there is a long and involved process before they let you get your hands on any kids. Despite my criminal past (even burglars are entitled to a family) CM and I are invited for an interview. Mindful that it is important to make a good impression I have planned to shower and shave in the morning ensuring that I am not only pleasingly fragrant

---

[56] I have never perpetrated a heist of any kind.

but equally appealing to the eye.

The morning of the interview I know something is amiss the moment I try to lift my head from the pillow. I cannot do it for the pain. It runs right down my neck and deep into my shoulder, from there extends down my right arm such that it is difficult to use it for any useful purpose, such as washing and shaving.

I don't know what caused it, I couldn't blame the police for this one, I was outside of Northumbria's jurisdiction and of course South Yorkshire Police are beyond reproach in all matters.[57] I just put it down to a bad night's sleep, perhaps I was stressed at the prospect of the next day's scrutinising.

We arrive in the offices of Sheffield Council Adoption Service; CM smart and business-like, I walking sideways with my stubbled chin glued to my collarbone, my right arm limp and useless by my side and my face contorted with the pain of climbing the stairs. It is difficult to say who has the most peculiar expression, me squinting around my left shoulder or our interviewer, wide eyed and aghast that a woman of CM's obvious standing should have hitched herself to the Hunchback of Notre Dame.

"Have a seat Mr Modo."

"Oh please, call me Quasi."

Bizarrely, she is happy to recommend us as potential adoptive parents, so I don't know what that says about some of the other candidates.

---

[57] All that business with the miners' strike and the Hillsborough disaster was just a long catalogue of misunderstandings I am sure.

## Crohn's Disease

The summer of 1985 and I am in Lodge Moor hospital having just started treatment for my recently diagnosed Crohn's disease. One of the first things I learn is that no one is certain what causes it[58]. The key words I learn are *inflammation* and *autoimmune*. The first I have heard of and seems self-explanatory, the latter is a new one on me. It seems the body's defences can mistake its own cells for foreign invaders (bacteria, viruses and the like) and subsequently set about beating them up. Brilliant result, I have a stupid immune system.[59]

The good news, in so far as my stay here is concerned, is that I don't have TB, bovine or otherwise. In fact, I am not in the least bit infectious and henceforth I can leave my cell. It also means that my visitors aren't required to dip into the dressing-up box when they turn up.

Those patients capable of doing so have taken to eating communally in the corridor; I decide to join them. There's not a lot of room, but it relieves some of the isolation. It is here that I meet my next-door neighbour. Not the number shouter, the quiet one on the other side. He has contracted an infection that has eaten away one of his heart valves which now requires

[58] Over thirty years on and medicine is still in the dark on this point.

[59] The term "autoimmune" seems at that time to have been used as a catch-all explanation for diseases where the immune system goes a bit over the top. For many the term now does not apply to Crohn's in a strict sense since it is believed to be an over-reaction of the immune system to an external antigen (such as a bacterium) rather than to the body's own cells.

Just to confuse matters there is also a case for immunodeficiency, that is an underperforming immune system, to be at the root of it!

replacing. He isn't very happy about it.

"What happens if I get into a fight?" He asks me.

"Do you get into a lot of fights?"

"I live in Longley."

He has a valid concern; I don't think I can help him. If it was me I think I would be more perturbed about the impending open-heart surgery and consign duking-it-out down the park to the back burner. I am jumping to conclusions here, but I suspect he was a bit miserable before his diagnosis; he has that air about him. One of life's natural melancholics. He could look at it from the other direction and think: *aren't I lucky that this has been spotted in time and that medicine has a fix for it.* But he doesn't. Perhaps when he has gotten over the shock he might see it differently, though I doubt it; some people are just dyed-in-the-wool mopers. Mopers don't make for good company by the way. But all that is very easy for me to say, I'm not facing the knife am I?

In contrast to Heart Valve is Sugared Custard. Sugared Custard is African. He doesn't say much, his English is rudimentary and so I learn very little of him. He has the blackest skin I have ever seen and he keeps it in tip-top condition by cleansing and oiling his body every evening. This is not the image of black Africans we are used to in 1985, having been fed on a diet of famine appeals and Idi Amin. I have never known a man who moisturises his face let alone his body. The closest I can think of are those Channel swimmers on telly and slapping on an inch of lard is a far cry from the fine oils and unguents in action here. Surprisingly, he has magnificent teeth too, which are on display a lot because he is quite the smiler. I say *surprising*ly because he has what seems to me to be an abnormally sweet tooth. He puts sugar on everything, even custard. Why are his teeth in such good nick? We have custard every night here, they should be shot through with amalgam like mine.

On a couple of occasions, and without explanation, we are ushered to our rooms and all doors and curtains are closed. The matron in charge of the ward is a stickler for protocol and doesn't let on but my guess is that someone down the way has pegged it and they are in the process of wheeling the body-bag away. This is confirmed by one of the nurses, she speaks in a hushed voice, not so much out of reverence as from fear of being heard by Matron.

Heart Valve has gone, and not in a bag if that is what you are wondering. In his place I have a new friend, N... who has a mystery condition. He is my age and has been in and out of hospital for one thing or another for years. He is quite a contrast to Heart Valve and despite his deadpan voice it is obvious he can see the funny side to his hospital career. He tells me a story about how he had a test that required him to have a full bladder. He held on so long that in the end he couldn't actually go and was left wracked in pain; eventually a nurse helped him into a warm bath and coaxed it out. I'm hoping I never have to be in that position, that big, moustachioed nurse is desperate for an excuse to leer over me. N... has a number of interesting medical stories; someone should compile them, it would make a good book.

Happy that I am on the mend I am sent back to the bosom of my family. Because of the steroids I have to carry what looks like a wartime ration card in case I'm in an accident[60]. It is not a good idea to stop steroids suddenly; it makes you poorly.

---

[60] In addition to wearing clean underpants.

We have an impromptu holiday, three days in a Whitby B&B. It leaves me with an abiding memory of delicious fish and chips; of which I consumed prodigious amounts.

I am starting to get spotty. A result of the steroids. This is annoying since I have only recently got shot of my home-grown plukes. For some reason that I have since forgotten I am given a course of metronidazole[61], an antibiotic. What I have not forgotten is the effect it has on me; I spew my guts up. I don't know why because I have had it since with no problem.

My weight is back to normal in a matter of weeks, in no small part down to the Nutrinel cartons which I am going though like a plague of EN locusts.[62]

## Cysts

A cyst is a closed sac that develops within tissue, rather in the manner of a bubble forming, and is filled with fluid or air or some or other gunk. I have had a few cysts, none of which (I am glad to say) were cancerous. Cysts can, supposedly, disappear of their own accord but mine don't seem to. They just get big and cause trouble.

My first one of note is on my jaw line, it starts out as a small pimple-type lump which resolutely refuses to be squeezed. Soon it is the size of a two pence piece in length and egg shaped. It alters the outline of my face which now has a prominent lump on the left-hand side. To make matters worse it is a hairy lump as no amount of gurning and skin stretching can make the thing shaveable with my Braun micron[63]. After

---

[61] Street name Flagyl
[62] Elemental Nutrition
[63] The knobbly one that was supposed to look like a Porche driving in a spiky landscape

about a year of this I finally seek medical advice which results in a charming lady at Newcastle's Freeman Hospital cutting it from my numbed-up face using a pair of scissors. I can't see what was going on, but it rasps in a way you would imagine scissors cutting through gristle ought to. I still have a faint scar along my jaw if you look closely. Not that anyone ever does.

Next, I move on to my eyes and on two separate occasions grow cysts on my eyelids. One in the region of the lash on a lower lid, the other smack in the middle of an upper one which produces a gritty, scratching sensation across my eyeball every time I blink which, I am told, humans do fifteen times a minute on average.[64]

I'm not looking forward to the removal of these. Anything to do with eyes adds another dimension to my fear. Perhaps because they are so integral to the way we interpret the world? And they're so damn delicate; at least they feel that way. I remember as a small child hearing stories of people rolling up an eyelid on a matchstick in order to remove a bit of grit. The alternative being to get a friend to stick his (or preferably her) tongue in and lick the mote out, which was the practice employed in the steelworks hereabouts. Both prospects sounded horrific to me. Despite being drawn to the scent of Optrex, I've never been able to properly use an eyebath, try as I might I cannot open my eye in that little blue chamber. Preciousness about my eyes stayed with me and so the thought of someone going at my cyst with a blade was a bit scary. What if they sneezed half-way through and stuck me one bang in the orb?

As with many procedures the anticipation is far worse than the event. The cutting was nothing, a mere flick of the scalpel; the

---

[64] More if you are on *the pill* or if you are a natural sceptic.

eyedrops that proceed it are the most unpleasant part.

Mid-thirties and the next port of call for the carbuncle cruise is my back; my left shoulder blade, just above what remains of my main youth hostelling scar (see "Audi Coupe"). This one, it was apparent during the initial *growing period,* was going to beat my personal best as far as diameter was concerned, outstripping my chin cyst in days. Soon it is clear that this baby is progressing to a new level. It is beginning to look angry; bright red and hot to the touch. Add to this the pain it is kicking out and you don't need to be Kildare to realise there is infection going on. This presents a bit of a pickle for me; ordinarily a dose of antibiotics would be prescribed but antibiotics have a destabilising effect on the guts. I avoid antibiotics where possible, preferring to tough things out rather than risk a Crohn's flare-up.

Another four days and the good news is that there is a faint yellow hue just below the skin in its centre. The bad news is that just touching it hurts like buggery and even dosed up on whisky and 'brufen the pain of squeezing is intolerable. And, for that matter, ineffective, as the skin at the apex doesn't show any signs of giving. The thing that really hastens my recourse to the GP is that I feel so ill! Really bad; febrile, weak, nauseated.

I explain my aversion to antibiotics to the GP and he takes my point.

"I can lance it for you?" he says.

"I thought you'd say that; yes please." I am so pissed off with the state of me I would have been just as amenable to: *I can take it off with the angle grinder if you're game?*

I have since (via the miracle of YouTube) watched a number of lancings and they all seem to begin with a series of Novocain injections in and around the offending lump. I wasn't offered any of that, it was shirt off and dig in. And when I say *dig in*, I mean *dig in!* I had assumed it would just be a case of nicking the surface and releasing the pressure but no. There's a whole load of probing and sawing involved followed by several minutes of squeezing. Of course, with it being on my back I can't see what is going on, but I see the cheesy gunk on the numerous swabs applied and I am shocked by the volume of it. My biggest surprise, however, is how quickly I start to feel well. It is almost instantaneous. I have gone from feeling like a walking corpse to perfectly well in a matter of minutes. It was like, I imagine, being cured by the spirit of Jesus at one of those evangelical affairs. Satan's poorliness was driven from me! I felt like dancing home.[65]

The good thing about an infected cyst (and it is the only positive I can think of) is the joy of seeing all that cheesy, bloody, soupy crud exuding, and it was a bit of a disappointment that I couldn't get a decent view. I felt for poor CM too, as I know she would have relished the experience going on how much she enjoyed my cheesy chest hole (see "Dermo"). Luckily, just like CCH, a decent sized infected cyst is a gift that keeps giving and by the end of the evening it has refilled sufficiently to provide the missus with a decent bit of sport to round off the week.

Whilst my cyst had been drained, it hadn't been excised, that is to say, removed, and when the wound heals there still remains a small, raised area under the skin. Nothing significant, about the size of an almond and completely painless. It stays that way for about seven years and then out of the blue starts to grow again. Growth becomes infection as the cyst reverts to its previous angry form. Off to the GP again, this time a different

---

[65] I didn't; can't be doing with all that Billy Elliot nonsense.

practice as we have moved house in the intervening years.

"You'll probably need antibiotics." I'm told

"Rather not; couldn't you just lance it?"

"I don't think it's quite ready. Come back in a few days."

I return three days later to be told it is still unripe. Three days after that he (grudgingly) agrees to stick it. This time I am lain on the examination table, face down, head on hands while he goes about stabbing and squeezing. A lot more squeezing than the previous lancing and it took twice as long, presumably because it wasn't quite full-on juicy. Nevertheless, he gets a good crop of gunk out of it, so he isn't chopping for nothing.

All well and good you might think. Well, yes, except that when I try to get off the table I have lost use of my right arm. It is completely numb. So much so that I can't make it move in any way. It just hangs limply at my side.

"Probably just a bit of pins and needles." I am assured on pointing out my problem.

"I don't think so. It doesn't feel like pins and needles. I really can't do anything with it!"

"Pins and needles. It will go in a minute."

Why don't some people listen to what you are saying? I leave feeling a little panicky and wondering how I am going to drive the truck home. Luckily, from the driving aspect, it is my right arm that has gone AWOL and so I can still change gears and I manage to get myself home one handed and without hitting anyone or anything. It's actually quite difficult to get out of a car with a dead arm, particularly on a drive as narrow and steep as ours. I have to reach across myself to the door lever[66] and open it by transferring my weight to the right at which point my lifeless limb falls out of the car dragging the rest of me with it. Not very edifying.

CM looks at me like I am a lunatic when I explain the situation and demonstrate by using my left arm to hoist up and subsequently drop its lazy sibling. Although on the face of it I am making light of the thing, inwardly I am getting quite worried; it has been an hour since the lancing.

After two hours I begin to get a little feeling in my fingers and shortly after that regain control of my hand. Three hours and my whole arm is responding to the signals my brain is sending it, though, it has to be said, not with the same enthusiasm I had come to expect of it. It is as if I am learning to use my arm again. By the evening it is responding tolerably and I am just about able to knock a squash ball around a court. By morning it is its old self again.

What had occurred remains a mystery; I still maintain the pins and needles diagnosis was flawed. The only thing I can think of is perhaps a pinched nerve in my neck or shoulder caused by lying on my front, perhaps due to the position of my head. Who knows?

Now that my dead arm is back to normal, I can get on with the business of enjoying what remains of the abscess. This episode is even better than the previous one. Where before the

---

[66] I have since learned that this manoeuvre is now known as the Dutch Reach and is the recommended way of exiting a car in Holland. The premise being that it gives you more chance of spotting cyclists who would otherwise splatter themselves on the inside of your door. There are a lot of cyclists in Holland.

refreshed gunk eased out with a steady flow (like squeezing a tube of Primula cheese spread) this time it fires out like a bazooka. I can shoot a glob of bloody-yellow matter a good seven feet across the room. I delight my wife with it, perplex my kids and, when I perform it in the shower at the squash club it sends four grown men running in naked fear.

This is not the end of story. Years on Old Yellow returns. In the interests of the narrative I have saved that account for later. (See "Wow that's a big 'un!")

# D is for...
## DALM
See "Under the Knife"

## Dark Arts

There is a period, relatively early in my Crohn's career, when things are looking less rosy than I might have hoped. I've had a few flare-ups and have received the usual prednisolone treatment which, for the most part, has worked. However, by the summer of 1986 this methodology seems to be failing; the illness waxes and wanes, I struggle to function, and weight falls off me. It is a time of disillusionment with the medical profession, particularly for my mother, and I have a vivid memory of her referring to Dr McK... as *a twat*. Which is quite unlike my mother and a bit unfair on the doctor, but it reflects the strength of feeling at the time.

In light of conventional medicine's floundering my mother

goes proactive; she joins NACC[67] and takes herself to Southey Library in search of knowledge; in particular, alternative therapies. If you are expecting aromatherapy, hypnosis, reflexology or homeopathy here then think again; my mother's research was more Denis Wheatly, Aleister Crowley, Samantha Stevens[68].

The theory, as I understand it, requires that the evil (in this case Crohn's disease) can be transferred to another host which is subsequently interred. As the new host corrupts so does the bane. One might suspect that this requires a degree of occultic shenanigans; incantations, full moons, transmigration of energies and the like. Not so. My cure consists of rubbing a rasher of bacon on my belly and then burying it in the front garden.

My situation improves. Could the rasher be responsible? Or is it the recent introduction of azathioprine? Who knows? I shall not gainsay the black arts; no doubt they employ mechanisms far too enigmatic for our staid, mortal minds to construe. However, I have a strong suspicion that Barney (one of our dogs) dug up and ate the bacon within a week of it going under the sod.[69]

## Death

We have all, I am sure, at some time or other, made reference to *feeling like death*, or *feeling like I was dying*, or some other

---

[67] National Association for Crohn's and Colitis; now called Crohn's and Colitis UK. I still have a little printed card assuring that the bearer is *non-contagious and desperate for a dump*; I paraphrase of course.

[68] As played by Elizabeth Montgomery in the sitcom *Bewitched*. Coincidentally Elizabeth Montgomery died of colon cancer.

[69] Spookily, Barney died barely fifteen years after this event!

trope along those lines. Obviously in the vast majority of cases this is just hyperbole; not something to be taken literally. There have been plenty of times I have felt awful and used such phrases but on none of these occasions did I *actually* feel like I was stepping aboard the last train to glory.

Crohn's disease does not, as a rule, kill you; that's one of the few positive things I can say about it. Of course, it can have its complications and it can pave the way for other things such as cancer which can certainly send you into the arms of Abraham but in general terms it is not a terminal illness. So far, and I consider myself fortunate in this respect, I have steered clear of anything where there is a good chance that I might pop my clogs. However, I am now in my sixth decade, a quinquagenarian, which statistically speaking makes the prospect of that "...we have some bad news Mr Lenity..." conversation ever more likely. I am not sure how I feel about that.

What will I do when it comes to the crunch? When I face death? Do I devote myself to some worthy cause? Or do I maximise my time with the people I love and inflict myself on my family? Alternatively, I could take the hedonist route and dive headlong into a world of sin.[70] I cannot say. I suspect that I would carry on much as before and try not to think about it too much. That all assumes that I am afforded some degree of warning. What if I am hit by a train? Or if I jump out of a window in my sleep?

---

[70] I suspect a steep learning curve awaits me. I'll start with leaving the toilet seat in an upright position and see where Satan takes from there

(Again!) What if a sniper takes me out with a head shot?[71] Is that better than a slow demise? I have often heard people subscribe to that view, but I am not sure it is necessarily right in this age of sophisticated pain management. *Different strokes for different folks* as the Americans say.[72]

And are we actually discussing death here? Or are we looking at the journey towards it? Is it, then, really the thought of getting there that gives us the willies. What happens when the last breath leaves us; is that worth worrying about? Is there something else on the itinerary or do we simply just end? Is there an afterlife or is that just something we have made up to dull death's sting? And if there is an afterlife, is it worth bothering with? An eternity of harp plucking and clean living is not doing it for me I have to say. And as for the seventy-two virgins; imagine what a pain in the arse that lot would be!

I quite like the Biocentric approach to all this, which postulates that time is just a creation of animal consciousness and as such death does not exist. To quote Dr Robert Lanza: "… at death, we reach the imagined border of ourselves…", which seems way too deep for this book; a work in which the recurring theme is of a middle-aged Yorkshireman having a poo.

## Dermo Stuff
(see also "Shingles")

That is to say, my skin and its tribulations. I am quite made up when my first teenage pimple appears. It is on my chin. Although it provides little in the way of sport, at the age of

---

[71] I never sit in exposed windows or light more than two cigarettes per match. It's not worth chancing.

[72] This has nothing to do with cerebrovascular accidents, swimming or onanism.

thirteen it represents a signal that manhood is on the way. Bring on the ladies!

Had I known that this first, insignificant blemish was just a pre-curser for the tide of volcanic custard that would ensue I doubt I would have been so enthusiastic. At first, coverage is nothing significant, I am averagely spotty. Then I make the mistake of growing my hair long which, as you will become aware (see "Follicular Issues") is very thick at this juncture. Thick and with a propensity to develop into ringlets. If I'd had the foresight to go to a decent barber I could have had a sexy Marc Bolan thing going on, but I don't; I leave it to its own, feral devices. Part of the problem is that I rarely wash it because a dose of shampoo turns me into Hair Bear[73]. Untamed, greasy and hanging over my face and shoulders, my locks allow the pimple hordes to run wild. Face, neck and shoulders are covered and it takes me two years to see sense and get a haircut, after which my skin miraculously clears up. Thankfully, and despite my own poor judgement, I manage to get through the traditional acne years without significant scarring.

*Ha! I pity the fool,* as B. A. Baracas would say[74]. Not to make too fine a point of it, steroids bugger up your skin. It doesn't need the assistance of long greasy hair; Prednis-alone is sufficient[75]. Within weeks of starting on steroids the zits begin to appear and fairly soon have taken over my face, neck, chest and back.

---

[73] Help!…It's the Hair Bear Bunch, a Hanna-Barbera cartoon from the early Seventies. Set in the Wonderland Zoo and featuring three hippy bears who live in a luxury cave and ride around on an invisible motorbike. Based on a true story. See also "Tingly Brain" re. Bob Ross.
[74] Mr T actually trademarked the phrase.
[75] Clever word play there. I wonder if anyone else has used that one.

The larger pustules are an absolute joy to squeeze which I suspect only helps to propagate them. Often, they pop of their own accord and many mornings I get out of bed to find blood and pus on the sheets. They persist even after I've stopped taking steroids which seems a bit unfair. In an effort to dry them up I try a topical benzoyl peroxide cream which is not without success. However, that stuff is really only for your face. If you plaster it all over your torso, as I did, you find that your shirts rot away.

Because of the risk of upsetting the bowel I generally avoid oral antibiotics which is a standard treatment for acne, however topical versions are available. These, particularly clindamycin, I find work quite well, particularly if combined with a bit of sunshine. If you are the sensitive type and choose to go down the phototherapy route, I recommend the privacy of your own back garden rather than stripping off on the beach at Bournemouth as I did. People can be quite hurtful at times; even complete strangers. But then I did look like I had been attacked by killer bees, so it was only to be expected.

As a postscript to my steroid-induced acne periods I am left with some scarring, though thankfully nothing that I would call pockmarking. The only residual effect of note was a cavity in the skin over the centre of my breastbone. Without ever looking angry or raised this little cave was full of thick, creamy matter which was readily exhumed by a little gentle squeezing. If this wasn't prize enough, the stuff also smelled very strongly of cheese. It is a great joy to my girlfriend (soon to be wife) that her man should be in possession of such a wondrous gift and she looks forward with relish to our weekly cheesings. Yes, correct, *weekly* cheesings. My blessed chest cave has the ability to replenished itself; a bit like Wolverine but slower and more dairy-fied.

This phenomenon no doubt pushed us towards getting hitched; CM must have realised that if she didn't get me tied down[76] pretty sharpish some bitch would move in and the deeds to the cheddar mine would be whipped from under her nose.

Sadly, these days, my gift lies dormant, we have had no gunk from it in years and I have to rely on sexual prowess alone to keep our marriage together.

I have always had something of a tendency to flush, particularly after a jar or two. There is one old photograph taken in a sweaty bierkeller in Birmingham which illustrates this clearly; a red mask across the top of my cheeks and nose. As I enter my forties, I notice that this red mask is becoming a permanent feature. Am I developing a drinker's flush? That's what it looks like to me and also (I know) to some of my more judgemental relatives. I have the misfortune to require a new passport around this time and the photo that lies within is testament to the degree that this took hold; I looked like I've been scalded. Indeed, after a time my cheeks became permanently tender, bordering on painful. Small pimples are opening up on my nose and despite the sport to be enjoyed from popping them I know action is needed. It is time to consult a physician before my conk turns into a huge strawberry.

Acne rosacea is the verdict, rosacea for short and I come away from the surgery with a prescription for a topical antibiotic gel, metronidazole to be precise. One might infer from this that rosacea is a form of skin infection, after all antibiotics are for killing bugs aren't they? But this doesn't seem to be the case.

---

[76] Matrimonially speaking, not literal restraint or anything like that

The causes of rosacea are unknown and the previously named culprits (alcohol, exercise, hot and cold environments) are merely exacerbators[77]. Metronidazole's efficacy is thought to come from its anti-inflammatory properties. Not that it was particularly efficacious to me, that is.

This reference to inflammation strikes a familiar chord and I do a little more digging on the internet. Indeed, a link to IBD has been proposed but little beyond that. In the absence of a sure-fire cure I decide to remove or restrict the potential irritants. According to my limited and unscientific research the main triggers cited by sufferers are: cosmetics and skin care products, spicy food and cheese (i.e. my diet), saunas (which I love), alcohol, tea and coffee (my three favourite addictions). I decide to embark on a process of elimination, opting to ditch cosmetics and skin care products first and pray it does the trick. I begin washing my face with water only and eschew shower gels and shampoo[78] in favour of old-fashioned soap for the rest of my bod. It works within a couple of weeks and I celebrate by taking a sauna then going on a prolonged beer and curry binge.

Whilst we are on the subject of cosmetics, for years now I have avoided underarm deodorants. Like every other fool who believed the lie that it is unnatural to smell like a human being I went for many years caking my pits in the stuff. I never fell for the one about anti-perspirants, though; you've got to sweat from somewhere after all. My change in habits happened suddenly in the mid-nineties when I start getting sore pits. It

---

[77] I always thought *The Exacerbator* would make a good name for a wrestler.

[78] Not a big shampoo user these days.

is probably contact dermatitis[79] and once I have ditched the roll-on it clears up. I never go back. The weird thing is that I seem to have less b.o. smell without deodorant than I do with a daily application. These days I go at them with a flannel as and when required and give myself a squirt of magnesium oil and a puff of talcum to round off the job[80]. Seems to work.

## Diabetes

There seems to be a general consensus (amongst those that know about such things) that we are on the cusp of a diabetes pandemic. That is to say, of the Type 2 variety, the one where insulin stops working as it used to.[81] Once considered a western disease the combination of genetic factors and increasingly affluent diet is bringing T2D to the rest of the world.

Although we in the UK are routinely tested for diabetes once we hit middle age my particular route in came through an investigation into the underlying reasons for my recurrent urinary tract infections (see "Prostate"). I have what is termed the A1C test which, to chop out the detail, gives you an average

---

[79] I think this was probably the reason for my cracked hands during my pie making years. See "Callouses and Cracks"

[80] It seems I need to make a correction here. What I have called magnesium oil, that is Epsom salts (magnesium sulphate) in water, is not strictly accurate. True magnesium oil is a solution of the chloride. Apparently, this is absorbed through the skin more efficiently though I am not sure why since they both consist of the same magnesium ions in solution.

[81] Rather than Type 1 diabetes whereby the body does not produce enough insulin. There is also a Type 1.5 or Latent Autoimmune Diabetes in Adults (LADA) which is less well publicised partly due to its association with shit Russian cars.

of your blood sugar over the previous couple of months. This shows nothing out of the ordinary. I also have a fasting blood sugar test which measures glucose level at a single point in time immediately after fasting. I am told at the time that my results are nothing out of the ordinary.

Months later I receive, completely out of the blue, a letter telling me to attend the GP surgery to talk to a nurse about diabetes. This is a bit of a surprise. I attend and am given a brief explanation of my test levels and asked a few questions. Apparently, someone had been going through my notes and has now decided that I might be pre-diabetic.

"Do you eat a lot of sweet foods?"

"No."

"Do you do any exercise."

"I play squash three times a week, lift weights, walk the dog every day, occasionally run."

"Good. Can I weigh you?"

"Sixty-nine kilograms. How tall are you?"

"Five ten or thereabouts."

She uses a ruler to plot my BMI on her little chart.[82]

"That puts you right in the middle of the healthy weight range. That's good."

"Correct me if I am wrong but I don't think I necessarily fit the criteria here. Could the test be wrong?"

She looks me up and down.

"I see what you mean. We can repeat it."

We do. I am still Pre D. I am encouraged to join a diabetes workshop.

I decline. Without wanting to sound like someone who

---

[82] Body Mass Index

propagates stereotypes, there is no way I am sitting in a room full of morbidly obese people being told to cut back on things I don't eat anyway and encouraged to perform activities I am already performing. And what sort of message does it send out to the other workshoppers? They will look at me and think: *What's the point? Even if we get as thin as that boney bastard we're still not out of the mire.*[83]

The nurse quite understands my reticence and instead steers me towards online resources. Because I don't eat anything much in the way of what we traditionally think of as sugary foods, biscuits, cakes, sweets, chocolate and the like, if I have been sending myself towards T2D then it must be through some other source. Beer springs to mind, there are plenty of calories in that, and then there are starches, I really enjoy my carbs, having a good old bowl of porridge every morning, and I can eat rice and pasta till it is coming out of my ears. Fruit has natural sugars and I do eat a couple of apples a day, a banana and a handful of dates with my breakfast. It would seem, then, that if I do need to cut back on something there are plenty of options at my disposal. But do I need to cut back?

My pre-diabetes diagnosis is based on the fasting test results; all the AIC results, (i.e. the ones that are low) are ignored. And this is my argument: surely an average score is more representative than a snapshot in time? No one seems to listen;

---

[83] I know, it's perfectly possible that I am a TOFI, that is to say thin outside fat inside. It's the fat built up in the liver and pancreas that causes the problems; multiple chins and bingo wings are just the outward signs. However, there is a lot of biochemistry at play here and I don't think it is as simple as just accusing people of being lazy and greedy.

they just keep trying to push me towards the workshop again. I might be wrong, but I think this has all stemmed from money. A pot of cash has been found from somewhere; there are always initiatives to push something or other and in this case it was probably T2D screening.

I do try cutting back on a few carbs, but it doesn't last very long and I daresay there is merit in revisiting the idea at some time but back then, the winter of 17/18, my concerns were focussed on tooth, and then bowel problems and the issue of by pre-diabetes is kicked deep into the long grass. It is still there.

## Diagnostic Imaging

In the old days this was the X-ray department. There was little reason to call it anything other than the X-ray department[84] as the choice of techniques available to doctors were a bit limited then. However, once ultrasound and PET and CT and MRI and all the others turned up then "X-ray" just didn't cut it anymore. Instead, the phrase diagnostic imaging was adopted, which means just what it says, creating pictures to use in diagnosis.

Considering how much reliance is placed on these techniques now it makes you wonder how much guess work went on before they were available. When I was first diagnosed with Crohn's disease, Sheffield, as far as I know, did not have either an MRI or CT scanner. I was, though, given an ultrasound which seemed like a novelty at the time; it was then just something that pregnant women, not teenage boys were subjected to. That said, having a jellied belly and an instrument that looked like a sawn-off hair dryer rubbed over me was perfectly pleasant and I had no complaints. Years later I have

---

[84] A case could be made for the use of *Radiology* or *Roentgenography*.

an ultrasound to look at my bladder (see Prostate), which for the duration of the scan needed to be full to bursting; that was less pleasant.

Because of the difficulty in negotiating a colonoscope around the various obstacles in my bowel (see reference to strictures in "Growing (Further) Up") I am given a CT scan to take a look at what is lurking beyond the bottlenecks. To be perfectly honest, I don't remember too much about this. I think I take laxatives beforehand but that is about it. I lie on a bench, then told to hold my breath whilst a large doughnut moves back and forth over my tummy. That is to say, the equivalent of me being inserted into a ring. I do remember it is relatively quick, completely painless and, all in all, not much of a story but I include it in the interest of completeness.

The MRI scan, however, is a much more interesting experience. If memory serves me I've had three MRIs, two to look at inflammation in my ileum and one to have a gander of my prostate.

For the bowel MRI I am required to drink a couple of pints of what I think is contrast medium, in this way the inside of the gut shows up better on the scan. It is not a pleasant taste, a bit metallic, but I have had worse. Unfortunately, the stuff has a real laxative effect on me, and within minutes I am running to the toilet as if my life depends on it. Contrast medium is also pumped into me through a canula, presumably to look at blood vessels and the like.

In comparison to the CT scan, where the instrument (doughnut) moved around me, with the MRI it is I who does the moving. Neither is it doughnut shaped; it is a thick-walled tube that the bench on which I am lying slides into. The first thing that strikes me is how claustrophobic it is; I am on the verge of a minor panic. All quite irrational too, I am going in feet first and my head never comes close to being inside and yet there's me sweating like anything. I think it is the sensation of not being able to move, my arms are by my sides as I slip in and I am required to hold my breath for periods during the scan which all combines to give me the sensation of being restrained. On this occasion I am lying on my back, for the prostate MRI I am on my front which is physically uncomfortable but not nearly as claustrophobic. I wonder whether being on my back conjures up some deep fear of death as there is a decidedly coffin-like atmosphere to being in the thing.

MRIs take ages. Well, in comparison to the CT scan they do, although the sense of time may be stretched due to any discomfort or irrational fears you may be experiencing.

They are loud. Really loud! A series of whirrs, screeches, clicks and clangs that would be deafening if it wasn't for the headphones you are wearing. It put me very much in mind of the Berlin based experimental music group Einstürzende Neubauten[85] but without the Germanic vocals. It's very *industrial sounding* but there is a distinct rhythm to aspects of it and by the end of the scan I have really got into the groove.

## Diarrhoea

Of course, this comes as part of the IBD package but for me (prior to surgery) runny poo[86] has never been my biggest problem. Obviously, this is just my experience; I know some people's lives are blighted by it. That's not to say I haven't had

---

[85] Which translates as *collapsing new buildings*

[86] I am speaking anything from Bristol Stool Scale 5 upwards

my moments, i.e. flare-ups, but for the most part when they have happened, I have managed to cope with the urgency. I consider myself very lucky in this respect.

See: "Lethargy", "Crohn's Disease", & "What it's like to have no colon".

## Dry Socket
See "Teeth"

## Duvets
See "Nocturnal Emissions"

## Dysplasia
See "Under the Knife"

# E is for...
## Earache
As a child I suffer regular bouts of earache. What this is down to is anyone's guess. I am prescribed antibiotics because in the 1970s patients are always given antibiotics whether the ailment requires them or not. These antibiotics came in the form of a pink syrup which despite its sugar content still leaves a residual, foul-bitter taste in your mouth. I dislike taking it and as soon as the symptoms show sign of abating, I stop. Not only do I receive numerous courses of unnecessary drugs (we have drawers full of clear plastic medicine spoons) I also compound matters by never actually finishing any of them. Antibiotics can kill off gut bacteria as well as their intended targets and I wonder what sort of effect all that medication had on me long term.

Although no explicit link is cited the general consensus of all my ear examiners is that I have a surfeit of earwax. I knew this anyway because it is flagged-up by the nit nurse during my first year at infant school. My poor mother is mortified when she comes to pick me up and I am standing in the school yard looking vacant and waving the same yellow, "further action needed...", slip of paper that all the smelly kids are clutching.[87]

I think I have inherited my wax generating propensities from my father who was forever poking around in his ears mining the stuff; his handkerchiefs always had that yellow/brown camouflage to them.

Although, in the main, it has been only an aesthetic issue for me, there have been times, I think due to compaction, when it has left me a little deaf in one or both ears. Nothing debilitating, just akin to the sensation you feel when swimming underwater. In order to alleviate this I am recommended olive oil. Apparently, a small amount poured into the ear canal can loosen things up; I deem it worth a go. CM agrees to help, and I lie on the bed while she hovers over me with the bottle of extra virgin. What I need is a tiny drizzle, a barely discernible tilt of the bottle, so it is probably a mistake to enlist my ham-fisted wife in the operation. I cop for about half a pint; it is seeping out of my eyes and nose; I can taste the stuff. I persevere with the therapy staying perfectly still for about an hour, my earhole brimming with olive oil like some sort of gristle-sided infinity pool. Eventually it becomes obvious that it isn't going to dissipate and so we mop it out with a towel. Next time I shall

---

[87] You'll probably point out that headlice actually prefer clean hair. Well that may be, but I know what I know and the kids with the slips were the ones who smelled like hamster cages. Possibly because the parents of the other kids did something about it when the scratching started.

use an eye dropper.

On one occasion I have cause to get my ears syringed. I know nothing about the procedure and, being cowardly, I am apprehensive; there's something about the word "syringe" I think. I have no need to fear. From the name you would imagine a procedure whereby a wad of gunk is sucked out of the side of the head, emerging with resounding pop. What actually ensues is the insertion of a small probe through which warm water is pumped into the ear canal. It has a mild hammering action which dislodges the wax allowing it to drain out into the bowl on my shoulder. It is a thoroughly pleasant sensation and I am surprised it hasn't been adopted for recreational use. See "ASMR."

## Elimination Diet
See "Flare-up"

## Embrocation
Whatever happened to embrocation? For that matter what about unguent and unction? Liniment anyone? Actually, they are still around but the names have been changed; they have just fallen victim to marketing. We still rub things into our flesh but these days they are called gels or muscle rub or massage oil. Modern terms that do not make the sufferer feel like they are being treated with something that was designed to remedy a damaged fetlock. I refer here to Dr Sloan (he of the soup-strainer moustache) and his famous liniment which was suitable for both humans and horses and claimed to treat pretty much everything. Along with Players No.6 it is one of the abiding smells of my childhood, my parents and grandparents were practically pickled in the stuff.

My favourite embrocation is Fiery Jack, which is another Lenity tradition albeit with a less pungent scent and as such has tended to occupy a less prominent position in my olfactory memory. Fiery Jack was basically Vaseline laced with napalm[88]. It was sold in a little old-fashioned tin which, in case there was any doubt about its potency, carried a picture of Satan on the lid. It was made by a company called J Pickles in Knaresborough. If you can think of a pharmaceutical company more stereotypically Yorkshire than that, please let me know. Sadly, it has been discontinued; I'm not sure why.

My first encounter (dermatologically speaking) with Fiery Jack comes when I am a child. I have been suffering with a twisted ankle or heel pain or something along those lines; it is the kind of thing that an adult would just run off or learn to live with. Naive that I am I take my complaint to my mother (the same one that tried to cure my Crohn's with witchcraft you will recall) and she offers to massage it with Fiery Jack. I agree and I lie on the settee, my foot across my mother's knee, thinking what a pleasant experience it is to have this stuff applied. The problem with Fiery Jack is the delay; the heat doesn't kick in straight away. By the time I start to feel the burn there is a half inch coating of grease across my ankle, foot and calf; she must have gone through a full tin! Why she put so much on I do not know, unless she has used so much of it on herself that she is now inured to the effects, but that scarcely excuses plastering it on her young, capsaicin virgin of a son. I am in agony! I try to wipe it off with bog roll which is no help because it clings like anything. And sitting on the draining board with one foot in the kitchen sink dousing it under a torrent of cold water is equally ineffective because grease-based embrocation acts like

---

[88] Actually capsaicin, the active ingredient in chilli peppers

dubbin; my foot has never been so waterproof! The only remedy is time, and I spend the evening and part of the next day waiting for the pain to go. On the positive side it really takes the mind off my original ankle problem.

Strange though this may sound, this situation repeats itself years later. CM suffers with back problems and one evening when she is at a particular low ebb, I suggest a dose of the old FJ. She agrees, and I duly perform a brief massage with the embrocation which, with hindsight, is probably applied a little too liberally. I don't know what I am thinking; I have completely ignored my previous experiences with the substance. Neither do I consider CM's notoriously low pain threshold. We finish up hosing her down with cold water in the shower which I tell her is a waste of time, but she is having none of it. Her back is a sheet of scarlet. I look back on that evening and wonder if I have a touch of sadist to my character because despite the pathos of all her sobbing and mewling, I can't help but laugh. Not something I am proud of. That said, she was in no danger and as with the ankle of my childhood, it did put the pain of original affliction in some sort of context.

## Erectile Dysfunction
See "Old Age and Getting There"

## Eyes
IBD can affect the eyes in a couple of ways: through inflammation associated with inflammation in the gastro-intestinal tract, and through secondary routes such as the prolonged use of steroids or vitamin deficiencies following gut resections. My first term at university and I notice that, at times, I am struggling to focus visually; I put this down to either steroid use, or from looking at baked beans down

microscopes for hours on end.[89] I am wrong on both counts; it turns out that I just have crap eyesight.

See also "Cysts", "Head Size"

# F is for
## Fainting.

Also known as syncope, from the Greek to cut off, since fainting is caused by a shortage of blood and thus oxygen to (i.e. it's cut off from) the brain. I get a mild form of this at times when I stand up quickly as my blood pressure is occasionally a touch on the low side. However, I have never gone the full way and flopped over doing that so I shall skip it in this instance[90].

As far as I can remember I have (so far) fainted four times: once as a child with a stomach bug, once aged nine-ish through prescription drugs, once with a back problem (see "Lumbar"), and once when I hit my elbow with a large rock and convince myself that it's broken[91]. It isn't and why that should set me off with a dose of the vapours I don't know. The drug episode is funny (in a way) since it happens at the breakfast table and leaves me face down in my Rice Krispies; I nearly drown.

For anyone who hasn't experienced fainting, there is a lot of confusion, strange sounds and swirly lights. I find it thoroughly unpleasant (and at times embarrassing) and I don't recommend it.

---

[89] Microfossils, specifically ostracods which look a lot like baked beans

[90] Not enough salt in my diet I have been told. I'm not sure if this is due to Crohn's, surgery or just a lack of bacon sarnies.

[91] My elbow, not the rock.

## Farting
See "Wind"

## Fasting
See "Yoghurt, Fasting and Staying Well"

## Feet
I take a UK size 8 to 8.5 in a shoe which I am led to believe is about the average in such matters. This is not surprising since I am of average height, 5 feet 10 inches in my twenties, but less these days. It has always perplexed me therefore when I have been accused of having small feet. It is only since our eldest daughter Bruce started growing up that CM and I have worked out the reason; small toes! She has my toes, which are small and stubby. I have never noticed it before but stubby toes, when juxtaposed with the rest of an otherwise normally sized foot have the effect of making the whole appear smaller than the sum of the parts. Bruce, alas, is far worse off than me because the rest of her foot actually *is* quite small and in shape matches the broad, swollen, troll-style sported by her mother. Thankfully, what she lost on the aesthetics she gained on the VAT; she still takes children's sizes which are zero rated. In addition, the short surface area allows her to scale steep slopes. Like a goat.[92]

Our children have all been a little short changed when it comes to foot genetics. I have bony crests at the top of my feet (See "Bunions") which our youngest daughter F... has copped for; although she doesn't have the stumpy toes. If anything, her toes are weirdly long. Our son D... has inherited his mother's

---

[92] If you want an idea of what Bruce's feet look like why not try Googling Chinese foot binding.

pods in spades and his feet look almost as wide as they are deep, and nearly cuboid. His uncle had a similar issue and was offered surgery to remove his little toe and the bones extending down the side. A bit like planing down a door to make it fit the jambs. He declined the offer.

One thing my children don't seem to have inherited is my propensity for the humble verruca though these days I believe the term is plantar wart which is such a shame; verruca is a great word (see "VD"). The opportunities to catch them have dwindled somewhat; there are no school swimming lessons and no one showers after PE these days (see "Erectile Disfunction") as ogling teachers are deemed more of a risk to children than ringworm. Which may be appropriate, I don't know; do you still get smelly kids in schools?

At the moment, I have a verruca on the outside edge of the sole of my left foot, although there is a school of thought that says it is a corn. My point is, it has resided there for years without giving me very much in the way of grief. On the occasions that it does irritate I simply shave away the surface with a razor blade and all is well; you wouldn't know it was there. This is very different to the verrucae of my youth.

My verruca years run from around 1977 to 1980 (or thereabouts) during which I advance from a complete one ruke novice to a full time sole-scraping, crud-footed  cripple. Everyone at my school, it seems, gets a verruca at some time. I say this based on my observations of people getting out of swimming on the weekly trips to the municipal baths at Upperthorpe. It feels like a minor rite of passage to get one, and when it happens, I am, in a way, rather pleased. I am one of the gang. I fully expect to float through the experience in a couple of months the same as everyone else does. However, no one tells my verruca this, he has designs on total world domination; well, total foot domination at least.

Within a month the tiny, tough little crater has doubled in size and its *insides* can be seen. It is soon half a centimetre in diameter and the little black specks, (what everyone said were baby verrucae) can be discerned below the whitening surface. They are not baby verrucae by the way, they are tiny, blocked blood vessels.

To make matters worse, this burgeoning wart is right on the ball of my foot so it's painful every time I walk, and I compensate for this by walking a little on the outside of my foot. Round about this time the secondaries appear, and I get one on the ball of the other foot which results in me developing a Charlie Chaplin walk.

Soon I have dozens of the things, most notably the two ball-of-the-foot monsters which are the size of two pence pieces. Not to be outdone, a number of the smaller ones begin to join forces and a few even migrate to the top of my feet and toes which seems to be adding insult to injury.

After various visits, the GP gets sick of seeing me and I am referred to the hospital. I am given what I think is an antiviral foot-soak. Every evening I have to soften my feet in hot water, scrape the spongy surface of my verrucae with a penknife then soak them in my medication. This takes a good hour and half and the treatment lasts for about two years during which no one in my family ever complains that my routine is affecting their enjoyment of Coronation Street or Minder or Blake's Seven or whatever, which in retrospect is very tolerant of them because it's not a pretty sight.

In addition to my nightly travails, occasionally I am required to turn up in clinic, stick my feet on a cushion and have the verrucae surfaces burned off with liquid nitrogen. The thing that sticks in my memory about this is the tartan thermos flask that the stuff is held in; an incongruous receptacle for such a space-age treatment.

Eventually the varuccae disappear, and I revert to a normal gait. I don't know whether it is the treatment that does the job or if the things just go of their own accord. For a while I have a strange feeling of loss, there is something comforting about a chronic pain. I have noticed it with toothaches and stomach pains also; you miss them when they are gone. Weird stuff.

## Fever

A fever, I believe, is defined as any increase in temperature above the normal range. One of the symptoms of Crohn's is fever. There is a lot of sweating involved; especially in hospital where waterproof mattresses are the norm. It is all very nasty and draining and uncomfortable and all the rest, and every flare-up I've had has involved fevers and night sweats to some degree. But I want to make a distinction here, there are little fevers and there are big fevers. In my case Crohn's has only blighted me with what I would term little fevers[93].

This section, then, is about big fevers. The ones that conjure up images of David Livingstone dying under a mosquito net, or wild-eyed, hallucinating mad men having to be restrained by doting, crinolined nurses. Once you've experienced big fever you can be forgiven for regarding everything short of it as a case of just "feeling a bit hot".

I am not one to blow my own trumpet but (if you will excuse the

---

[93] I don't want to play these down; they can stick around for ages and really get to you.

pun) I am red-hot at doing fever. I have had some beauties. The first one of note occurs when I am a student, 1989 to be precise and I am living in a damp shithole in Fenham, Newcastle upon Tyne.[94] I can't nail it down to anything in particular, no doubt a virus of some kind, but it knocks me for six. With the virus comes a fever. I am freezing cold and shaking under my duvet. Not little shivers but real, wild, uncontrollable shakes. My teeth are chattering! I must look like a cartoon. Then the sweating starts. I never knew there was so much liquid in my body, it just flows and flows. Every so often I drag myself downstairs to quench the raging thirst, which only brings on the shaking again, and when I return there is only the prospect of a saturated bed to look forward to. There is no refuge in a single bed, no dry half; you have to bite the bullet and splash in. Thankfully, all this passes in a couple of days and I am left with a pile of washing to do which no doubt I get around to at some point, I don't recall precisely, domesticity is not a big thing for me at that time in my life.

You might imagine that having a fever with a loving wife on hand, to tend to your every febrile need, is preferable to having one as a lonely student in a single bed in Fenham, in which case I am here to disabuse you. Yes, it is nice to have drinks, drugs and wot-not brought to you when you need it, and it is nice to know that there is someone there to answer the phone, feed the dog, etc. but marital fevers are not without their challenges. It cannot be nice to have a sweating, shaking body beside you in bed all night and anyone that has to put up with it has my utmost sympathy and admiration. Good to know all that *in sickness and in health* business still carries some weight, then?

---

[94] 5 Belsay Place. It's quite an attractive residence these days.

Yes, but, the sanctity of the marriage vow, it seems, counts for little in comparison to the sanctity of the best bedding. I can see her point, I have a tendency to leave my mark. Our duvet cover has a permanent imprint of my body; it's like the Turin Shroud but with spectacles. And we have a king-sized wool duvet which is difficult to wash and even more difficult to dry. If you thought that CM's displeasure is to be avoided it is nothing to the lengths I have to go to avoid her mother's wrath. It happens one Christmas, we are in Filey at my parents in law's holiday home and I am suffering the full deal again. This time I've just started on methotrexate and so running a fever has an added frisson of mortal danger[95]. For CM, however, the risk of her husband's admission to a small, coastal hospital takes a back seat to the risk of her mother finding out that the sponging son-in-law was yellowing her bedding. And I am, I'm really going for it, or perhaps it just seemed worse because all the bedding there is kept meticulously snowy white[96].

Everything has to be kept secret; as far as anyone was concerned Jon's got a bit of a sniffle. I have to be cleaned up, dragged out periodically to show my face, then I limp back upstairs and violate the linen again. I even cook Christmas dinner. If I drop dead in the sprouts all well and good as long as my transgressions betwixt the sheets remained undiscovered.

Hallucinations. Now there is a real sign of your fever

---

[95] Perhaps that is over dramatising things a touch; fever can be a sign of toxicity to the drug.

[96] In order of dirtying potential, we go on holiday with dog, kids, pet rats and me, so a practical choice of colour there.

credentials. I've had them a couple of times and I have to say they do break up the monotony of lying in bed for days on end. That said, I have only had the briefest of flirtations with them and I am happy to leave it at that; anything beyond that and it starts to get a bit scary. My hallucinations tend to happen in that grey area between sleep and consciousness which has always been a danger zone for me (see "Audi Coupe", "Sleep Paralysis", "Under the Knife"). I recall one of my fever episodes; I am alone in the house and the phone by my bed rings. I answer it and have a brief conversation with Satan about something or other. In reality it is the father of one of my daughter's friends phoning to arrange the little girls meeting up. I don't know what he makes of it; he's very polite, all things considered. Ironically, they are quite a Christian family I think, so it was good of him, when I later proffer my explanation, to be so understanding. But then forgiveness is a Christian trait I believe.

## Fissure
See "Back Passage"

## Flare-up
Crohn's is a chronic disease; it does not go away. Rather, it waxes and wanes in the fashion of a grumbling volcano. These periods of volcanic activity are generally referred to as flare-ups.
I know for some people the baseline level is a pretty unpleasant starting point, but I have been lucky; for most of the time my Crohn's has been manageable. Flare-ups are never far from one's thoughts however, they are something of a sword of Damocles, a constant worry. You never know if that slightly looser stool, or that bit of lethargy is a precursor to something

more sinister. That has always been the way of it with me; the symptoms build. I have never been well one day and full on IBD the next, it has always been a slow descent.

And so it is with my first flare-up after initial diagnosis. I have been discharged from Lodge Moor hospital in the summer of 1985 on a diet of sulphasalazine, prednisolone and Nutrinel. After a few months I am weaned off the latter two, leaving the sulphasalazine as a long term "maintenance" drug.[97] I am still plotting this course in early 1986 when I start to feel ill once again. It is the same story, loss of appetite, lethargy, loose bowels, pain, and I soon find myself in Lodge Moor Hospital once again. Same ward, same room, although my number-screaming neighbour had gone; I don't like to speculate where. And it snows. Tons of the stuff! The drifts are up to the windows. My parents have a job getting the Chevette through. It must look impressive on the moors here, unfortunately all I can see is the inside of the quad formed by the intersection of Lodge Moor's endless corridors; it's pretty enough but if you've seen one quad you've seen 'em all.

After a quick hit of steroids I begin to feel more myself and avail myself of Lodge Moor's fine cuisine. My regained appetite is about to get a slap in the face however. There is a school of thought that says Crohn's may be linked to an allergy to certain foods and the team want me to undertake an elimination diet. Starting from a bland base I will introduce individual foods on a fortnightly basis and see if any of them make me ill. It sounds hellish but my lovely dietician, she of the gentle voice, delivers the news and I cannot help but be all for it.

---

[97] It remained as such until it is superseded by Asacol in the 1990s. This, in turn was superseded by Pentasa around 2010.

Out of the window go my fry-ups, and chips, and tea and coffee. In come lamb and potatoes[98]. The rest of my nutrients I shall get from the Nutrinel cartons which I quite like so I don't imagine it will be too arduous.

I am wrong of course.

L and P for breakfast, L and P for lunch, L and P for tea[99]. I will be honest, it gets to be a real ball ache in a very short space of time, and this is from someone who is quite fond of both lamb *and* potatoes. Imagine if it was boiled fish again?

After a couple of weeks in hospital I am sent home with a list of foods and a schedule for their introduction. It's weeks until I get a cup of tea and I cannot see beer on the list at all. Next up is a bit of butter for my potatoes which, and I don't mean this sarcastically, is something to look forward to.

Buttered potatoes are a big hit but my thoughts are moving ahead to white bread. Oh the sandwich possibilities! Potato sandwich, lamb sandwich, lamb and potato sandwich. Plain bread and butter even! Will I ever get used to this rock and roll lifestyle?

I am still ages from trying tea and coffee and I am pig sick of drinking water. I think the problem with water is that I don't particularly like the taste. It's my own fault really, I drank almost exclusively milk and pop as a child and then segued into tea and coffee and ultimately beer. The only exceptions were the occasional Horlicks, and a brief flirtation with advocaat. I decide to push my luck with my parents and request fizzy water, which in 1986 is Perrier and is a bit on the pricey side.

---

[98] Both quite easy to digest apparently.

[99] I am pretty sure it was mutton on a couple of occasions, but it didn't seem to make a difference to me

There isn't anything else like it as far as I am aware, and it's regarded as a bit of a yuppie affectation. I still buy fizzy water but these days it comes in a two-litre bottle and cost less than twenty pence. It is also available without the bubbles which is anathema to me; why would you pay for something you can get free by turning on a tap?

I get through a fair bit of Perrier until T and C come online, after which I neither want it nor can I justify the expense.

My comparatively good health lasts until late spring when I start to feel signs that another flare-up is on the way. Tiredness in the main, with the odd loose stool, not diarrhoea as such, just loose. And of course, wind; Crohn's makes you fart like a trooper.[100]

I embark on another course of prednisolone but the steroids don't seemed to be working with same efficacy as they did before. I'm not getting that superman buzz that I have come to expect. I'm just getting sicker and sicker. My poor mother is in tears with the situation and neither me nor my father know what to do with weeping women[101]. I am all for persevering and trusting that the medics will sort this out. All she can see is her best-looking son turning into a loosely assembled skeleton. It is at this point that she refers to Dr McK... in the most unflattering of terms (See "Dark Arts") leading me to suspect she was losing faith in him.

All this has come at a bad time for me (see "Yoghurts, Fasting

---

[100] An interesting idiom this, I wonder if this comes from trooper as in cavalry horse rather than trooper as in soldier. Presumably *swears like...* and/or *smokes like* a trooper come from the latter because horses do neither of those things.

[101] I'm still in the dark on that even now. What does one do?

and Staying Well") I am about to re-sit my A levels and I am determined not to make the same mistake as last time; even if they have to wheel me in, I am going to sit all the papers. Examining boards make no allowances.[102]

I sit my exams; I don't think I've done myself justice, the whole experience is thoroughly brain-fogged. But I do it and I can now concentrate on getting well again, which I intend to make a start on during my holiday. We have a week in a caravan in Hubbert's Bridge which is close to Boston in Lincolnshire. Hubbert's Bridge is well named in that there is a bridge there and poorly named in that it ought to have an apostrophe. But this is a fishing, not a grammar holiday so no one minds at all. In truth there is no other reason to go to Hubbert's Bridge other than to fish. It lies on the Forty Foot, which is a drain famous amongst the Sheffield angling fraternity; there is even a Forty Foot pub in the city.

Engulfed in the same fog that saw me attempt maths and chemistry, my fishing is a bit of a let-down. It surprises many people when I say that fishing can be tiring, it is down to the concentration required I guess, and in this instance I have none to spare. By the time I have carried my tackle from the caravan, and down the bank I am a spent force.

To avoid the trekking, on another occasion, my father loads up the Chevette and we drive to a different stretch; a farm where we can park close to the water. A sweet little mongrel puppy, presumably belonging to the farm, follows me to bank side. The *peg*, or *hole* that I am fishing is lower than the main bank, closer to the water line and I struggle to lower first basket, then

---

[102] Well they didn't at that time; I cannot speak for these enlightened times.

rods and, finally, myself into it. I take off my coat and have a breather, leaving it lying on the bank. At this point my little canine friend shows his true colours, sticks his head into my coat pocket and lifts out a whole half pound bar of Bourneville chocolate. As soon as he has tugged the confection free he's off and by the time I have inched my way up the slope he is a figure in the distance, struggling to run with a huge red rectangle sticking out the side of his head.[103]

Half an hour later the little bugger returns, this time with an older accomplice. With all the cheek in the world they stand there wagging at me, awaiting the next course.

"This is the one Uncle Fido, you distract 'im while I go fru 'is pockets."

Days after my holiday, I am in Lodge Moor once again. My weight is down significantly, I have a good deal of pain, and not to put too fine a point on it I feel thoroughly shagged out.

On the plus side, I make a new friend; a bald bus driver by the name of D..., who is an ardent socialist, Wednesdayite[104] and Ry Cooder fan. I've never heard of Ry Cooder; unfortunately, I have heard of Sheffield Wednesday who, in 1986, are undeniably better than United. Dark times!

D... has been admitted with a variety of symptoms, none of which anyone can immediately pin down. After a fortnight of

---

[103] You will note the reversion to my previous strategy of living on dark chocolate and yoghurt. Although I did not know it at the time chocolate is toxic to dogs and that quantity probably did for the bugger. That'll learn 'im!

[104] A follower of Sheffield Wednesday

testing[105] he is diagnosed with a rare bacterium, the name of which takes three seconds to pronounce. He commits this to memory and now has a conversation piece for life.

D... embarks on a running feud with Matron. He tells me it is political, that she is a Thatcherite and ideologically opposed to everything he stands for. He refers to her as the *Gauleiter*. As far as I can tell she is just being the same old martinet that she has always been. I suspect D... just doesn't like being told what to do. He is reading a biography of Mao Tse-tung; he says it is just to annoy her. I am not sure it is working. If anything, her reaction to him is slightly coquettish; I am too inexperienced at this stage to understand, but in retrospect I reckon there was a bit of sexual chemistry there.

I am to get a colonoscopy, which is a procedure whereby a camera is inserted up my anus and into my colon. It sounds like an extended version of the sigmoidoscopies I've had in the past; which is no recommendation at all. Like the barium enema, I am required to drink gallons of laxative; at least this time I get to squit it out in a real toilet and not a commode. That said, it's further to travel. I do several Le Mans starts before I run dry.

This test comes with a free canula, which is basically a little plastic access valve inserted into a vein in my arm; it allows various potions to be administered to me as and when needed and without all the fuss of needles. First off, I assume the knees up position, and a brief fingering ensues. After that I think some form of grommet is inserted in, though it's hard to be certain what is going on back there. This is presumably to make the passage of the camera easier.

---

[105] No doubt arrays of petri dishes were analysed under a microscope- I've watched Quincy, I know how these things work.

Having a colonoscopy is a fairly uncomfortable business; a lot of pushing and twisting of the apparatus is involved. It can be quite painful at times, I think due to the bowel getting stretched. I start the procedure without any drugs but within a few twists I am feeling it and am given buscopan via my canula. Buscopan relaxes the bowel, this is the reason it is used to treat irritable bowel syndrome. In the case of colonoscopies it reduces some of the resistance to the progress of the scope. The effects are swift, a quick squirt into my arm, I go dizzy briefly, then refocus. My mouth is suddenly very dry.

During the procedure, this happens with barium enemas too, air is pumped into the bowel to stretch it out and get a good gander into all the nooks and crannies. Often this is painful. On this occasion I am offered a sedative which I accept. I'm glad I do, it's great! I can feel it as it enters my arm, a slightly cold sensation moving up to the shoulder and further into me, then...wham! It's like getting all the benefits of skin-full of beer without having to put the hours in. Suddenly I am the jolliest person in the room. I am laughing, slurring a bit, generally loquacious. The doctor asks me if I would like a look at what is going on. Of course I do, and he turns the screen around and talks me through it. I am surprised by how green it all looks. I think biopsies are taken, I don't remember; I am just blown away by the scene. Me on a table, out of my head on drugs and looking up my own arse.

Inflammation is found at various sections of my plumbing which is no surprise to anyone. Since the steroids don't seem to be working, trying them in combination with a different drug, Azathioprine, is proposed. As we mentioned, Crohn's is thought to be caused by an overreaction on the part of the body's defences, it follows therefore that anything that can dampen down the immune system could be used as a treatment. Steroids act as immunosuppressants working by reducing inflammation and moderating the work of white blood cells. Azathioprine is classed as an antimetabolite, also an immunosuppressant but works in a different way to the corticosteroids.

Within a couple of weeks I see an improvement which may or may not have been in response to the Azathioprine as the drug is supposed to take a couple of months before it kicks in. Who knows? The important thing is that I am back on an even keel, which is timely; I have about a month to get myself well enough to leave home for university.

## Fleas
See Parasites.

## Follicular Issues
The Lenity clan, I am sorry to say, can boast slap-heads going back deep into the realms of time; father's father's father's…and all that. The continuance of the tradition was something of a foregone conclusion and no matter how many times I canvassed my mother for reassurance that it would not be the case, both my brother and I knew that the clock was ticking.

We are fortunate to live in an era when a close-cropped pate is perfectly acceptable, sadly, my father was less fortunate. The sixties and seventies were a time of long hair and the only famous men with chrome domes are Telly Savalas and Yul Brynner. More often than not, a gentleman will adhere to the fashionable length despite being ill-equipped to do so. It is the age of the combover, and Bobby Charlton is its poster boy. Combovers fool no one and this is especially so with my father's which consists of barely a dozen threads which, for most of the time, stick out of the side of his head like some strange spidery appendage. It is a source of amusement for us as children[106] even if it is tinged with anxiety for the future.

There is some hope in that I have a particularly thick head of hair, the type that is difficult to drag a comb through,[107] so when male pattern baldness does make its move it's going to meet some resistance. A war of attrition. With a bit of luck, I thought, I might make it to my forties without developing a monkey's arsehole[108]. Oh, how I laugh when, at the age of nineteen, it falls out overnight.[109]

When I say *falls out overnight* I don't mean to imply that it *all* went AWOL. It is just a comparatively small area, although it might just be the start of something more extensive, which worries me. About the size of my thumb the clearing extends backwards from just below my left temple, which strikes me as a bit of a random place for it to happen.

There is some debate as to whether this is due to the Crohn's, Azathioprine, Prednisolone or some combination therein. No consensus is reached and I get the sense that no one views it with the same level of concern that I feel. Perfectly understandable in the grand scheme of my general wellbeing; after all, a few weeks earlier the disease was unresponsive to any drug therapies and I was wasting away.

It doesn't help that I have a rather unsympathetic hairdresser, G..., the girl next door, who on discovering it, laughs her head off, points and shouts:

---

[106] Still is.

[107] In my early days I looked like the feral kid from Mad Max 2.

[108] Bald-spot

[109] Actually, I didn't laugh at all.

"Ha! Jonathan's goin' bald! Look everybody Jonathan's goin' bald!"

Beckoning the other members of her family into the front room to join in the merriment. This probably breaches some hairdressing code of ethics, but I don't complain; a free haircut is a free haircut after all.

Clearly, I am the only one taking this issue seriously and so I set about seeking a cure. There is talk of a relative who used to wear a poultice of onion and garlic in the hope of regrowth. A quick look on the internet tells me that this belief still persists and in fact the treatment may have some benefits. My instinct is that this is nonsense not least because the relative in question was as bald as a coot.

Anyway, I have no intention of going around reeking of pungent vegetables. Instead I propose to adopt a high-tech approach. Cutting edge. Which in 1986 means popping down to Boots and picking up a bottle of Silvikrin Hair Tonic. I put a great deal of faith in this since (I am told) my father had used it in the early sixties and had succeeded in cultivating a layer of peach fuzz across his previously barren cranium. It must have looked ridiculous on him but, I speculate, it might do a job for me.

It does not. If anything, it makes it worse. It has a kind of varnishing effect, so instead of having a small bald-spot at the side of my head I have a small, *shiny* bald-spot at the side of my head. The stuff's adhesive qualities, however, do prove useful and my miniature version of the Lenity combover is well secured.

Moving to Newcastle I come under the care of Doctor L... at the Freeman hospital and, pulling aside the carefully teased concealment, I point out my affliction.

"Probably alopecia," he opines, "I can refer you to a dermatologist if it bothers you."

Doctor L... is quite bald and somehow it seems churlish of me to make a fuss over a square inch of visible flesh when he's sat across the desk from me glinting away in the morning light. Despite my self-esteem issues, I decline.

Some months later as I am weaned off the Azathioprine there is an anticipation that my bald spot might shrink away, but it never does. I sometimes wonder if all that rubbing with hair tonic abraded the life out of it the way that years of sock wearing forms a shiny high-tide mark on a man's ankles[110]. In the long run it matters little as the rest of my barnet joins it in oblivion.

It is easy to say that baldness doesn't matter and that as afflictions go it is pretty small beer. This is perfectly true, but if you are young, a bit self-conscious and on the lookout for love then a barren pate is a real handicap. No doubt less-confident men are less likely to appeal to women but the main reason, I suspect, is that thinning hair does not fit in with our concept of physical beauty. It's a generalisation I know, but girls don't go for baldies[111]. Neither do they go for shorties, weedies, uglies, farties (sadly), goofies, bozzeyes, chinnies or the chinless to name a few. Thankfully there are two ways to combat this:

1. Become incredibly wealthy, or;
2. Learn to accept your physical appearance for what it is and meet with alacrity the limitations it brings.

---

[110] Having spent a lot of time on building sites I can vouch that safety wellingtons have a similar effect.

[111] Does the same apply for gay men?

Either way you will buy yourself a more comfortable ride through life

# G is for...

## Ganglion Cyst

Some time in my forties I develop a ganglion cyst on the second toe of my right foot. Whether it came along gradually or whether it popped up overnight I cannot say, I just happen to take a look one day and there it was. It is quite different in appearance from the other cysts I have had (see Cysts) and for that reason (and because I am short on ailments beginning with G) I have afforded it a separate section.

It looks very much like what it is, a translucent, fluid filled sack forming under the skin on the joint of my toe. Occasionally painful, for the most part I am unaware of its presence. The exact cause of ganglion cysts is not known but they seem to be associated with weaknesses or flaws in tendon joints. Mine is quite squidgy to touch and very tempting if you are into that sort of thing. Which I am. I have a go at popping it whilst we are on holiday in Paris[112]; all I have is a pair of nail scissors, but I manage to make a little rent in it. It is a bit underwhelming actually, all I get for my labours is a wee globule of clear jelly that looks like something you would put on a mouth ulcer. No high-pressure squirting, no blood, no stinking custard; rather disappointing. The cyst filled up again within days. It's still there.

---

[112] Oddly enough, I discovered later, I was spotted at distance in some or other arrondissement by both my gastroenterologist (Dr J...) and his wife (Mrs J...). Apparently, I don't look Parisian. Who'd have thought it!

Historically, ganglion cysts used to be known as Bible bumps or Bible cysts as the standard treatment was to give it a whack with a heavy tome which for most households meant the family Bible. Times have moved on of course and this is no longer the prescribed approach; these days the Guinness Book of Records is the preferred option.

## Garlic

I cannot remember where I heard this, probably from my mother which should have sounded warning bells bearing in mind some of the other things she told me. Nevertheless, I get it in my head from somewhere that in the days of the Roman Empire, the legionaries would stuff garlic into their sandals for its medicinal qualities. This set me wondering if garlic, or some component therein, could actually be absorbed through the feet. I take a look on the internet and, it seems, it can; within a short while of smearing it on the pods you can taste the stuff on your breath.

I decide to give this a go and pack crushed garlic into my socks for a couple of weeks. Whether it shows up on my breath is hard to say; I eat so much of the damn stuff anyway. And besides, if you walk about with garlic on your feet it does tend to make everywhere stink.

It also rots your socks.

## Gastroscopy

Sometime in the noughties I develop a funny feeling in my throat; nothing much, just a sort of roughness on swallowing. Because Crohn's can affect things from the mouth to anus (and beyond), when I mention it to my gastro consultant he thinks it best to have it looked at and I am booked in for a gastroscopy. It is not an experience I look back on with any fondness and I wish I'd opted for the sedative rather than taking the advice of the nurse who told me that a big strapping lad like me wouldn't need it. For a kick-off the tube is surprisingly substantial and swallowing it is like a form of medieval torture, trial by gagging. Imagine the worst puking retch you have ever had and triple it. Once the scope is in, the process is not too bad but getting there is like drowning. Getting it out is not much better, although sweetened by the prospect of the ordeal being over. Afterwards I am left with a throat ache (if there is such a thing) for about a week. Incidentally, nothing sinister was discovered.

Some years later CM is forced to have one. She leapt at the offer of sedation and fell asleep before it was even in her mouth. She has no memory of it. Lucky cow!

## Growing Up

In the autumn of 1986, I exchange family life in Sheffield for student life in Newcastle upon Tyne. It may not be independent living in the true sense of the phrase, student life is a comparatively cosseted one, but I like to think it is on the way to being a grown up.

Because I am still recovering from a bout of Crohn's that summer (see "Flare-ups") I miss freshers' week[113]. In addition, due to my restricted diet I am allowed to go straight into a self-catering flat rather than the halls of residence that the majority of first years are billeted in. Socially speaking, all this leaves me at a bit of a disadvantage; everyone knows everyone else, often biblically, and I confess to feeling a little out of place in these

---

[113] A week of introductions prior to term starting in earnest. Essentially seven days of drunken debauchery as hordes of eighteen-year-olds are let off their parental leashes.

first few weeks.

There are other factors at play. I am really spotty; standard plukes due to the steroids and a strange rash-like covering of tiny pustules which I think are due to the azathioprine. As, I believe, is the chunk of hair that has fallen out of my scalp leaving me with a bald patch just by my left ear. (See "Follicular Issues"). Suffice to say I don't see a lot of action that first term.[114] On the plus side I have regained my weight so at least I only look terrible from close up.

Socially I am experiencing the Perrier effect again. Because of concerns over what booze might do to my system I abstain from it, not to the full, fizzy water extent but I limit myself to drinking pints of shandy instead of pints of beer. At least that way I won't stand out from the crowd. It's awful! All that gas! And it's impossible to get drunk on shandy; God knows I try! Better, I conclude, to eschew student events where possible.

I am still far from fully-functioning; I feel really tired and I eat a lot of Mars bars in the hope that it will give me a boost. I sleep a lot too. This I now put down to the azathioprine, having subsequently experienced similar symptoms with other immuno-suppressants. At the time, though, I assume it to be a manifestation of my Crohn's.

I have another issue which, whilst it might sound minor, is actually quite debilitating. I have a sore arse. That's amusing is it? Well, for your information, no it's bloody well not. There are some days when I can barely walk for it; which is bad news for field trips (I study geology) of which there are a number. My

---

[114] I have a memory that it was called Michaelmas term although looking at the University website that seems to have been dropped in favour of Autumn. It is quite possible that I just imagined it.

immediate reaction is to slather the area in Germolene, which seems like a reasonable medication to choose based on its haemorrhoid credentials. This has limited success and has the drawback of always leaving me smelling "medicated". It is quite pungent stuff.

I take my problem to Newcastle's Freeman hospital, home of my latest gastro consultant, Dr L.... (he of the shining pate) who advises me to avoid medicated creams and instead wash with un-fragranced soap, and rinse thoroughly. It is good advice and this protocol continues to serve me well in what is a recurrent problem to this day[115]. Something else he said which really set me thinking, and I don't recall the specifics of the conversation but the phrase he used was this:

"...we can't wrap you in cotton wool..."

Cotton wool is exactly what I have been wearing for the last two years. Every time I have an inkling of Crohn's coming on, it dominates my head space. It occurs to me that perhaps my attitude to the thing is part of the problem? I take stock of my actions to that point.

If I have a loose poo, I worry about it for days. I sometimes retain stools for as long as I can through trepidation, not wanting to see what would come out of me. Crazy behaviour that only serves to create further stress.

I deny myself food in the belief that in doing so my symptoms will abate; which they never do. The more I deny myself the more my appetite perishes. There might be a case for giving the gut a rest and allowing it to recover but living on Bournville and French set yoghurt is not the way to go about that; it just leads to malnourishment.

---

[115] More prevalent following surgery.

And what role does stress or anxiety or tension, call it what you will, play in all this? At the time it is a widely held opinion amongst sufferers that stress has a significant impact, but this does not appear to feature heavily in the thinking of medical professionals[116]. From a personal perspective I was with the laymen. All my flare-ups, if not necessarily caused through stress, were certainly exacerbated by it. (See "Yoghurt, Fasting and Staying Well") If I were less uptight about the prospect of flare-ups then perhaps, when they occur, they might not be quite so severe. To come to the point, I decide that Jonny might benefit from a little fun now and again. Aside from the boost to my health it would mean that I get a slice of the cake everyone else is wolfing down.

In the first instance I relax my diet. I've been living on pretty bland fare for the first term; plain pasta with butter and black pepper was a favourite, boil in the bag fish, corn beef, frozen peas. There is a weekly visit to the chippy[117] every Wednesday and, of course, French set yoghurt abounds. It is suggested to me by the other two English lads that share the flat, that we might pool our cooking skills. This, of course has many

---

[116] It was, for many years believed that IBD was a psychosomatic disease and that there were certain personality types who were more susceptible to it. Indeed, therapies were developed on this basis and in extreme cases IBD patients were even lobotomised. By the 1980s these theories had been abandoned and I suspect that there was something of a backlash to them such that the psychological aspects of the disease were, to a degree, poo-pooed. No pun intended.

[117] Which was a great disappointment. Having been raised in Yorkshire I never realised that fish, chips and peas could be so mistreated.

advantages: it is cheaper, I would only have to cook every third day, and I wouldn't need to walk into town to the supermarket as both of them have cars.[118] I accept, and whilst we never push any taste boundaries with our attempts (a lot of minced beef is involved) in spirit it is a leap forward for Lenity.

I give up on the shandy too. I remember the day well; it is a field trip to Whitley Bay and several of us have stopped in a pub for a sandwich. I have a pint of bitter, fully intending to go back onto the shore and smash rocks for the rest of the afternoon. However, someone suggests having another. Which turns into another, etc. the upshot being that precious little work is done. However, the trip is not a complete waste, I have proved to myself that I can neck a couple of pints and not finish up wracked with pain or rushing to the loo continually.

So successful is my Whitley Bay trial that I expand the programme. I eat and drink what I like, in whatever quantities I can manage. I smoke spliffs. I keep unsocial hours. I do and

---

[118] There were four other members of the flat none of whom were suitable to join our cooking circle. They consisted: an older German postgraduate who kept himself to himself and lived exclusively on things that would spread on toast, a Thai chap whose cooking was so spicy it burned just looking at it, and a pair of Hong Kong Chinese who shared a tiny room they had illegally sublet from the genuine tenant. They had a penchant for frying dried fish at ferocious temperatures which smelled for all the world like someone had just pissed on the hob. If that sounds racist let me assure you that our opinions were more than reciprocated by their disdain for our eating habits. I quote: "Ha ha, only English put vinegar on fish!" Apparently, it's hilarious to do so.

say stupid things, mostly under the influence of alcohol. The cotton wool is well and truly off and if you are reading this thinking that it sounds like a descent into hedonism well, you are probably right; carousing is the order of the day. Of course, academically it is unfortunate but in terms of my Crohn's it has no adverse effect whatsoever. I don't have a single flare-up in the three years I spend there.

## Growing (further) Up

1991 and I find myself back at my parent's house in Sheffield picking over the bones of a failed relationship. Jobless and skint my only consolation is that I'd got custody of the dog.

I feel rather sorry for myself. My diagnosing current wife would probably describe it as a depressive state but back then life is less technical. In the end it all amounts to the same thing; melancholia, ennui, down in the dumps, take your pick.

I have a lot of time on my hands, I become nocturnal, drinking homebrew and watching Alain Delon films until the early hours of the morning. I sleep until mid-afternoon then repeat the process. Within a few weeks I am suffering a flare-up. I make every effort to eat as normally as I can (as is my mantra by this point) and I manage to maintain a moderately healthy weight, but the pain and the diarrhoea are as bad as anything I have experienced. The nadir is when, after emptying my bowels of seemingly pints of foul-smelling liquid, I look down to find that it consists, in the main, of blood. Like anyone else there have been times when I have considered myself to be up *Shit Creek*[119], but this was the first time I thought I might actually be

---

[119] Islay, 1988 see Wife Swapping Nazis of the Inner Hebrides, available on Amazon if you can be bothered.

the source of that famous tributary. It is shocking, even though I am fairly inured to that sort of thing; you will recall the pearl of wisdom I had been given years earlier: *a little blood goes a long way*. (See "Back Passage"). I am prescribed prednisolone by my GP but the pain and diarrhoea continue to the stage where I am hospitalised again; this time the Northern General. The Northern is one of the biggest hospitals you will find anywhere and quite a different environment to Lodge Moor; for a start I don't get a private room. I know some put great store on personal space, but I cannot say that I am bothered one way or the other. I don't want to come across as touting my *man of the people* credentials but there is something wholesome about mucking in. There is a camaraderie, especially amongst people with a common cause. I soon make a little friend[120] by the name of J... who is a Crohn's sufferer himself, although his problems centre on the small intestine whereas I'm more of a colon man. He is looking at surgery to remove a section of his ileum which he seems to accept with alacrity. He is a very philosophical individual; were I in his position I doubt I would be so laid-back, but I suppose everyone finds their own way of dealing with things. Besides, I am determined not to have surgery despite the constant warnings that most Crohnies, at some stage in their journey, will get chopped up to some degree.

I am given a big hit of prednisolone and this seems to stop the rot without resorting to azathioprine again. I'm quite pleased about this as I am still coming to terms with my first bald patch without starting work on another. I begin to get my appetite back and take full advantage of the seemingly endless supply of

---

[120] He genuinely was both *small* and *friendly*

bacon available at breakfast. The food is pretty good, and that is not just the steroids speaking, it is. '91 is a good year to be scoffing institutionalised food[121].

A colonoscopy is performed as it's been a few years since my insides have been properly looked at. Dr R... is at the helm and I am told that he is a dab hand at this kind of thing. I am dosed up with Buscopan to relax my tubes. This is quickly followed by the *happy drugs* as it becomes apparent that this is going to be far from pain free. I don't remember much about it (I am pretty spaced) but it is curtailed when Dr R... hits a narrowing of the bowel. Such a narrowing is known by the term *stricture.*

This was the first indication that I had a stricture although I had read about them. Strictures develop as scar tissue builds up in areas where the bowel has been damaged by prolonged inflammation. They vary in severity and in extreme cases can block the passage of food completely. Mine is left under a watching brief and it does not rear its ugly head until some four years later when I have my next scope.

In the intervening years I undertake a master's degree at Bournemouth University and set about raising my pleasure quota once more. A month in and although I am as fit as a flea, my back and neck look like rhubarb and custard[122] and so I register with a GP. We go through all the prelims:

"Abdominal pain?"

"Very rarely."

"Good. Bowel movements?"

"Once a day, sometimes twice."

---

[121] Alas, the glory days of the hospital fry-up seem to have passed (See "Under the Knife").

[122] The pudding rather than the cartoon

"Good."

"Solid and buoyant too!" I add.

"Good."

"Feeling well in yourself?"

"Oh yes, definitely."

"Good."

"Do you smoke?"

"No." Not cigarettes at any rate.

"Excellent. Alcohol?"

"Just a bit of beer."

"OK. And how much, would you say?"

"Per week?"

"If you like."

I'm on my guard here, he's found my Achilles heel. I deem it appropriate to shave my estimate a wee bit.

"Dunno, thirty? Thirty-five?"

"What! Pints?"

"Yes."

"Fucking hell!"

That is the only time a doctor has sworn at me in a medical context. I have to say I warmed to him.

It is now 1995 and although I am living closer to Huddersfield, in the interests of continuity I remain under the care of the Northern General Hospital in Sheffield. This suits me as I am working in the city at the time[123]. My gastroenterologist is Dr L..., my first lady specialist, which, seeing as I have been at the IBS game for ten years and travelled around the country a fair bit, is probably a sad indictment of something or other. She is

---

[123] Digging holes for the University

quite attractive, in an older woman sort of way; a classy dresser with a rather appealing foreign lilt to her voice[124].

By the late nineties my stricture starts to become the centre of attention. Dr L... has performed a couple of colonoscopies on me and has repeatedly drawn the same blank as Dr R... did in 1991. The issue now, it seems, is uncertainty. No one knows where exactly the stricture is or how far it extends or what the bowel is like on the other side. For my part I am comfortable with this, which is probably naive of me, but I am, on the whole healthy, and although I've had the odd flare-up it has responded well to prednisolone and I am, generally speaking, sailing on an even keel; pooing once a day, turds big and (to maintain the nautical theme) rather buoyant.

A barium enema is suggested as a way forward which, again, is fine by me as, remembering my previous experience of the procedure, it is a lot less painful than the scope.

I have the enema as planned which makes me quite unpopular with the people at work since I leave a slick of unflushably-dense, grey gunk in the bottom of the office toilet. It is there a week before the cleaner plucks up the courage to deal with it.

Once the photos have come back from Truprint (or whoever the NHS use) Dr L... gives me the good news, I have not one but two strictures, one in the region of my splenic flexure (the bend at which the transverse colon becomes the descending colon) and one in the descending colon itself. Both were incredibly tight. There is also a bit of inflammation, but no signs of anything truly sinister which to me sounds perfectly frabjous. Not so with Dr L... who spells out the diagnostic limitations of the barium enema. She also makes the point that the risk of a

---

[124] Possibly Italian?

blockage is high since my gut is so narrow that by rights, I should not be able to pass stools.

"But I do pass stools; big and buoyant ones."

"Hmm." She looks sceptical.

"Honestly I do. I should know!"

"The strictures are really very narrow."

"Does that make me special?"

"No."

I think I notice a hint of frustration in the good doctor's countenance. There is a sense that we are reaching a bit of an impasse here; she must have felt it too and suggests that I have a chat with a surgeon to see what they can offer. A sort of free, no obligation quote if you like; the kind of thing you get from replacement window salesmen. I agree; if it stops all the nagging it will be time well spent.

# H is for...
## Haemorrhoids
(See also "Back Passage")

It is notoriously common, especially since the advent of the internet, for a person to present with a series of symptoms and, based on them come to completely the wrong conclusion. Allow me to offer you an example.

My mid-forties and despite my IBD I am living a very normal lifestyle: I play sport, I eat whatever I like, I drink beer and so on, and so forth. Aside from the ongoing Crohnie things like the rumbling guts, and the constant foul-smelling farts I am as fit as ever. However, over a period of about a week I begin to notice a little tenderness around my back passage. Anyone who has engaged in the art of carousing to any degree will recognise the feeling; it is normally attributed to piles[125] brought on as a consequence of drinking beer. I think nothing of it at first but notice over the next few days that it is slowly worsening to such an extent that it is uncomfortable to open my bowels. To be specific, it feels as if my bumhole is being twisted out of shape in some way.

This anal torsion progresses for a couple more days and I decide to have a proper feel around there; something beyond the basic probing one does in the course of wiping and washing. My discovery causes both shock and relief; I don't have haemorrhoids at all. The cause of my distress are winnets, aka clag nuts, aka dangleberries, aka grogans. You may be squirming at this point and wondering: *how could the dirty sod let himself get into such a state?* and I understand your consternation. But, in my defence, these are *clean* winnets. I've been washing them for a week without realising that they were actually add-ons.

This is a side-effect of the constant farting; if you have any sort of crevice undergrowth it's going to pick up its share of debris as the draught shoots through. The answer of course is washing; showers and bidets and the like, however there is that rare occasion when one slips though the net, as it did in this case. Having been showered and wiped numerous times it had developed into some form of Gordian cleft-knot that had now left me with a distorted gurn for an orifice.

The question is: what do I do about it? It has gone beyond the washing phase, I am now looking at surgical removal. The thought of going at it with nail scissors does not appeal; working blind in that region is courting grief to say the least.

---

[125] Well, it's well known within my carousing circle at any rate.

Nor can I ask CM to get involved as there would be every chance that I might lose a leg and/or my gonads in the process. As I see it there are three options: burn it off, wrench it off or let the dog have a nibble. The first is a non-starter; I am soaking wet and even were I dry the risk of the conflagration spreading to the rest of my simian body is too great; a lot of combustible gases down there too! The dog, unfortunately, has this insane habit of chewing rocks which has left her virtually toothless. It takes her a week to get through a rawhide chew so heaven knows how long it would take her to deal with my bird's nest. Which assumes that she would agree to take on the task in the first place. Hobson's choice it is then...brute force!

I don't suppose it actually made any noise but in my head there was the sound of cordage ripping. It is painfully nautical but just about worth it for the instant relief from the constraint. A little shaky, I regain my breath as the winnet, looking like a mouse's toupee, floats past my feet, tarries momentarily in the plughole eddy before disappearing down the drain.

## Hard Nips

About the age of thirteen I experience a strange sensation in one of my nipples, a sort of hardening. It passes, but before long I experience it again, this time on the other side. It recurs a couple more times around about that age before disappearing from my life forever. *Presumably a puberty thing*, I think.

I am right, it is called gynecomastia and occurs when the maelstrom of teenage hormones induces breast tissue to develop. Once hormone levels are stabilised it goes away.

I never thought much about it until I shared a flat with a mechanical engineering student from Cumbria who had a penchant for lifting weights without his shirt on. He had quite prominent nipples[126] and was persuaded (I think by his girlfriend) to have them looked at. He had gynecomastia that had never receded; he finished up under the knife.

I recently did a search for images of gynecomastia on the internet and it struck me that a disproportionate number of the men with it seemed to have rather chiselled torsos, much like my friend had. I know this is casting the empirical method to the four winds, but could it be that the desire to engage in shirtless weightlifting is due to a hormone imbalance during puberty?

## Head Lice

See "Parasites"

## Head Size

I have a small head. I don't realise quite how small it is until I start to lose my hair and so resort to the standard, close-cropped, skinhead look. Without hair it suddenly looks tiny. It doesn't help matters that I am married to a woman with an abnormally large head; I think CM's ancestors came from Easter Island.[127]

My father had a small head, smaller than mine in fact but he was much shorter and stouter than me with a round face so he could get away with it. He also had a moustache which may have had a bearing.

The only issue I have with my small head is spectacles, which are an essential part of my life. And I mean *essential!* If I drop my glasses and no one else is around I am scuppered; think Velma from Scooby Doo. Unfortunately, the distance between

---

[126] You could hang a coat on them.

[127] It's a nightmare at junctions when she's in the passenger seat.

the back of my ears and the bridge of my nose is a bit on the short side and as a consequence, standard specs are too long in the arms; they poke out the back of my head like the wings on Asterix the Gaul's helmet. I can get children's glasses on, but they look as if they are disappearing into my face and they also tend to come in those jellybean colours which is really not me. Luckily there is salvation in that spectacles aimed at teenage girls are available these days which, it seems, fit me perfectly. I say perfectly, actually, *no* glasses fit me perfectly because my ears are on different levels. Specs are always a little skew to my eyes but aside from that, teenybopper glasses are just the job.

## Helminths
See "Parasites"

## Hemi-colectomy
See "Mrs Lenity as Proxy"

# I is for...
## Immunosuppressants
This is a rather sweeping term but for the interests of this book I am referring to a group of drugs known as antimetabolites; specifically: azathioprine, mercaptopurine and methotrexate, which I have listed in the order in which I made their acquaintance.[128]

Back in the eighties I credited azathioprine with bringing me through an episode of inflammation that was refusing to respond to all my previous treatments. (see "Flare-up") With hindsight I wonder if this really was the case since I started to

---

[128] We have discussed prednisolone, a corticosteroid immunosuppressant, elsewhere in this book

recover before the benefits of azathioprine might be expected to manifest themselves. I may be doing the drug a disservice here as it could well be the reason that I avoided a rapid relapse. Of course, I have no way of telling. What I do now recognise is the degree of tiredness it left me with which, back then, I had put down to the disease itself.

Years later (2013), inflammation is found within my terminal ileum and it is suggested that an immunosuppressive drug is the way to prevent this developing further. These are preferred to steroid treatments due to the side effects associated with long term use of the latter. My consultant suggests azathioprine and I point out to him that it had made my hair fall out. He looks at my noggin and says, in that blasé way that men with a full head of hair have:

"Well, that's just a man thing, you know."

Yes, I do know; obviously it's a man thing and I am resigned to it going naturally but the hair loss with azathioprine is random. What I don't want is a bloody patchwork quilt of depilation. People will think I have mange. I am going to make this point to him, but he's moved on and is offering me mercaptopurine.

"Go on then; I'll give it a whirl."

It begins with a series of weekly visits to the hospital for injections, after which I am given pills to take. Because of the risk the drug poses to my liver and pancreas I need to have regular blood tests. I take mercaptopurine[129] for something in the region of twelve months and it is a pretty miserable year. It makes me feel tired all of the time and I find myself resorting

---

[129] Street name 6MP

to frequent Worsleys[130]. However, based on my next colonoscopy it does seem to be working, so my consultant is keen to continue along this route. We try something similar, if one drug doesn't suit me then perhaps another will.

After the initial injection phase, methotrexate is just one tablet a week followed by a vitamin tablet (folic acid) a couple of days later. There are a number of potentially serious side effects and once again I require regular blood tests. On a couple of occasions, the blood tests flag up an issue with liver function and I need to lay off the drug for a week or two until things return to normal.

In terms of how it makes me feel, I don't think it has much more going for it than mercaptopurine. In some respects, it is worse; it makes me feel nauseated a lot of the time and I still need the occasional Worsley. Worst of all is the way it effects my cognition; it sends my brain into a fog-like state. It's hard to describe actually, not slow-witted as such but a feeling that some of the sharpness has been worn away, abraded if you will. I think with hindsight the methotrexate was on borrowed time because of the brain fug alone; Crohn's-wise I was in no urgent state and it was questionable whether the benefits to be gained are worth living my life as a slack-jawed dope. Ultimately the decision is made for me when I am struck down by a spontaneous urinary tract infection (see "Prostate") which develops into a long running issue; it takes about a year before the water works were anything near normal and two and a half years before I am signed off by the urology boffins. The advice with nasty infections, fevers and the like, is to lay off the

---

[130] An afternoon nap. Named after a customer of mine to whom I could not deliver pies between the hours of 2 and 4.

methotrexate for a while, which I do, but such is the longevity of the new problem that I never go back on it. To my mind methotrexate was the smoking gun; the drug had compromised my immune system and I had an infection as a result. My gastro consultant didn't think this was likely, my urology consultant though, thought it might be; take your pick. I started on methotrexate late in 2014 and it lasted through to the summer of 2016 when I got my first urinary tract infection; I have not taken it since.

## Isolation
See "Bovine TB"

# J is for…
## Johne's Disease
Johne's disease affects the guts of ruminants (sheep, cattle, goats and the like) and is characterised by diarrhoea and wasting. Many people have made a connection between this and Crohn's since the two diseases have a number of similarities.

Johne's disease is caused by the bacterium *Mycobacterium avium paratuberculosis;* paratuberculosis meaning tuberculosis-like and you will remember that when I was first admitted to hospital it was as a suspected case of bovine tuberculosis.

Aside from the clinical similarities there is one obvious coincidence that no one has noticed; the names of the diseases sound very similar. Well, for me this is the clincher providing you are prepared to ignore the fact that Dr Johne's was German and pronounced his name "yow-ners". And that Crohn's might reasonably have been called Dalziel's disease or Dalziel's

syndrome after the Scottish surgeon Kennedy Dalziel[131]
Incidentally Dalziel noted the similarity with Johne's disease
way back in 1913.

## Joints

Inflammatory bowel disease can produce joint pain, most
commonly when the gastrointestinal tract is in active flare-up.
This may include swelling of the joints (arthritis) or it may not
(arthralgia). The good news is that this is unlikely to result in
permanent damage and usually abates when gastro symptoms
improve. However, one condition also associated with IBD,
ankylosing spondylitis can produce permanent damage to the
lower spine.

Although I have had stiff joints in the past and a fare bit of
trouble with my lower back I have no reason to believe that this
had anything to do with Crohn's disease.

# K is for...

## Knees

See "Old Age and Getting There"

## Knocked-out

To date I have been knocked out three times. That is to say,
actually lost consciousness, not just gone a bit woozy, but
genuinely on the canvas.[132]

The first instance, I must have been about seven, and acting (as
seven-year-olds are wont to do) like a dick. I am chasing my
little brother around Sheffield General Cemetery which puts it
in December because that is the only time my wreath-toting

---

[131] Pronounced *Dee-Yell*

[132] Canvas was not involved on any of the occasions.

parents make that particular trip. To cut a long story short, I run into a tree branch. You know, like they do in cartoons? My little brother is short enough to go under, but I hit it full on with my forehead and the next thing I know I am looking up at Mum and Dad's concerned faces. Even at that age I recognise a cliché when I see it.

On the subject of clichés, I once slipped on a banana skin and it is true, they really are treacherous; not quite as bad as dog turds but pleasanter. Once I drove a pick-up truck into a Scottish cow! I know this is not the same thing, but I wanted to get it off my chest[133].

KO number two was more conventional. Scotland again, though totally unrelated to the cow/truck incident, and I am punched by a dwarf outside a ceilidh. I am unconscious, so my companions tell me, for about thirty seconds. It's bad enough that I have to go to a ceilidh without getting chinned afterwards. I shall not go into details here, if you are interested, an account can be found in "Wife Swapping Nazis of the Inner Hebrides" by J. F. Lenity, available on Amazon.

The last time (I hope it is the last time) occurs at the Goodwin sports centre which is part of the University of Sheffield. I have played squash with a group of friends and we are showering afterwards. The showers there are those standard, communal type; a tiled room with four shower heads protruding from the walls. In addition, and I can only surmise that this is for the benefit of shy people, are a pair of curtained cubicles squeezed into the corner. All other showering points being taken I avail myself of the cubicle at the end.

My eyesight is not brilliant at the best of times, in a steamy,

---

[133] The cow was completely unharmed I hasten to point out.

confined space I become a menace to myself. This particular cubicle houses some or other pipe run and in the interests of hygiene it has been boxed in. Rather than extending the boxing up the full length of wall, it finishes in a very sharp apex about chest height and is custom made for a half-blind fool who has dropped his soap to duck into.

It is not so much that I dive for the soap or move especially rapidly; I think the damage is done because I hit it at the apex of the box work, the force is concentrated on one small point. Luckily (ha!), because I was bending down, the drop to the floor is limited and no Hitchcockian wrenching of shower curtains ensues.

Rather like my graveyard experience as a child the first thing that comes back into focus is my audience. In this case, instead of my parent's consternation I awake to see four sets of soapy genitals hovering above me.

Blood is streaming from the strange puncture wound in my forehead; it is still producing the odd spurt when I am in the pub. I suspect that necking a couple of pints probably runs counter to the accepted medical wisdom in the event of mild concussion but my trips to a public house are such a rarity that I cannot afford to waste one.

## Knuckle
## See "Broken Bones"

# L is for…
## Lethargy

This has genuinely surprised people when I have said it[134] but of

---

[134] It also surprises people to find my favourite food is salad

all the many symptoms of Crohn's disease I have found tiredness to be the most difficult to deal with. This is only *my* experience of course and for others it may be the pain or the streaming diarrhoea, or the gas, or whatever. As I have mentioned earlier, Crohn's does not necessarily affect everyone in the same way or to the same degree; we are all individuals after all.

I have coped well with loose bowels and never suffered significant dehydration, and pain has (generally) been managed effectively. That is not to say that it doesn't hurt when I get a flare-up, it does, in spades, but a lot of the time it ebbs and flows whereas the tiredness will stay with me constantly and no amount of sleeping helps.

When I say *tiredness,* this is perhaps understating matters; lethargy, fatigue or lassitude are better terms. It is both a physical and mental inertia. Everything is a trial. The body is leaden and gets progressively more leaden as you lose weight. The mind is slow, and often it feels as if the head is filled with a dense fug; the cogs turning at half speed.

Claims of lethargy, as sufferers of chronic fatigue syndrome will attest[135] don't always garner as sympathetic a response as they deserve. It is better now than it once was, there is a little more general awareness, but I fear it will always be tainted by a whiff of malingering. Everybody feels a bit tired from time to time, don't they?

I remember explaining my condition to an A level tutor back in 1985, his response was: "well, you don't look ill." If that sounds uncaring it was nothing compared to the attitude of the

---

[135] Or Lyme disease or depression or hyperthyroidism or chronic fatigue syndrome to name but a few.

Department of Health and Social Security (DHSS) which, once upon a time, was the body responsible for administering unemployment benefit. Perhaps you recall the queue scene from the film *The Full Monty*; I had to *sign-on* in the same building. Except that in 1985 the queue is longer; it extends out of the room, down the staircase, outside and halfway down West Street. Some weeks you are waiting a couple of hours to make your mark, which is bad enough at the best of times but when all you want to do is lie down, it truly drags.

It is worse if your claim involves any divergence from the norm. Because I have lost so much weight none of my clothes fit me; there is room for two of me in my trousers, one down each leg. This means I am entitled to a small grant to buy new ones. However, the guidance cites colitis as a qualifying condition but does not make reference to Crohn's disease and the DHSS with their customary benevolence refuses my claim. It takes several letters from doctors (who frankly have better things to be getting on with) before they relent[136]. Even then I have to practically process the claim myself, trekking back and forth between West Street and Sorby House (an outlying office). It's not a great distance (1.2 miles according to Google Maps) but when you are dead on your feet you can really do without it. It is months before the cheque arrives, by which point I have put the weight back on.

## Limes

Although this anecdote did not affect me in a direct medical sense, I have included it because it is so damned interesting.

---

[136] This is where my designation of Crohn's colitis came from, a kindly and pragmatic doctor.

Back in 2009 or thereabouts CM and I are operating a little food business. The bulk of our produce is pies although this is supplemented with a number of condiments. Two of these condiments require a high proportion of lime juice, which at that time, means sitting down with a big box of the little green fruit and squeezing away like billio.

On this occasion CM is on the case and, wooden juicer in her right hand she allows the resultant liquid to run over the fingers of her left on its way into the bowl. CM is blessed with Hibernian blood and has inherited that typically pasty-white complexion that God chose to bestow upon the Irish. Not a skin to take out in the sun, so obviously being a woman who always heeds good advice, all it takes is a break in the cloud and she races out of the blocks and into the garden, deckchair under her arm.

The dangers of toasting the Irish under strong UV are well documented, the consequences of doing it after first marinating in lime juice are less so. Within an hour or so CM's left hand is swelling horribly and we prudently, though with some difficulty, remove her jewellery which is in danger of being subsumed into the throbbing red sausage meat of her ring finger. At this point we are at a loss as to why this is happening but when the rings are removed, they leave a white band in their place. The likely explanation is that whatever is causing this had not gotten to the skin under the rings. The only things the hand had been doused in were lime juice and sunshine and since her right hand had had an equal amount of UV it was reasonable to assume that the limes are the culprits.

I get on the internet, as I usually do, to see if there is any background to this theory. Sure enough there is, I find numerous examples of people burning up after handling limes.

Admittedly not many of them are in Yorkshire but that is neither here nor there; we have monsieur Limon Verde bang to rights.

CM's hand is starting to blister so she gets on the blower to NHS Direct and explains the situation to the doctor there who chooses to disregard the fruity aspects of the conversation.

"You were in the garden you say?"

"Yes."

"And your hand has swollen up?"

"Yes"

"It sounds like a bee sting."

"It's not a bee sting, I've been squeezing limes all afternoon."

"Do you have any antihistamines?"

"It's not a bee sting; we've found it on the internet it's lime juice. Why would a bee sting leave a white band where my rings were?"

"I think you probably need to go to A&E."

"Clearly!"

I have since found out that this a recognised condition. It has a name and everything; phytophotodermatitis, or Berloque dermatitis or sometimes (for the obvious reason) margarita dermatitis. Perhaps, had we been armed with this at the time we might have received a more appropriate response from NHS Direct.

She didn't go to A & E, she went to the local walk-in centre instead; much good it did her!

"You sure you've not been stung by anything?" CM is asked as she presents what looks like a bright red wicket keeper's glove. The blistering is so bad now it could have been a chemical burn and CM is in considerable pain. Still no one is prepared to entertain the lime theory.

Eventually, and grudgingly, she is given steroid cream which, if nothing else, it stops the rot. She is sent home and told to take paracetamol and avoid anything buzzy with stripes.

It is days before the swelling goes down and weeks before the blisters (which were huge) heal and the redness recedes.

## Lumbar

Everybody pulls something in their lower back from time to time; it is symptomatic of the modern, "sedentary" lifestyle and the disservice it does to posture and movement. I am no exception and was familiar with that "twanging" sensation followed by sudden pain, after which you have to go around a little gingerly for a few days. That was my perception of a bad back, until I got one for real.

It would be quite wrong to place the blame for this on having to drive a pram backwards and forwards through steep woodland every day. Plenty would kill for such a picturesque school run and would gladly push around a double buggy into which are squeezed a pair of hefty twins[137]. The root cause of my back problem is not this at all, but it certainly doesn't help.

We are elaborate biomechanical entities; nerves, muscles, bones, tendons, etc. all working together; interrelated. It seems to me that nothing works in isolation and if one part is too tight to facilitate a movement, then other parts of our anatomy have to bear some of the strain in order to accommodate this. In this instance, if my legs are too tight when I bend, then more of my back is brought into play, and if there is a similar lack of flexibility there then something will

---

[137] I put this squarely at the door of the maternal line; my wife comes from a long line of densely boned Irish

eventually give.

Flexibility, particularly in the hamstrings, is the name of the game and it seems that I am bereft of it. My youngest daughter (not surprisingly the one with all the back and shoulder problems) is the same. Neither of us can progress much further than our knees when asked to touch toes.

2006 and sciatica, that is to say, pain along the sciatic nerve, is the first sign that something is awry. The sciatic nerve (strictly speaking it is a collection of nerves) originates in the lower spine and extends through the pelvis and down through the legs to the toes. It is the longest nerve in the body. I'd had sciatic pain in my buttocks in the past which I'd always managed to "walk off" but this is different, it originates in my spine and extends down my right buttock into the leg. I take a couple of paracetamol, apply some embrocation and sit around with a hot water bottle stuffed into the waistband of my tracksuit bottoms. Although there is something comforting about applying warmth, physiologically I doubt it makes a blind bit of difference. If anything, I am getting *less* mobile.

We've arranged to go out for a family meal that evening and I take my hotty-botty with me, cleverly concealed below a long shirt. Since paracetamol seems to be a waste of time, I try more traditional methods downing a few jars and, upon returning home get into bed and augment the beer with single malt[138]. I don't have a good night, the pain worsens, shooting down my leg every time I move. As a consequence, I remain more or less immobile until the morning.

I wake with a slightly thick head and a straining bladder. Getting out of bed is a trial. Stiff and with pain shooting down

---

[138] 10 year old Isle of Jura

my leg I shuffle to the edge of the mattress, roll to my left and flop to the floor. Pulling myself up using the bedside table, I hobble towards the en-suite as CM watches on from the bed. I empty my bladder; happily, and more through luck than judgement, it goes into the toilet. As I shake off the drips a shooting, paralysing pain hits me down my right side and is closely followed by a wave of dizziness. I regain my composure but sense it is coming again so, carefully, I descend to the floor to avoid cracking my head on the porcelain in the event of a collapse. I call over to CM who is engrossed in Homes under the Hammer:

"I think I'm going to pass out!" I tell her

In fact, I am certain I shall, and lie down in preparation adding: "I'm going!" meaning, *I'm going to pass out,* as intimated in the previous sentence. CM, however, interprets this as: *I'm going...to the netherworld."*

To compound matters I let out a gurgling groan consistent with the throes of death, which confirms the theory for her.

I come around to see CM hovering over me, saying my name and telling me the ambulance is on its way. She has gone into emergency mode, the twins are lined up on the bed, ably martialled by Bruce who, like all five-year-old girls, finds that bossing people around comes all too naturally.

I remain on the floor, unable to move. I have a sudden recollection of Norman Tebbit's attempts to retain his dignity within his pyjamas as he is carried out of the rubble of the Grand Brighton Hotel. I call on CM to fetch me a pair of pants. She presents me with what looks like a posing pouch; I've no idea where it has come from. The paramedics arrive before I can send her back for a pair of boxers and so I am stuck with it. Boy Twin is ridiculously excited by the arrival of the paramedics and is bouncing up and down on the bed. Girl Twin, perhaps with a presentiment of what awaits her in her stiff thighed teens provides succour, coming over to me on the floor and holding my hand. She doesn't know what is going on and for years after she asks me:

"Tell me about that time you fell off the bed, Dad."

The paramedic, having got over the initial shock of seeing a man in a posing pouch/dress combi[139], starts attaching things to my chest. I tell him that I have passed out from pain and that the heart attack was my wife's idea, but he is having none of it. There are procedures to follow, motions to go through, which means that I am strapped to stretcher and shipped out to the van.

The hospital, after several hours on a trolley, sends me home telling me I have hurt my back. One young doctor talks to me about loss of consciousness associated with a sudden drop of blood pressure when the bladder empties. Micturition syncope I believe it is called and it is all very interesting but not helping the situation re. pain and immobility.

"Oh, there are a lot of really excellent pain killers these days," he tells me.

He doesn't give me any, he just tells me about them.

My GP refers me to the physiotherapy service. Unfortunately, the waiting time is running at about six weeks and in the meantime I shall have to manage with a crib sheet of stretching exercises and paracetamol. If you have ever had a really bad back you will be all too aware that oral paracetamol is classed as a FAU medicine[140]. At home I find some ancient painkillers

---

[139] Nightshirt actually but it's a frock in all but name.
[140] Fuck-all use

(diclofenac) which are left over from my wife's operation. Quite against the received wisdom I began taking them to help me through the night but they gave me a strange tingling sensation around the undercarriage and so I desist. I know this sounds out of character, but it really was less pleasant than you would think.

Because of the pain of moving I spend most nights in one position which, come morning, leaves me effectively locked-up and it takes me several minutes to actually get out of bed. At my request CM buys me one of those wide-necked urinal bottles which are surprisingly difficult to use if you are unable to sit up. My technique is to roll over on to my left side and poke out over the bed. After a week CM stops setting the alarm clock as the noise of my piss hitting plastic is more than sufficient to wake her in a morning.

Having dealt with urgent bladder issues I can go about rising at my leisure. Well *comparative* leisure; there is still the matter of getting Bruce to school on time. The most difficult part is getting off the mattress and I found that the least painful method is to roll to my left (as per piss bottle) but to keep rolling and allow gravity to do the rest. It hurts but is preferable to the agony of trying to sit up. The next step is to roll onto my back, inch up my knees and start swinging them from side to side as per my crib sheet. After that it is on to the front where I perform ten reps of a sort of back-bending press-up, hips and groin stuck tight to the floor. Ten minutes later I am loose enough to get to my feet, and I can start the pacing. I say *pacing*, a better description would be *slow mincing* as I make a point of trying to incorporate a bit of lateral movement into it. Bear in mind I am still wearing a dress at this point.

Then downstairs. By wedging open the door I can get a good

long mince through the hall, past the staircase and into the kitchen, wave at the family, grab a pikelet[141] and mince out again, returning forty seconds later for a slurp of coffee.

It does the job and once I manage to get the fat little buggers into the pram, tie the dog to the handle and remind Brucey to hold on tight or risk a horrible, mangled death, we are ready to cross Ecclesall Road and descend into the woods. Three hours from waking to getting out of the house; a new personal best.

This rigmarole continues for months such that it becomes my normal way of being. Movement is the key, as long as I'm walking about, I'm comparatively comfortable. However, short of sleeping on a treadmill, you have to allow inertia to creep in at some point. Long car journeys are the worst and exacerbated by our ridiculously steep drive which makes getting out of the car extra tough. Ordinarily I would hold open the door with my right arm, swing my legs to the right and lower myself down onto the slope in a controlled and measured fashion, catching the swing of the door with my left hand and locking the beast with a nonchalant, over the shoulder shot from the key fob. However, without that core strength to support me, such moves are right out the window. Exiting is like jumping from a moving train; a leap of faith and a hundred rapid, tiny, agonising steps until I reach the decelerating softness of the grass verge at the bottom of the slope.

Low point of these lumbar months is a long-planned visit from friends. Mindful that my state might put a damper on things I decide to take another delve into CM's surplus drug stocks and give codeine a go. Now, I am aware that codeine has a

---

[141] Local word for crumpet.

reputation for bunging you up a bit[142] but my reasoning is that a couple of pills to get me through the weekend should be okay; how much damage can it do? Besides, quantities of ale were going to be involved so I theorise that the congestion of one will be counteracted by the liberating effects of the other.

I am quite wrong of course. The whole lot just seizes up and even if I could have managed the beer, I doubt it would have shifted what lurked within. The bloating is terrible, no doubt made worse by the strictures within my colon, all I can do is lie down. This inertia, in turn, exacerbates my back problems such that the only way I can get comfortable is to drape myself over a bean bag. This is the most immobile I have been, and CM takes advantage of my corpse-like state. She is merciless! Unable to intervene she buys a new lawn mower (which we didn't need) and indulges in the middle-class affectation of engaging an Uzbek cleaner (also not needed).[143] She has free rein, complete control over me; I feel like James Caan in Misery. I have to do something before she bankrupts us. I have to force the issue.

Forcing the issue is easier said than done; I am sat on the loo, pushing away for hours. At least with childbirth there is the option of forceps, I have no such assistance. CM is out of the question (see "Earwax") and what kind of host hands a guest a pair of oven tongues whilst he pops his feet into the stirrups? I am on my own for this one.

I have been told, or I read somewhere, or something or other, that sitting on a loo, elbows on knees is not the optimum

---

[142] O.I.C.:opioid induced constipation

[143] To clarify, that is a cleaner from Uzbekistan and not something for sprucing up tarnished Central Asians.

position for coaxing out obstinate turds, they prefer a more upright posture. After all, it's a lot easier to go fast in the long straights than in the chicanes. With this in mind I adjust my posture as much as I can and press on but with a straighter back. Alas, this yields no benefits[144]. I have to go one step further. I have to stand.

Having had the misfortune to use a French hole-in-the-floor toilet years earlier I have my misgivings. That particular episode had not gone well; I left that toilet looking like a cell at Long Kesh[145].

I strip off everything below the waist including my shoes and socks as I have a disturbing premonition of shitting on my own foot. I take up position, legs either side of the bowl and, in the absence of a decent bombsight, dropped a test turd made of scrunched up bog roll. Happy that my aim is there or thereabouts I begin to squeeze. I can see myself in the mirror and it is not a pretty image; I look like Bruce Banner when he's on the turn.

The straining goes on for ever, and I have to remember to breathe every now and then or risk blacking out. Eventually it emerges but I am so knackered by this point I cannot push through to a conclusion. I have to take a breather, which is a strange sort of half-in, half-out limbo state, I can tell you. Eventually I show up for the second half and score within seconds.

No more codeine for me that weekend.

---

[144] Because it is nonsense; squatting, knees elevated above waist is favourite.

[145] Scene of the IRA dirty protests.

# M is for...
## Mental Health
See "Yoghurt, Fasting and Staying Well"

## Migraine

Migraine is one of those terms that is so commonplace, that we are so familiar with, we have probably lost concept of what it really means. I, in the absence of any first-hand knowledge, had always assumed it was just a hyperbolic term for bad headache. Yes, it is that, but it can be a host of other things as well, either with or without the headache. It can include: nausea, vomiting, dizziness, light sensitivity, sweating and even a dose of the shits.

No one really understands the cause of migraines, something going awry with signals in the brain in response to stimuli; of which there are a number. My particular trigger seems to be physical activity. My migraines only ever occur after a vigorous game of squash. At first, I'm not sure what is happening. I have driven home, cracked open a beer and am sitting in front of the telly suffering whatever baking/dancing/skating/apprenticing drivel that is in vogue with the Lenity ladies this month, when I noticed a zig-zagging shimmer in my vision. I move my head and it happens again. The best description I have of it is the flickering movement of the camouflaged alien in the Predator movies. However, rather than rush off and cover myself with jungle mud[146] I draw breath and allow reason to climb on board. Of course, this is no Predator, if it were we would all be dead meat by now. Using my well-honed analytical skills, I deduce

---

[146] As Arnie did in the film to mask his thermal image. I don't think it would have worked, the mud would have warmed up in no time.

that it must be something else.

In the absence of headaches (which I assumed was an obligatory symptom) it is a long time before I come up with migraine as a culprit. What I experience is a migraine aura or ocular migraine and not once have I experienced it alongside headache. I am glad to say it always passes within half an hour or so and consequently, I have done nothing about it.

There is another squash player I know who also gets them; he's done nothing to remedy it either.

## Mrs Lenity as Proxy

The early noughties and various attempts have been made to get past my bowel strictures, none of which has any success. This represents something of a problem for my gastroenterologists since they are very keen to know what is going on back there. Pursuant to this I am referred to General Surgery to see if they have any thoughts. As you know I am terrified at the prospect of being cut open, but I go along anyway. It seems only right that I should hear their pitch.

The first thing that strikes me about Mr A..., the surgeon, is his moustache; very Stalinist, I think. Not that there is anything dictatorial about him; quite the opposite, he is a good listener and takes on board my rationale for not being cut open, which is this:

I am young, in my thirties, the strictures cause me no problems and the Crohn's is relatively dormant. I accept that there is a risk of cancer but cutting out the strictures just on the off chance that there might be something going on further up seems drastic. I'm not comfortable with prophylactic surgery. Also, if we leave it a few years who knows what new techniques will become available. At the time there is talk of a swallow-able *pill camera* and I have half an eye of that becoming mainstream.[147]

Mr A..., no doubt suspecting that cowardice is at the route of all this, does his best to sugar-coat the surgical options, drawing me a nice little diagram of my colon and where he intends to chop. This only serves to dissuade me further because, in my ignorance, I have assumed that surgery would involve nipping out the strictures and stitching the ends together leaving me deficient of just a few inches of tubing. Apparently not. There is an issue with blood supply, cutting out sections of bowel willy-nilly can leave other parts off-grid, so to speak. When you think about this it's quite obvious, the colon needs blood to function just like any other organ. And since it is so long, by necessity this means a number of different blood vessels. This is why DIY surgery is such a bad idea; there's so much more to it than you think. The solution to the blood supply issue is to take a much larger section of the bowel out. This is known as a hemicolectomy; hemi being from the Greek meaning half. This doesn't appeal to me at all. Mr A... further entices me:

"I could do it keyhole if you like?"

It's still a big "no" from me, but I keep that bit of information in my locker for future reference. We leave it there; he has apprised me of the risks I am running and I leave him in no doubt about my yellow streak. He shakes my hand, looks me in the eye and says:

"We understand each other then?"

It feels like I have just negotiated an arms contract.

2005 and CM is experiencing bleeding. No stranger to a dose of farmers she pays little heed to it expecting it to go away. It does

[147] The use of capsule endoscopy (pillcam) was pioneered by Prof. Mark McAlindon at Sheffield Teaching Hospitals.

not. In fact, it worsens and after seeing her GP she is referred to a specialist. Quite by chance the doctor, Prof S... does more than the basic scoping and as he delves deeper finds a couple of polyps. A polyp, in case you do not know is abnormal tissue growing outward on a stalk from (in this instance) the lining of CM's colon. Further investigation reveals that her colon is a mass of them, and when I say "a mass" I make no exaggeration, apparently there are so many it looks like a mushroom farm up there. Chief amongst them is a huge beast loitering on the corner of her ascending and transverse colon.

CM is booked in for her polypectomy (operation to remove polyps) which, via a colonoscope, involves looping a wire around the neck of the polyp and burning the bugger off. This goes well and yields a good crop of fungi, however, the big one proves a little stubborn. Sheer size and its position right on a bend mean that the wire loop won't go over it. It remains in situ and CM is referred back to Prof S... to talk about surgery. He recommends an extended right hemicolectomy, a version of the operation I have been swerving for the last few years. I think that is called situational irony.

Prof S...will perform the operation himself and explains the procedure in detail, telling her it is quite routine, and that she will function perfectly adequately afterwards, albeit with a large scar down her middle. CM takes it stoically, although I know she must be shitting bricks.

Something is niggling at me, however. A couple of years earlier Mr A... had mentioned keyhole surgery as an option for my colon. I didn't pay it a lot of attention at the time because as far as I was concerned, I was having *no* surgery, keyhole or otherwise. I know CM is worried about the size of the wound and I put it to her that it might be worth asking if something

similar could be done here. She gets on the phone to Prof S...
who is game, and a brother surgeon skilled in the technique, is
dragged down from Newcastle to show him how it's done.
According to CM she is the first person to have this type of
operation in Sheffield, but I don't see how that can be true if I
was being offered it years earlier.

The surgery takes hours and I sit around the hospital worrying
myself sick. Eventually she is wheeled onto the ward still
asleep, waking momentarily to ask me if they have done it? I
take this to mean: "have they done it laparoscopically?" (i.e. by
keyhole). I confirm all has gone to plan with which she shuts
her eyes and goes straight back to sleep. CM later maintains
that she was asking *had she been given an ileostomy?* which as
far as I recall was never a great issue. Funny how the memory
plays tricks, is it not?

## MRI
See "Diagnostic Imaging"

## Muscle
Playing squash one evening and moving to the T from a
backcourt length I feel a sudden impact on my right calf. It's
just like being hit with the ball, which of course is impossible as
the ball is on its way to the front wall. As soon as I put any
weight on my leg, I know something is amiss. I can't support
myself; there seems to be no connection between my foot and
my knee. Thankfully it is only a ruptured muscle rather than
torn ligaments or Achilles tendon, so the debilitation is
relatively short-lived; I am off the crutches in a week.

The interesting thing about this episode is CM's reaction to me
hobbling home.

"That's it now," she says, "you'll have to stop squash."

She is alarmingly quick with her diktat; almost as if this is just the opportunity she has been waiting for. It makes me wonder how many other secret plans are lurking in my matrimonial future.

# N is for…

## Nerves

See "Cricked Neck"

## Nocturnal Emissions

I recall some time in my youth when a fellow pupil missed a day's schooling and word got around that his mother had phoned in to explain that the poor chap was distraught at having had a wet dream the previous night. This caused so much hilarity amongst the throng that nobody sought to question how the information was leaked. Suffice to say when the child in question did return to school he was greeted with appropriate levels of sympathy and understanding. Schools, like Turkish prisons and the French Foreign Legion are no place for sensitive souls.

Wet dreams are just part and parcel of being a male adolescent. They happen and, yes, they are embarrassing, mainly because of the mess they cause. Youths requesting that their bedding needs a wash is a bit of a giveaway. There is the option of leaving things in-situ but if one is a regular wet dreamer this runs the risk of poor mum trying to fold a sheet of corrugated cardboard into the twin tub.[148]

---

[148] Back in the days of twin tubs only women and Chinese did laundry. These days of course, Western man is perfectly comfortable with the DAZ which is why the Lenity family's clothes are all the same pinky-grey colour.

Aside from the embarrassment, a nocturnal emission is not an unpleasant experience; after all, an orgasm is an orgasm and not to be sniffed at.[149] One caveat to that would be the dream aspect. Dreams as we all know are a law unto themselves and I imagine it would take some deep thought to rationalise having shot one's load over a close relative or pet for instance.[150] I once had a wet dream where I ejaculated drinking chocolate,[151] which was strange, and I had a lady friend who orgasmed in her sleep (the female version of a wet dream) after being soundly pumped by Rolf Harris which, in 1992, was strangely prescient.

I had assumed that wet dreams were something I had left behind as I entered adulthood, but I was mistaken. For some reason they started again in my mid-thirties only this time they rarely have an erotic dream associated with them which leaves a man feeling quite short changed. All the mess and none of the cocoa.

I was at a loss to explain this at first until it occurred to me that after all my *accidents* I would wake up on my back. I am, it would appear, something of a duvet rapist. The received wisdom states that nocturnal emissions do not generally come about via mechanical stimulation, but I am here to question that. If I sleep on my side, they don't occur. I can fall asleep on my back on the settee without making a mess but as soon as I

---

[149] Sound advice figuratively and literally.

[150] If you are a Christian it may help you to know that according to the doctrine of St Augustine, wet dreams are not regarded as sinful since they are involuntary. If you happen to be Jewish the bad news is that, according to the Torah, you're just a dirty bastard.

[151] It may have been cocoa, the dream was a little vague on this point.

get under anything with a decent TOG rating, I am like a splurge gun[152].

I no longer sleep on my back.

# O is for...
## Old Age and Getting There

I recently began reading a book on aging, the premise of which was that we should embrace, not fear the aging process. At least I think that was the gist of it because I gave up on it after a while; why it takes a hundred and fifty pages of pretentious flim-flam to say: "cheer up, you old bastard!" is beyond me.

I don't think we should fear getting older, but that does not mean I am looking forward to it; I stopped doing that once I reached the legal drinking age. There may be many benefits attached to being of advanced years, but I cannot imagine that they make up for what has been left behind. However, I accept it. What choice do I have? Getting old is one of two options and the other one has an even worse reputation.

Age, I think, is to some degree a state of mind and I could probably bang out a few paragraphs discoursing on that but for the moment I am more interested in the physical changes that have occurred to me over the years. I say *over the years* because that is how such processes work, they quietly erode at us until at some point the change is too stark to ignore. It is the work of decades but as far as our cognisance is concerned it happens overnight. I know it is a cliché but some time in my forties I looked in a mirror and an old face was looking back at me. Shaven headed and with grey stubble I looked like an elderly chimp in spectacles. The last time I looked I was a beautiful

---

[152] From the film Bugsy Malone

youth![153] What happened?

Hair loss I have covered already (see "Follicular Issues") and as you are aware it came as no great shock to me. That is to say *baldness* in the common meaning of the term, i.e. on the head. I was not at all prepared for baldness on my legs. There was a time I had a rather shapely, hirsute and manly calf, these days I have a shapely, bald and not at all manly lower leg. All the hairs, it seems, have been polished off by years of sock and trouser abrasion. My brother and I as children would mock our father's pallid, varicose vein embossed legs on every occasion he exposed them[154]; *corpse legs* we called them. It never occurred to us that we would inherit them. I think we assumed that they were a result of pre-war deprivation, like rickets.

It is not all depilation however; my ear and nose hair are out of control. I have tried those little electric trimmers but they are simply not up to the job and so I have resorted to burning them off with a cigarette lighter.[155] I even tried it on our dog, who is a martyr to ear irritation due to the excessive wool in there and it went off like a wildfire. Thankfully, she has floppy ears, so it was just a case of dropping the flap and starving it of oxygen.

My pubes have got in on the act too; they grow to an unfeasible length. Left to their own devices, in a couple of weeks my genitals would have disappeared inside a huge raft of wire wool. Unfurled, my Rubiks would stretch down to my knees. Why this happens I do not know; it is hard to see any evolutionary advantage to rampant pube growth. Unless it is to

---

[153] Strictly speaking a *beautiful (but spotty) youth*

[154] Not very often: he was never a great shorts wearer.

[155] Just the ears, nose hair seems a step too far. There is a video of me in action on my Facebook page if you are interested.

do with the cushioning effect of all that tightly curled hair? That could certainly be the case with mine; you could ping a house brick off them.

Whilst we are in this neck of the woods let me introduce my testicles. Years ago, I was flattered to receive a compliment on my knackers from a lady friend on the occasion of our first physical union[156].

"Ooh, nice balls." She exclaimed.

Although she had one of those voices that made everything she said sound sarcastic, going on the gusto with which she threw herself into our subsequent lovemaking, in this instance, I believe she was being sincere. I dread to think what she would make of them these days! I have half a mind to part my pubic jungle, take a photograph and send it to her but caution tells me this is probably not a good idea. You know how it is with sending pictures of one's genitals to people; there is always someone that gets the wrong idea.

My nuts no longer seem to have anything restraining them and on the rare occasions that I have sex, my climax is often marred by the right one popping into my body cavity which, I have to say, takes the gloss off it all for me. I resort to standing on one leg wiggling around until it drops into its pocket again. I mentioned it to the doctor but after a thorough juggling all he could offer me was:

"Yeah, feels a bit loose."

Which I suppose is actually the root of the problem. I have lost my elasticity.

Lack of elasticity is not restricted to my unruly scrot, the rest of

---

[156] The same woman that Rolf Harris brought to climax (see Nocturnal Emissions)

my skin is affected too. There is no spring to it and it seems so thin, like crepe paper. Obviously, aging skin loses elasticity which is where all the wrinkles come from. And this is especially so if you have been a bit slapdash with your lifestyle; drinking, smoking, sunbathing, they all take their toll. It strikes me that we skinny types are hit worse than most; there is nothing much on our bones to stretch out the slack, no padding. Now that is something they don't tell you in Cosmo; if you want to avoid wrinkles, just get fat.

Both my mother and her mother suffered from dementia, so it is not surprising that I succumb to the odd moment of panic whenever I fail to recall something or other. I have always had a good memory[157] and set great store by it so quite aside from the thought that I might be showing early signs of losing my marbles it bothers me that my recall can now be a little sluggish. Does the mind slow with age? I keep reading about how the brain, rather like a muscle, needs exercise to keep it performing to its potential. I have taken this on board, sort of, and when I do stumble over some fact that I really should recall rarely do I resort to Google in order to set my mind at rest[158]. I keep working on it until it arrives, which eventually it does. Either that or I forget I needed to remember it in the first place.

A man's sex drive certainly fades with age, it is linked with testosterone levels which drop as we get older. Is that such a bad thing? Well, the prospect of not being able to generate a stiffy when I need one is obviously going to be a

---

[157] But not for anything of value. The phrase: *Mine of useless information* could have been penned for me.

[158] This is partly because I don't have a smart phone.

disappointment[159] but being a slave to desire as I was as a teenager (and well beyond) I do not miss one bit. And it is nice to be able to sit at the back of a bus and not worry about the vibration from the engine. I was terrible, I dread to think what proportion of my time, since the onset of puberty, I have spent nursing some degree of tumescence. I suspect this contributed to my poor academic performance; starving my brain of blood or something like that.

The most difficult time was in P.E. We had sadistic P.E. teachers[160] who decreed that underpants would not be worn beneath shorts for the purposes of physical education. Apparently, it was a hygiene issue or something[161]. My problem was that without pants to keep it restrained my manhood had a tendency to get animated. The slightest brush of nylon short against German helmet and I was in pan handle mode. Which is not ideal in a changing room full of your naked and semi-naked peers; it gives the wrong impression. I would sit hunched over, concentrating until my brain bled. Trying not to move and praying for flaccidity before I had to go out and start diving around on a frozen rugby pitch. I never noticed anyone else that had this trouble; perhaps I was the only one? Perhaps they had a different technique for disguising it?

And whilst we are on the subject of stiffness, I will mention joints and muscles. I may well change my tune in years to come, but at the moment (early fifties) I don't feel a lot different in this

---

[159] I am some way short of that at the time of writing

[160] Is there any other sort?

[161] Without intending to make a pun, the pendulum has swung back the other way, my children don't even shower at school these days; school sends them home stinky.

respect to when I was in my twenties. This may be a reflection of the lack of physical activity I was engaged in back then, but I don't think it's the whole story. I get the same aches and pains now as I did in the 1980s; my knees hurt in the same way, my muscles are just as painfully stiff a day or two after exercise, and stretching is still the same tedious and uncomfortable chore even without the leg warmers.[162]

Where I have noticed a difference is in getting going, I cannot leap into action from a sitting start[163], I have to ease into physical jerks these days. Also, my recovery time has lengthened; I take at least twice as long to recover from twists and sprains as I did in my prime. It doesn't take long to stiffen up either; round-robin squash brings this home to me and the five-minute breaks between games leave me running around court like Forrest Gump in his callipers.

I think I have been lucky in that I haven't suffered much in the way of wear and tear. I have always been relatively light boned and other than being a bit creaky[164] I believe my joints have stood up to the rigours of time quite well. Early days though.

I think I am getting nesh. This is probably not a word you are familiar with since it is very much in the dialect category; it means to be susceptible to the cold and I have yet to find a better word to describe that condition. I have always had a healthy respect for cold weather, I'm not saying I go to football

---

[162] I have never worn leg warmers.

[163] Why would I need to?

[164] When I bend down my knee groans away like Leonard Cohen. My neck feels like a pepper mill when I turn it, and on rising in a morning my first few steps are so clicky that it sounds like a game of dominoes. That's it, run out of similes.

matches in February wearing nothing but a vest, I'm not a
Geordie! Far from it, February for me has always meant the
wearing of a coat of some sort. Generally speaking, that was
sufficient; I never needed to be swathed head to toe in
insulation as I do now. CM on the other hand has suffered from
the cold terribly. There were times, out and about, when she
could barely move for all the layers of clothing she would be
wearing. She looked like the Michelin Man; less smiley
though.[165]

These days our positions are reversed, CM is starting to suffer
from the odd hot flush, and I get so cold that I cannot function.
There are times when I lose feeling in my feet, and my fingers
turn first white and then blue. I am fine if I am moving;
walking, gardening, that sort of thing but as soon as I stop, the
chill sets in rapidly. There is a condition known as Raynaud's
phenomenon and I sometimes wonder if I have a dash of that
going on. I hesitate to take this to the GP because, frankly, they
must be sick of seeing me and also, according to Wikipedia, the
primary treatment is avoidance of cold and I don't need a
professional to tell me that.

It may sound counter-intuitive, but my icy extremities
prompted me to adopt the practice of taking cold showers. I
had a thought that cold water might improve my circulation in
some way; making the heart work harder or something. I don't
know whether this has any basis in medicine, it was just one of
those things one does on a whim. See "Yoghurt, Fasting and

---

[165] Whose real name is actually Bibendum (a drinking reference?).
Incidentally, he's slimmed down over the years, given up cigars and
now wears contact lenses. Unlike the current Mrs Lenity, Bibendum
has never sported a nose.

Staying Well" and "Garlic"

There is a long tradition of cold-water baths and showers and it seems that they are experiencing something of a renaissance; they are becoming fashionable, with beneficial citations including: improved circulation, a reduction in uric acid, helping with depression, burning fat, releasing endorphins and becoming more like James Bond[166].

A quick caveat here, I don't generally do daily showers. My philosophy with showering is this: I don't get involved unless I stink. As my late father said: "Only mucky people wash." This has led to questions about my personal hygiene, particularly from my wife and daughters who are obsessed with showering and yet smell far worse than me.[167] As a consequence, they douse themselves in so much scent that I can barely breathe in the mornings. If I were a badger they would need a Defra licence to do that to me.[168]

If it wasn't for my punitive toilet flushing (it confuses the shower thermostat and momentarily scalds the showerer) the Lenity womenfolk would happily spend an hour under the hot stream. This, I believe, is in no one's interests. Firstly, our fuel bill is horrendous and down mainly to daily bathing, boiling five litres of water to make one small cup of tea,[169] and having the heating on full whack whilst lounging around the house in

---

[166] James Bond famously took cold showers although his ritual involved a hot shower after which the temperature was immediately reduced whereas I go in cold from the outset. Which of us is the real man? Answer me that.

[167] Discounting the farts.

[168] Department of environment, food and rural affairs

[169] And then not drinking it!

skimpy clothing. A stranger to Schloss Lenity would be forgiven for thinking they had wandered into the Playboy mansion.

Secondly, there are environmental aspects. We are continually told that we must all do our bit for the planet, a mantra that my kids are quite happy to recite at me when it suits them. Putting this into practice, however, they seem to struggle with. As I said, I'm nesh and it doesn't take much for me to get chilled bones, I often fall victim during the day. Once the kids get home though there is no problem, I am constantly working up a sweat, up and down stairs closing doors, turning off lights and radiators, etc., etc.

Thirdly, I'm not sure washing is all that good for you. It can't be natural to rub chemicals all over your body whilst dousing it in hot water for an hour every day! At best it must strip out some of the body's natural oils and whilst we are, nowadays, aware of the importance of maintaining gut bacteria, might not the same philosophy apply to our skin's natural flora?

# P is for...
## Pain

One of the reasons for this book was a conversation with someone about the worse pain we had experienced. The upshot was that I could not come up with a definitive answer. Pain, it seems, is a rather subjective experience and the sensation of pain relies as much on the brain's attitude to it as it does to what we would traditionally regard as the source. Pain is not an absolute then, it is whatever the brain makes of it, which makes my conversation, and this section, in many respects, somewhat meaningless.

Nevertheless, I have a list:

Tooth abscesses.

Post-surgery.

Sudden blunt trauma.

Shingles.

Cystoscopy with a swollen prostate.

Slipped disc/sciatica.

This of course makes no distinction between chronic pain and acute pain. It omits emotional and mental pain. It takes no account for age; would my crushed finger feel as painful today as it did when I was seventeen? Is there a situational aspect to things? Do we feel more pain when we are miserable? Does the shock of receiving an unexpected blow, say, increase the pain or lessen it? One Christmas I had the misfortune to slip on a pool of frozen sick whilst out walking my dogs. I flew into the air and landed on my left thigh on a flight of stone steps.[170] The pain when it came through was horrible, I felt like crying! However, I hadn't done a great deal of damage, I was left a bit achy and bruised but I was ok. Yet that brief period lying on the stones was like the world was coming to an end. Would it have been worse if someone had seen me? Does embarrassment help or hinder?

Here is another strange aspect of pain, and I have noticed this on a couple of occasions, when pain is removed, that is to say,

---

[170] I put this in Sudden Blunt Trauma alongside the weight dropped on my fingertip. In this case I narrowly averted disaster; the shock was such that I let go of both leads and if it hadn't been for their impulse to have a nibble at a bit of frozen diced carrot the dogs would have carried on into the traffic

longer-standing pains, for instance when a tooth is fixed up, or when bowel pain suddenly starts to respond to treatment, part of me misses it! See "Feet"

Does pain hurt more if you can see it? Based on personal experience I would say yes. I once had a cyst removed (see "Wow that's a big 'un") which left me with a gaping hole in my shoulder. This required *packing* with specialised dressings on a daily basis. The nurses charged with this task kept telling me that it looked painful and enquiring of my pain management regime of which there was none. The fact was it didn't seem to hurt and I wonder if that would be the case if could see all those bits of rag being pushed into the wound's crimson maw?

Thus, I elaborated on my failure to name a definitive pain which I think left my interlocuter (who'd once had the misfortune to step on a three-pin plug[171]) wishing he'd kept his musings to himself.

## Parasites

Fleas

I have never had fleas in the sense that I have had human fleas, aka house fleas or *Pulex irritans* to give then their posh name. My mother did once catch a flea from a tramp who sat next to her in Birmingham's Digbeth bus station, but I don't think she kept it and it was never tied down to a particular species. My experience of fleas is second hand, from pet dogs, although perhaps this should read third hand as most dog fleas are in fact cat fleas (*Ctenocephalides felis*), or so I have been told.

The source of our strife was a wire-haired miniature

---

[171] Which, my caveats notwithstanding, is a bloody painful and peculiarly British injury.

dachshund by the name of Rudi. Ru had a number of unpleasant characteristics, one of which was that he was a flea Shangri-La. I think it had something to do with his coat which was in fact two coats; a longish, coarse outer and a soft and downy inner. It was the latter that these alleged cat fleas found so appealing.

Because Rudi was such a lap dog these visitors inevitably found their way onto the bodies of his owners, and CM and I were forever scratching up bites on our legs, torso, neck arms, you name it. The fleas don't thrive on human skin (not hairy enough) but they do hang around long enough to be a bloody nuisance.

I confess to being puzzled by the flea's modus operando in respect to human beings. The itchy lumps they leave in their wake tend to be in a pattern, often a line or discrete patch. What has to happen, I wonder, for this insect to decide it is time to chow down?[172] Does it amble around until it gets a tummy rumble, digs in for a minute then leaves, but within a couple of inches finds it hasn't sated its appetite so has another go, and so on? And at what point does it decide (being in an altogether unsatisfactory environment) that it's had enough and actually wasn't that mad on the flavour of the host anyway? There was nothing much we could do about our unwelcome guests; for some reason flea treatments didn't work on Rudi. On one occasion we tried one so potent that my parents, who were looking after the dogs at the time, got an allergic reaction. Their faces swelled and eyes closed up until they looked like one of those shocking news photos:

---

[172] It may seem an obvious point but I shall make it nonetheless, the flea feeds on the hosts blood.

*Elderly couple savagely beaten by heartless yobs!*

There is, however, a positive side to these interlopers, and if you have ever caught a flea you will know what I am talking about. It is immensely satisfying to crush the little bastards. There is bit of technique involved but worth mastering. Ordinarily the most difficult aspect is locating the beast but with Rudi this was never an issue; he only needed turning on his back and dozens could be seen busily to-ing and fro-ing around the open ground of his hairless underside. The trick to catching a flea is to use a little spittle on your fingertips, then, whilst maintaining the moist contact, shift it between thumbnails, and apply pressure. They give an audible crack if you catch them right and often leave a little ruddy smear to assuage any guilt one might feel at dispatching them. They knew the risks, they were caught bang to rights, blood on their hands![173]

Head Lice

I don't recall having head lice as a child, which is just as well because it would have been a bugger to treat on account of me being a bit of a Cristal Tipps[174]. I have to wait until my forties before catching a dose from my dear children which goes to show that having hair is not necessarily a prerequisite. At least I am spared the nit comb which is something.

I am glad to say we avoided any of the pesticide resistant super lice that Mumsnet is preoccupied with, and ours cleared up with the bog-standard remedies. Aside from the irony of a baldy catching them I have nothing else to offer on the subject.

---

[173] Fleas do not have hands.

[174] From Cristal Tipps and Alistair, an animated show from the seventies featuring a big haired girl with a dog. Very much of its day

Worms

As far as I know I never had worms as a child. This was despite going to school and associating with a few dirty kids. You know the type, the ones with the greasy hair and a permanent stream of snot marked out in a bright pink stripe twixt nose and mouth. The ones that always carried a general fusty aura with them and smelt like a wet Labrador every time it rained. Perhaps you don't, they aren't as common as they once were, but they still exist; university I.T. departments are a good starting point if you are interested in sourcing one.

My first experience of parasitic worms is at Bakewell cattle market, late seventies to early eighties, were I to guess. We had just adopted a puppy, which in those days was a much more laid-back (and cheaper) experience than it is today. In fact one didn't *adopt* a puppy, one just *got* a puppy. Puppy adoption seems like a gentrification of the process. We name our puppy Barney on account of him being born in a barn[175].

Nobody worries too much about worming or vaccinations then. Nor do we pick up excrement; you just wander off and think nothing more of it, but in this instance we, and a couple of Bakewellians are compelled to stand and stare at Barney's little present.

"He's eaten a load of elastic bands!" states my father, a man who is in denial about his need for spectacles. Clearly, they are not elastic bands; even when trapped in a foul-smelling dog turd an elastic band does not feel the urge to wriggle free and make

---

[175] We were simple folk relying on our own wit for entertainment

good his/her[176] escape. Poor Barney clearly has parasitic worms (aka helminths) and by shitting them out in a cattle pen he is doing his best to reintroduce them into the Peak District food chain.

What is this to do with anything? Well, I am trying to point out that the presence of parasitic worms (humans included) is a perfectly natural state of affairs. There is a school of thought which postulates that helminths, or more correctly the absence of helminths may be contributing to the rise in immune disorders in more developed regions of the world; diseases such as Crohn's and colitis. The *too clean* theory suggests that because our bodies have adapted to function in the presence of parasitic organisms, our immune systems are geared up to deal with them. When these parasites are removed (through improvements in hygiene and the like) the immune system has no one to legitimately take its aggression out on. In frustration it turns on the body itself. There are social parallels; in Britain National Service ceased in the early nineteen sixties which had hitherto provided a legitimate release for young men's aggression. And if you think that's just Daily Mail style reactionary dogma, well that's up to you but next time the local Teddy Boys give you a kicking don't come crying to me.

It follows, then, that if an absence of worms in the gut causes IBD then replacing the worms could be seen as a way of treating it. Indeed, I believe trials have been undertaken with some success. From a personal perspective my experience of hosting worms does not produce any noticeable improvement

---

[176] Most intestinal worms, I believe are hermaphrodites, that is to say both sexes in one. As for rubber bands, I couldn't say one way or the other.

in my situation, if anything I actually feel worse during my infestation. Though to be fair the conditions under which I became host had little scientific rigour about them; just a case of arse-scratching kids who never wash their hands. I, or rather we, since the whole family was infected, were in the grip of pinworms, which in UK worm terms are regarded as the usual suspects. And fiendishly clever little buggers they are too. They live in the large bowel, particularly the rectal area. At night the female worms pop out and lay their eggs around the anus. How they know that it's night time when they live in such a dark environment is anyone's guess. Along with the eggs comes an irritating secretion which causes the area to itch. Itches get scratched and eggs get transferred to fingers, from fingers to door handles, to kitchen surfaces, to sandwiches, teacups, etc., ultimately arriving in the mouth of a potential host. The eggs move to the small intestine, hatch and wriggle south to take up residence in the colon at which point the cycle begins again.

It's not difficult to see why pinworms are more common in households with young children. A. young children are in contact with other young children and B. young children have quite a cavalier approach to hygiene. For some time one of our kids (I won't name him) thought that walking up to a sink, waving his hands at it and saying "wash-wash, wash-wash" was a perfectly adequate ablution.[177]

It is very easy to kill pinworms; all it takes is a single pill from the chemist[178]. The difficulty lies in making sure they stay dead, which means lots of washing of surfaces and underwear and

---

[177] That is a perfectly (word for word) true story

[178] *Drugstore* in American

bedding and the like. The weight of domestic chores they bring with them is the probably the worst aspect.

As for benefiting my Crohn's, well, as mentioned, it doesn't do me any good at all, I get a mild dose of the trots for my trouble. But then, at that time I don't have any active inflammation to speak of, so I suppose that there was nothing much to cure.

## Physics A Level

A lab based practical, working in pairs we are required to drop an iron weight down the length of a retort stand and record some or other pointless guff associated with it. I can't remember exactly and it doesn't really matter as far as the story goes, the point is, one of us is timing and the other one is required to release the weight on command. My partner, being an idiot, lets go of the weight far too early sending it directly onto my left index finger. It really hurts, well you can imagine, and we have strong words over it.

Surprisingly (according to my GP) it doesn't seem to be broken which shows you that we are sometimes more durable than you might suppose. However, blood has pooled under the nail and it remains painful, so the GP suggests cutting the nail and relieving a bit of the pressure. He had several chops at it with a scalpel but didn't make much progress and I am creating such a fuss that he just gives up. Months later my black fingernail withers away under its own steam.

## Playground Doctors

2007 and CM is having problems with her hemicolectomy. She has raging diarrhoea, is losing weight, and getting weaker by the day. Despite her history the GP refuses to refer her to a specialist and continues to insist on a regime of gulping down loperamide[179], replacing fluid and crossing fingers.

At an absolute low ebb, we book an appointment with a gastroenterologist at a local private hospital. Dr J... is by anyone's estimation a handsome man; CM is visibly swooning every time he talks to her, which she tries to pass off as dehydration, but I know that dehydration doesn't make you blush, nor does it make you play with your hair and giggle like a schoolgirl.

He reminds me of a young Patrick Mower, and if you are wondering why my wife is attracted to a portly, xylophone-playing astronomer with a penchant for monocles, then return to your Google search and check your spelling.

Almost immediately upon hearing CM's symptoms Dr J... has a handle on the problem and prescribes something to deal with it[180]. Within a day of taking the medicine CM is on the mend and we are relieved but a little annoyed that we had wasted so much time getting to this point.

Back to my bowels now and after General Surgery had sent me back to Gastroenterology for not playing ball (See Mrs Lenity as Proxy) Dr L... decides she is busy that day and another consultant can have the obstreperous one. My hefty case notes land on the desk of Dr B... who, by chance, is the father of one of my eldest daughter's friends at pre-school. Dr B... is fairly sanguine about my situation and is happy to continue with just a maintenance dose of mesalazine[181] whilst I am still asymptomatic.

---

[179] Street name Imodium

[180] A problem to do with reabsorption of bile, the part of CM's colon responsible for this now being absent.

[181] Street name Asacol, the successor to sulphasalazine

There is talk of a procedure to widen the strictures rather than remove them. Strictureplasty, as it is known, involves making a cut along the length of the stricture and then stitching it up at right angles to that cut. Dr B... draws me a nice little sketch to illustrate this. It is very clear and reminds me of something from the Boy Scout Manual. It is still a little too *cut'em open* for my tastes and I commit it to the Mind Palace for future reference.

My association with the aforementioned Dr J... is renewed when I meet him one day in the school yard; one of his children, it seems, is in the same year as our twins. Coincidentally, it is around this time the he becomes my gastroenterologist. At his first attempt at a Lenity colonoscopy, he fares no better than anyone else at getting past my strictures and in view of my aversion to surgery goes along with the watching brief, informed by the occasional CT scan and barium enema. He tells me about a procedure whereby a balloon is inflated inside the colon in order to stretch and thus widen the strictures. Unlike Dr B..., he doesn't draw a diagram; I think because the procedure is pretty self-explanatory. Endoscopic balloon dilation is not without risks (as you can imagine there is a chance of rupture) and for the time being we leave it at the description phase.

I have a feeling that Dr J... fancies himself as *Cock of the Scopes,* so to speak, and still harbours hope of performing a successful colonoscopy on me. He wants to be the first to reach the promised land of my terminal ileum and suggests trying with a paediatric scope which is much narrower. I agree, at the same time wondering why no one had thought of this before. It works. Obviously, there is a good deal of discomfort due to all the twisting and turning required to get it around and the baby scope is shorter than the standard one and so Dr J... is elbow deep when he's finished but that is a minor complication. Dr J... cannot not hide the satisfaction in his voice when he says:

"Oh! I think this is TI.[182] It is, it's TI!"

Rather like John Hanning Speke on rolling up at the source of the Nile:

"Bugger me! Lake Victoria! Who'd have thought it?"

My colon is thoroughly biopsied and everything is found to be hunky dory.

2012 and Dr J... has got my scopings down to a fine art and my colon looks as good as it has done in years. There is even talk that the disease has "burned itself out." This is brilliant news! I give myself a pat on the back for declining surgery[183] all those years earlier, happy to carry on with this yearly confirmation of my fine health and rosy prospects. Right?

## Podiatry for Jonny Oddlegs

Round about the time that I am having all of my lower back trouble (see Lumbar) someone[184] notices that I have a bit of a pronation to my gait. A pronation being a rolling of the foot as you walk. The feeling is that I might benefit from seeing a podiatrist. At this time the podiatry service here is stretched to its limit it and it takes over a year before I get an appointment by which time I've forgotten why I'd been referred in the first place. Nevertheless, I present myself at Pod HQ, which is an inconspicuous little unit around the corner from the Crucible Theatre. If I hadn't been told I would never have known it was

---

[182] terminal ileum.

[183] For *declining* read *chickening out*

[184] In case you were wondering it is someone qualified (a physio), not just a bloke down the pub.

there.

A very nice young woman there reminds me what is wrong with me (pronation) then gets me to roll up my trousers and walk up and down, barefoot in the waiting area whilst she watches on. Yes, I do have a pronation and, further examination reveals, I also have one leg longer than the other. I've had knee pain on and off (nothing serious, more discomfort than pain) for many years and have always regarded it as a sporting inevitability. What I now discover is that the pronation (possibly hampered by my odd legs) might be the cause. I also have problems with my ankle, having fallen over on a child's shoe some months earlier. Although the initial injury has ostensibly gone, a bit of residual pain remains. This is added to my notes.

I am given a pair of black plastic arch supports to put in my shoes (the technical term for these is orthotics) and a wad of stiff foam to sit under my left heel to raise that leg up a tad. Arch supports can be pretty uncomfortable at first, but one gets used to them by stages until after a couple of weeks you wouldn't know they were there.

I think my orthotics make a difference to my knee, but the ankle thing remains. A few more visits to the nice lady ensue before someone decides that I am a waste of energy and I am passed up to a senior pod-bod who gives me a thorough going over and sends me for an ultrasound examination. He also refers me on to a consultant who has a name very similar to mine; Dr T... Nice though it is to be passed up the pyramid, I really get the feeling that Podiatry have had enough of me and the rigour with which this examination is undertaken is just to make sure there is no excuse for anyone to send me back. My referral letter no doubt contains some of that mysterious coded language that the medical profession uses, such as Plumbus oscillans, which is Latin for swinging the lead or PITA (pain in the arse).

I have my ultrasound and my visit to Dr T... and apparently there is nothing wrong with me. Even my odd-length legs had evened up[185]. My ankle still hurts though.

## Prostate

I cannot say that I knew very much about this particular organ until I became personally affected. I'd always associated it with old men and their bladders and at fifty I didn't put myself in that bracket, assuming prostate trouble was still years off. I'd an initial flirtation with it a few years earlier, but it was so brief and was resolved so quickly that I was never spurred on to investigate the subject in any depth. On that occasion, I would hazard a guess somewhere around 2005, I discovered an issue during one of our (CM and I) scheduled love-making appointments, the culmination of which was brown rather than its customary, milky white.

"That's not right!" announced CM perceptively.

"I know."

"What's it mean?"

"It means in future we'll have to change my secret gay fantasy from Hulk Hogan to Magnum P.I."

"What do you mean?...urgh you're a disgusting man! Go and see the doctor."

Which, assuming she was referring to my henna ejaculate and not my sense of humour, I do.

"Sorry but I'll need to do a digital examination." Says the GP.

---

[185] There may have been some disparity but nothing my gait could not accomodate

"Don't worry matey, I'm a Crohn's vet of some twenty years standing; you can twizzle away to your heart's content."

Which he did.

"I can't feel anything obvious," he reports, "it's probably nothing, chances are it will sort itself out."

Which it does, and I hear nothing more from the perfidious little bleeder[186] until 2016.

The summer of my fifty-first year and despite the encumbrance of methotrexate, I am feeling pretty good about myself. I have joined a squash club and for the first time started playing the sport without it being an excuse to quaff ale. I actually improve and manage to gain a promotion through a couple of the mini leagues therein. To be brutally honest I am punching above my weight and am scheduled to play T... who has wiped the floor with me on every occasion we have met on court. However, based on our previous duels I have managed to identify that he holds only two advantages over me: he's half my age (literally) and he's better at playing squash than I am. If I can, in some fashion, take those out of the equation then we'll really have a game on our hands.

Strategizing in this instance becomes irrelevant because the morning of the game I get a strange feeling in the end of my penis. Now T... is a good-looking fella but he's not handsome enough to persuade me to bat for the other side so, clearly, something is amiss down there. Initially I speculate that perhaps a little underpants chaffing has gone on or even a scratch from a zip fly but there are no obvious signs and as the day progresses the sensation increases. What had started out

---

[186] Meaning my prostate not my doctor. Even though he paralysed my arm (see cyst) I don't bear a grudge.

as a tingling is now an indescribable irritation and is coupled with the sensation that someone has inserted a potato up my arse. At this point I cancel my squash game as I am starting to feel quite unwell.

I want to wee. All the time! When I do, the best I can manage is a teacupful and even that is quite painful. It looks horribly cloudy, like that bottle of lemon barley water that has been sat in the back of the cupboard for so long that it has started to ferment.

By late afternoon, dosed up on paracetamol and 'brufen I try soaking my extremities in a hot bath which provides me with no relief whatsoever. It's like the sensation of an itch that can't be scratched, but it's amplified a hundred times. By now there are moments that, if given the option of a painless procedure, I would happily dispense with my manhood to spare me from this torment. And I don't say that lightly; this is an organ that I am inordinately fond of.

I resort to the tried and tested method of dosing myself up on whisky[187]. I say tried and tested, that should probably read *tried, tested and proven to be waste of time.* All it does is makes me drunk which was good value as a distraction once upon a time but now, beset as I am by middle-age, requires the payment of a surcharge for dehydration, poor sleep and blinding headaches. Between tots I'm off to the loo for a dribble, the last squirt of which now contains blood and is even more painful than it was before. Like pissing broken glass is the simile often used and I can confirm that it is an apposite one.

CM is away visiting a chum and in one of those bizarre coincidences that life throws up from time to time she phones

---

[187] Isle of Jura if you are interested

up with the news that her friend's husband has just had surgery for prostate cancer.

"Funny you should say that," I say. She doesn't laugh at all.

"You're touching forty degrees," admonishes CM, "I don't want yellow sheets again (see "Fever"), go to the fucking doctor!" She's right to be concerned, sweat is pissing from me. Ironically, far more efficiently, than *piss* is pissing from me. I have to do something; the pain and the arse-potato are driving me out of my nut. I'm lucky, I get an appointment that afternoon.

The doctor, whose name I think is O'C...[188] smiles at me warmly. He has strikingly blue eyes and looks very much like Harry Enfield.

"A UTI you say?[189] What makes you think that? they're pretty unusual in us chaps."

He's just typing: *...probably a chronic masturbator...* into my notes when I return from the toilet clutching my beige-coloured sample. There is so much matter floating it that it looks like a miniature lava lamp.

"Oh! I see what you mean."

He tests it with one of those multi-reagent strips which confirms both the infection and the presence of blood.

It's time for me to show my ignorance now and I suggest that I might have caught it from my wife who is a serial UTIer, getting one every time we have intercourse without fail. In fact,

---

[188] It might not be; I seem to see a different face every visit. I suspect they operate a rota system for the irritating patients.

[189] Urinary Tract Infection. Word to the wise, get your diagnosis in before they do; they always appreciate it.

just the mention of marital relations is enough to give her a dose[190]. Apparently, it doesn't work like that with these things. All the time I was being blamed (including a text seen by our teenage daughter which included the phrase: *...your dirty willy...*) it was her own bugs doing the damage. Admittedly, my fervid rutting probably helped with the distribution, but the underlying blame lies with vaginas. When you think about it it's a wonder there aren't more problems. They are permanently moist and have all these flappy nooks and crannies; perfect for growing stuff. It's a bit like that wobbly rubber flange[191] on a washing machine door, always trapping water, always growing gunk. Also, the opening to the urethra is bang in the danger zone, there's no wonder germs get pushed up it. Fannies[192] are so beset with design flaws it makes me question why I have expended so much time, money and energy over the years in trying to make their acquaintance.

Armed with my newfound knowledge I return home and explain the true mechanism of UTIs to CM but it is to no avail; I may no longer be holding the smoking gun but the rule that *...it shall be washed on a regular basis...* still stands.

Despite my antipathy towards them, I leave the surgery with a prescription for Amoxicillin, an antibiotic; there really is no other option. I start to feel the benefits of them within a day. A false dawn! Two days later I am back to square one and I am forced to visit an out of hours practice. More antibiotics, this time of a different hue, (Trimethroprim) because different

---

[190] So she says and I can't imagine why she would make something like that up

[191] Why are they always grey coloured?

[192] In the British sense.

bugs require different treatments and you don't necessarily hit the bull with your first dart do you? A sample from the lava lamp is sent away for analysis to nail down just what we are dealing with.

The new drugs work well, and I am back to normal, more or less; my weeing is not what it was, and I still struggle to pass any sort of volume. I assume this is due to a degree of inflammation somewhere up there in the pipework and that it will all slacken-off with time. Likewise, my arse potato, although that's not now the full-on King Edward that it once. Although it's still more substantial than a Jersey Royal; if pushed, my best estimate would probably be a Charlotte. Also, and this is the one I'm really looking forward to, I have been referred to the Hallamshire Hospital for a cystoscopy, which is basically a flexible camera inserted into the end of the penis, up the urethra and into the bladder.

I must be the youngest member of the, predominantly male, Urology waiting room. Arranged on rows of chairs facing the corner of the room we sit with our spouses in tow watching the telly screen high on the wall anticipating our name popping up there. Radio Hallam, hosted by some overly excited nitwit, is playing a selection of popular tunes none of which I recognise, so goodness knows what the rest of the old codgers here make of them. Urology needs to take a look at its demographics and retune the radio accordingly. This lot don't want Ariana Grande, they want Vera Lynn and Gracie Fields. *Sing as we go!* Except when we do go, nothing much comes out.

We are channelled into the secondary stage of the waiting process, into an area milling with clinicians. The nursing staff are gathered around a central station and the conversation is all about a stage version of The Full Monty currently playing at the Lyceum. Apparently: "....you get to see the lot!"

Somebody asks the question that springs to my mind and that is:

"Don't you see enough of willies, working here?"

The man immediately before me is called and ushered into a room. He returns ten minutes later looking embarrassed and apologising like his life depended on it.

"I never realised beetroot could do that. I'm so sorry!"

It happens all the time apparently, beetroot wee. They should put a warning on the jars.

My turn, and I am kitted out with the obligatory bare-arse smocks and green carrier bag. It's coldish in there so I keep my vest on; should be all right, they aren't interested in that part of my anatomy. I have a pair of black Chelsea boots on my feet as I shuffle through to the examination room. Any boots would look ridiculous but the fact that these have recently been polished and gleam impressively somehow adds to the incongruity. Inside is a young nurse who escorts me to the examination table. She is exceptionally attractive, the spitting image of the actress Sarah Alexander. And when she says the words:

"Could you lift up your gown, I need to wash your penis..."

you might expect my immediate reaction to be one of extreme elation, but it's not. The swabs are cold, deliberately so I suspect, and all the handling, drawing back of foreskin (see "Circumcision") and wiping, are performed using two pairs of steel tongs. It's like she's turning a sausage on a barbecue.[193]

---

[193] This may have been down to my state of nervousness or perhaps the clinical surroundings. I have since played out in my imagination the

There is nothing erotic to be had here.

The doctor arrives, we have a brief chat and he gets down to business. A quick digital exam (prostate a little hard) then around the corner to sausage street. Lubrication is the order of the day; it might not be a Box Brownie he's going to shove up me, but it will still need easing on its way. Having cold gel squirted up the inside of one's penis is not (for me at any rate) a pleasurable experience; it hurts. However, compared to the pain that comes with the insertion of the scope it is but the draught from a butterfly's wing. Dear God it is painful! And the further it goes the worse it gets, culminating in passage through the sphincter into the bladder. The trick here is to try to wee at that moment; first sign of a wink and it is pushed through. Fat chance of that, I'm in agony; close to tears with the pain and in no position to focus my mind sufficiently to pass water. It's difficult enough doing it in a public urinal let alone under these conditions. I try, but it is excruciating and to my shame I resort to profanity; *Fucking Nora!* if memory serves. No one seems bothered, the consultant carries on telling me about how healthy my bladder looks and pointing out the openings of ureters on the TV screen to the left of my head. I am not interested. All right, I am interested that there are no tumours up there, but the anatomy lesson can wait; I want this torture to end.

Withdrawal is also painful, though less so than insertion as I don't have to perform any sphincter tricks to facilitate it. Going past the prostate gives a sharp stab and it all looks very red around there. Don't know whether that redness is normal.

---

scenario of Sarah Alexander fondling me with a pair of tongs and found it to be most stimulating.

Removal of the cystoscope is a relief but not as much of one as I had expected, or would have wished for. I walk to the car like John Wayne heading to his horse. It takes a good day for the stinging to abate and I wonder why I have not read more about just how painful this procedure is. Is there no form of anaesthesia available? because, frankly, my brush with the cystoscope felt like barber-surgeon territory. At least in the old days the patient got something to bite on.

A week later and we are back to the fever and the pain and the bloody piss again. At the GP's is another new face. This fella looks like a rugby player; big and burley. A digital examination is offered now that the rota system has thrown up the doctor with the fattest fingers in the practice. Not that it bothers me; I've had worse stuff up there. He finds a hard, swollen area on one side of my prostate which, he tells me, may be nothing much, but to be on the safe side a PSA[194] test is undertaken and I am referred back to urology. Until then it is more Trimethroprim and a watching brief.

True to form I am trawling the internet looking for symptoms that match mine in order to make my own ill-informed and unqualified diagnosis. Bacterial prostatitis seems to be ticking a number of boxes although from what I can gather it's not as common as you might thing. My theory is that three and a half years of immuno-suppressants (mercaptopurine and then methotrexate) have left me compromised, and some common or garden bacteria seeing me with my pants down (metaphorically speaking) has snuck in and taken up residence in my prostate. The sneaky little bastard!

---

[194] Prostate specific antigen: a marker used in diagnosis and treatment of prostate cancer

Summer holidays and I am taking my daughters camping in Dumfries and Galloway; CM and D... have stayed back in Yorkshire on grounds that there are A. too many spiders and B. not enough computers. My malady, as yet still not fully defined, is comparatively dormant; no fevers or anything like that but the bum spud and urgency of urination are still with me. Neither of those issues makes for a very comfortable drive and it is over five and a half hours to Kirkcudbright when you add in all the pitstops.

The campsite is one of those big-old rambling, family-friendly types and not the back to basics, wash-in-a-trough kind that I normally favour.[195] When I booked it, I was fit and well and could cope with the long trail through caravans and campers to the ablutions; in my current state it is something of a chore. Ordinarily I would just pop behind the tent and relieve myself there, but the campers are jammed in here and everyone seems intent on staying up late into the night. There is no scope for surreptitious widdling. The obvious solution would be for me to remain in the tent and to piss into a receptacle of some sort. This should not be a problem, it's a big tent with different rooms and plenty of privacy but this cuts no ice with teenage daughters. The prospect of having to listen to their father micturating into an Irn Bru bottle is beyond repugnant to them. And I don't think they have even contemplated the thought that since we are separated by just a single sheet of canvass there is every prospect that, when I switch on my lantern, they will be treated to a spot of silhouette theatre to boot.

---

[195] A prerequisite for the girls coming along.

I am given no option but to use the camp toilets which are two fields away even via the quick route. Unfortunately, the quick route involves cutting through the vast children's play area which is literally swarming with Caledonian brats who never tire and whose parents have, seemingly, no concept of "bedtime".

There is no quiet period during which I can slip through, I have to run the gauntlet of snot-nosed terror. I traipse back and forth so frequently that I am in danger of being identified as a paedophile and I have half an eye out for any gangs of vigilante dads which may be gathering. I don't help myself at times; due to my bladder urgency, I'm walking in a mincing, slightly stooped fashion, often holding my crotch, which looks for all the world like I am trying to disguise an erection.

Back in Yorkshire I have a scheduled MRI scan to look at a spot of inflammation that has been hanging around my small intestine[196]. I have read about the use of MRI in diagnosing prostate conditions and, wise-guy that I am, I suggest to the GP that this might be a two bird/one stone opportunity. I am told *forget it matey,* there is no way on earth that primary care could liaise with three separate hospital departments at the same time. I am quite vexed but with hindsight I can see that they were just being realistic.

Urology at the Hallamshire once again and I have an appointment to see Professor C... He's a tall, jocular bod with a haircut to match mine. I've looked him up on the internet and he seems to be quite a big name in the field of all things pissy.

He recaps the story of my UTI's to date and then admits that it isn't obvious to him what is occurring. In fact, he says, a lot of

---

[196] The reason why I was taking immunosuppressants

what goes on with the prostate has medics scratching their heads. I'm scheduled for more blood tests (PSA), an MRI scan and (joy of joys!) a repeat of my recent cystoscopy. I'm pleased about the MRI because there are few things I enjoy more than being right, but my self-congratulating is tempered by learning that it is a bit of a specialised procedure and not something they can tack on to a routine session in the *big tube*.

Never mind, I give thanks for living in a town with access to a teaching hospital otherwise I would be looking a prostate biopsy which involves a big needle and sounds thoroughly horrid.

Another digital rectal examination and it is suggested that CM leaves the room whilst it is performed. I think that must be for her benefit rather than mine; I'm not shy in that respect, she can video it for her Facebook page as far as I'm concerned.

"I've spent a bit of time in the States," says the Prof, "they do it slightly different over there. If you could just drop your pants, spread your legs a little and lean over the bench."

He's showing off that he's been to America. For all I know it could just have been a week at Disney World Florida. I don't know why there's a difference, there might be clinical reasons, or it might simply be convention. Perhaps a straw poll? What's best, sideways knees to chin or touch-your-toes cowboy style? Answers on a postcard please.[197]

Notwithstanding the results of the MRI I am put on a prophylactic dose of Trimethroprim for twelve months with Cephalaxin, Nitrofurantoin and Ciprofloxacin on standby in the event of breakthrough infections.

---

[197] Showing my age there, email your answers to jflenity@gmail.com. Actually, don't bother.

The MRI (See Diagnostic Imaging), or the multiparametric MRI to be precise has shown something on my prostate that is causing concern. So says Mr C... the consultant who is about to perform my second cystoscopy. Sarah Alexander has given the old stormtrooper's helmet the once over with her tongs[198] and I am cleared for action. The end of the camera is lying between my legs waiting for the word to go. It's functioning, I know because the huge and menacing image of my nob-end is glowering at me from the TV screen by my head. I am filled with remorse for all the times CM has awoken on a Sunday morning to come face to face with that thing bearing down on her.

Mr C... rests his hand on my thigh, it's very warm and, combined with his softly-spoken, slightly accented voice I find myself having something of an ASMR moment.[199] Considering my previous experience of cystoscopy, i.e. torture, I am remarkably relaxed. I think some people are just supremely suited to what they do. Mr C... is a natural healer; it radiates from him.

He explains to me how the MRI scan has shown an asymmetrical enlargement on my prostate which could be cancer or could be a peculiar type of infection. The only reliable way of telling is to take a series of biopsies. Just when you think you've dodged a bullet a series of unfortunate *pings* behind you sends the slug ricocheting back and up your arsehole. Which, coincidentally, is where prostate biopsy is performed through. It's not all doom and gloom though, the cystoscopy reveals

---

[198] Poor girl; a day of washing old men's cocks- not much of an incentive to get out of bed in a morning is it?

[199] See "Tingly Brain."

nothing untoward and the procedure on this occasion is comparatively painless. Don't get me wrong, it's not pleasant, I wouldn't want to suggest that it is in any way a jolly experience but, compared to the previous one it's a stroll in the park. Mr C... at the helm perhaps had something to do with it (healing hands and all that) but I am inclined to think that my *front-plumbing* is just a lot less inflamed than it was in the summer. The day of my biopsy and I am standing in the doorway looking lost.

"Who's doing your procedure?" asks the nurse. I'm in my combination of bare-arse gowns and I must look like a small girl who has woken up in the middle of the night and stands before her parents, blinking in the light, her teddy bear hanging limply by her side[200].

"Mr C...," I reply

"Oh, you'll be all right then; he's lovely."

We chat as Mr C... gets on with things, taking what looks like a large sex toy and rolling a condom down its length. It gets a liberal dose of lube before I am asked to lie on my side and hitch things up. Mr C... comes from Tanzania and he tells me about physician density in his homeland, approximately one for ever twenty thousand people.

"Did the Tories get in over there as well?" I ask him, but he doesn't see the joke.

A prostate biopsy is performed by pushing a (big!) needle through the wall of the rectum and into the prostate, at which juncture a local anaesthetic is injected. That's the worse bit. All this is guided using ultrasound, you'll be glad to hear, they

---

[200] I don't have a teddy bear

don't just stab away until they hit the right spot[201]. Plus, the MRI scan gives them a clue where to look, these are not random biopsies, so they don't need to go overboard on sampling.

The tissue extraction itself is a weird sensation. A spring-loaded gun fires some sort of sampling needle (auger?) into the prostate and a core of tissue (ideally of a suitable length) is extracted and sent away for analysis. Imagine someone up your bottom repeatedly twanging rubber bands at you and you will not be too far away from the experience of a prostate biopsy. I get twelve "twangs".

We get the results in a few days' time and CM is frantic with nerves. For my part I am more sanguine. It's not that I have nerves of steel or anything like that, more that I have convinced myself that this is down to an infection. I've no grounds for that belief but it suits me to adopt it. Optimist/delusional idiot, it's a thin line isn't it?

Back at the Hallamshire and we are awaiting Mr C... The Current Mrs Lenity insists on holding my hand in anticipation of the news; I think she has got this from watching the contestants on Deal or No Deal. I have a secret suspicion that, given a choice, she would prefer my biopsy results to be revealed through Noel Edmunds unlocking a sealed box. I, for my part, prefer the soothing tones of Mr C...

"It's good news." Announces Mr C... cutting to the chase. CM's relief is palpable, the tension drops from her as all those concerns surrounding my death (how will I program the boiler? Boden or Fatface for widow's weeds?) drain away.

Of course, I am also greatly relieved, although as I think I mentioned, my money was always on a different nag. Phew.

---

[201] TRUS; trans rectal ultrasound

Three cheers then for the seldom-seen condition, granulomatous bacterial prostatitis. I am sent away with a series of yellow slips requesting PSA tests for the next year and a prescription for Ciprofloxacin, which is nice because I haven't tried that one yet. This antibiotic targets a broader range of bacteria and the course will last for four months. It seems that fixing infected prostates is something of a war of attrition; infections like it in there. As Mr C... (unknowingly borrowing one of my wife's stock phrases) put it:

"...it's not a very clean organ."

We are just about to leave when I look down at the prescription in my hand and notice that it has someone else's name on it. Mr C... apologises and makes the correction. A couple of days later and there is a nagging doubt in my head that, in addition to having some other bloke's prescription, I have his test results as well. CM phones the Urology department who assure us that my result is kosher; I'm still alive and kicking two- and a-bit years on, so I'm inclined to believe them.

My urgent urinations have gone now, though as I was warned it was a slow process and it took many weeks to get anywhere near normal. This is all well and good if you don't have to rely on public conveniences which, it seems, are on the endangered list these days. A couple of weeks after my all clear I was forced to descend into the stygian gloom beneath Sheffield's Orchard Square shopping centre which, as bogs go, is really just a token effort. It's little more than a cupboard. The pissing area is particularly cramped; just because you plumb in two urinals does not mean there is room for two men in there. I skittle down the steps, my hand already at my flies and shuffle into bay two, bay one is occupied by a fat, bald little man with a red face. He's shaking off the drips as I extract but I can't wait for him to finish; he will have to either wait or squeeze behind me to leave. Despite my focus being on my own stream I cannot help noticing from the corner of my eye that he is still in the drip phase and showing a distinct lack of concentration since his eyes are fixed on my cock rather than his own. At that point he looks up at me, grins and his drip-shaking takes on an altogether faster tempo. I look down and my fears are confirmed; his hand is a blur. And his breathing is getting rather laboured which is worrying for the both of us.

Well there is no way I can stop what I'm doing; at that point in the recovery process I am still very much in a Magnus Magnusson, *I've started so I'll finish*, phase. I just have to ignore him, get on with things my end and hope I beat him to the finish line. And if he thinks there are going to be any cuddles after the event he can think again.

It was quite flattering really, being an object of desire even if it is only a fat, bald short-arse who may or may not have had a chest complaint.

## Queasiness

As a child I am afflicted with car sickness. At its worst the nausea would be upon me before we had even got to the end of the road; the smell of vinyl car upholstery alone would set me off. It is quite a problem for me; and for the rest of the family too, because it takes such a long time for us to get anywhere on account of all the vom-stops. These always followed the same protocol with my mother insisting that she support my head allowing me to lean into the puke in a pose similar to that adopted by ski-jumpers. Whether this is to do with maximising distance or, more likely, a theory of my mother's that involves children's heads falling off through excessive retching is never explored.

Motion sickness, it is believed, is caused by the difference in the messages that the brain receives from different sensory regions. For instance, my balance was saying we were moving whereas all my eyes could contribute was the back of my dad's bald head. Why the brain gets narked by this sort of thing is open to debate.

For reasons I cannot explain, the situation resolved itself. I outgrew it perhaps, or maybe as I got taller, I could see more of the road and less of the comb-over which, perhaps, resolved some of the disparity from my senses. The more superficial of you might suggest that swapping cars, from an orangey coloured Moskvitch 427 estate to a Vauxhall Viva, was enough of an anti-emetic for anyone but I won't stand for that sort of talk. I have nothing but fond memories of that old Soviet bus.

# R is for...

## Runny Nose

Granted, this is not much of an ailment and, one would have thought, not worthy of its own section. After all, everyone has runny noses, don't they? Well not like mine they don't. There are times when you'd think I had a pair of glue guns working up there; it streams out. Not all the time; when I'm in a warm environment it is fine, a little drippy but not a problem but as soon as I get anywhere that is a little chilly, or if I exercise, the floodgates open.

Having got to the stage where my top lip was becoming red and permanently moist like those kids at school who had never been taught to use a tissue, I sought medical advice. Allergies were ruled out which I was glad off, I can do without those, but beyond that nothing much was established.

*You're a snot-nose matey, there's nothing more to it.*

I did have some fancy nasal spray which took the edge off it, but it all seemed like treating the symptoms rather than the cause and I gave it the elbow. After that I just made sure I had enough kit to soak up the flow which, until society deems nose tampons acceptable to wear in public, means a surfeit of handkerchiefs. Which is fine if you are in coat and trousers, less ideal on a squash court. Sports apparel being what it is the stowage of snot rags requires the use of sleeve cuffs and waist bands and the like. You get some odd looks from the gallery when, between rallies, you are pulling out different coloured handkerchiefs from various parts of your clothing. There was a point when I considered knotting them all together and announcing...*and for my next trick*...but you never know where that sort of thing will end. You don't fuck with the Magic Circle. I do wonder if people like me are prone to inflammation in general and that I am always going to suffer from an irritated nose, or rosacea, or bowel problems. Maybe joint pain is next on the list. Can't wait! I once mentioned my theory of integral inflammation to a consultant, but it wasn't well received.

While I was writing this, a horrible nose-related memory returned to me and in the hope of redemption I confess it here. As a small child I was an inveterate nostril miner and would sit for hours in front of the television picking away like billio. At the time we had a leatherette suite the arms of which had a thick piping seam running along their edges. It was under this seam that I deposited a seam of my own. Over a week I could cover the whole length of the arm in bogies. Periodically my father would chip off the accretions with a table knife. I don't understand how I was allowed to get away with this, particularly after my little brother caught onto the idea and effectively doubled production. This contrasts with my own parental bogey policy which is a bit intolerant and doubly hypocritical in that I am still partial to rooting out the occasional crow myself.

My nose picking habit had gone through something of a hiatus, by my teenage years it had all but disappeared; something reserved for emergencies. Then, following a drinking session in Manchester, I awoke having spent the night on a dusty carpeted floor. My nostrils were crammed full of desiccated goodies and as I set to work I was reminded what a satisfying hobby it was. My habit was resurrected.

Nose picking, then, is addictive. This is a fact. It can actually develop into an obsessive-compulsive disorder at which point it is afforded a posh name, rhinotillexomania. I am some way short of that, probably because I'm a bit mangled up there (see "Septum") and because my nose, for most of the time, is streaming liquid which, obviously, is not pickable. Oh, and in case you are wondering, I don't eat it, though perhaps I should because there is a school of medical thought which holds that snot eating is beneficial[202]. Mucophagy is said to prevent bacteria sticking to teeth and, according to Dr Friedrich Bischinger, an Austrian medic, can boost the immune system by introducing bacteria into the body that have already been sterilized by the nose[203]. Nose pickers, says the good doctor, are, all-in-all, a happier breed than those who abstain. Come on Friedrich luv, tells us something we don't know!

---

[202] Presumably this refers to eating one's own snot rather than "importing it in".

[203] I think this is just an opinion rather than results of any actual research.

# S is for...

## Sebaceous Cyst

See "Cysts".

## Semen

See "Prostate" and "Nocturnal Emissions"

## Septum

As mentioned in "Knocked Out" I had the double misfortune, back in 88, to find myself at a Ceilidh and to get clobbered in the process. A year earlier I had been head butted in a barroom altercation elsewhere else in Scotland[204]; no country dancing was involved. As a result, I must have suffered some damage to my septum. That is to say, the strip of soft tissue and cartilage that runs down the centre of the nose and sets us apart from all those mammals that only have a single nostril[205]. In my case the septum must have healed in a lop-sided fashion leaving me with one nostril larger than the other, though you can't tell without delving inside; which may or may not appeal to you. See "Runny Nose".

My wobbly septum restricts the passage of air slightly on my left but not by much and the only real drawback of it is that I can't fire a snot rocket from that side. I am nothing if not a trier and persevere, which explains the dried slug trails on the left shoulder of my coat.

## Shingles

Shingles is caused by the zoster virus, or to give it its posh name, the herpes varicella-zoster virus. It also causes chicken

---

[204] Loch Sween actually
[205] I can't actually think of any mono-nostrilled mammals

pox, and most people will have had a dose of it in their childhood.[206] I have no memory of contracting chickenpox, I was very young when my turn came, but I am reliably informed that I got it and the following serves to bear that out.

The varicella zoster virus (VZV) can remain dormant in the body after the chickenpox has passed and can subsequently reactivate. The virus then manifests itself as the disease known as shingles. My introduction to shingles came from seeing my mother suffering with it. She was unfortunate to receive two or three doses all resulting in fever, pain and rash. It was treated, I recall, with bed rest and Sloane's liniment.[207]

My personal experience began as a student when I was confined to bed on suspicion of shingles. I was, in fact, covered in a rash triggered (I believe) by the drug azathioprine; faux shingles. (See "Trapped Nerve"). I have to wait another two years to be treated to a dose of the real thing.[208]

I am living, at this time, in a small village in Warwickshire called Sheepy Magna, it's not far from Sheepy Parva in case you don't know it so obviously quite isolated and miles from any reliable source of Sloane's liniment. It all begins with a slightly strange, tingly feeling in my left ear which eventually develops into a nagging earache. Next, a string of blisters appears on my face, running from ear towards chin. I feel quite off too, and so take myself to Atherstone to see a GP.

I have to say I did not take to the fella, either personally or

---

[206] These days chickenpox is routinely vaccinated against; although not in the UK.

[207] Always Sloane's liniment

[208] Shingles that is, not The Real Thing, British soul band of the nineteen seventies.

professionally and throughout my many years of dealing with doctors he ranks as the worst. Despite me having pain in my ear he never looks in it and you'd think that the patently obvious pustule archipelago running down one side (note, *one* side) of my face would have given him some sort of a clue but alas no. I leave with a diagnosis of blocked sinuses and prescription for Sudafed.

Unsurprisingly, Sudafed is absolutely no help whatsoever; my symptoms get worse. I have fevers, I look haggard, I have no energy, but worst of all is the pain. The thing with shingles is it works along nerves and the nerves it was working along this time extended into my ear, face and teeth. After a week all three are agony. It is so bad that I can't touch my face and any hot or cold drink touching my left molars is excruciating. As a consequence, I take care when drinking not to let anything swish back there, but it is so easy to forget and on these occasions I almost faint from the pain.

I go back to the GP who this time makes a decent fist of it. That said he doesn't disguise his utter contempt for this tramp (I couldn't shave because of the pain) who has the gall to turn up at his surgery with illness. An illness! I am given a prescription for an antivirus medication which seems like a reasonable call but that isn't before I am lectured on how expensive this medication is and how I must, *must*, make sure I take it. Never mind whether stopping short affects the efficacy, no, the important thing is cost; if the stuff is a bit pricey you make sure you swallow the bloody lot matey!

It may or may not have done the trick, I don't know. I start to feel better over the coming week and am soon back to my normal self. Except for the pain. That stays with me for months, long after I leave Sheepy Magna. This is known as postherpetic neuralgia and is a common symptom. Nasty though it was, I have to consider myself lucky in that getting it in the face only left me with residual neuralgia and not paralysis, deafness or eye damage. (See "Pain")

## Shroud of Filey
See "Fever".

## Sleep Walking
See "Audi Coupe".

## Sleep Paralysis
See "Audi Coupe".

## Stroke
The late noughties and for some reason we have been persuaded to go bird watching[209] at Bempton on the North Yorkshire coast. It is full of surprises, firstly how bloody busy the place is on a rainy, late spring morning, secondly, that I actually enjoyed it and thirdly, that I have a stroke whilst I'm up there.

One minute I am happily observing what even I could identify as a puffin, the next I have lost all clarity of vision in left eye. My first thought is *I've had a stroke*, albeit a minor one as my limbs seemed to be functioning. I put my hand to my face to feel for any signs of paralysis and it is at this point, as my finger slips through the hole where the left lens of my spectacles had once sat, that my fears abate.

Fortunately, and despite the length of the grass, I managed to find the lens and slot it back home. I have had a further couple

---

[209] Bird watching you will note, not bird spotting. There is a big difference apparently.

of strokes since then prompting me to invest in a spectacle repair kit and some Araldite.

## Styes

I don't seem to get these anymore. I can offer no explanation for this other than that I require spectacles to do anything these days[210] and so I probably do less poking around my eyes with grubby fingers than I once did. As an adolescent and young man I have any number of the styes, a couple of which develop into cysts (known as chalazia, I believe) and require surgical removal. If you think that cutting chunks of eyelid away sounds gruesome, it's not. This is just a day case procedure and far less distressing than you would imagine. See "Cysts".

# T is for...

## Testicles

See "Getting Old"

## Teeth

I shall come to the point; I have rubbish teeth. I won't pretend otherwise. They are quite dark, riddled with fillings, a little bit irregular and in parts absent altogether. When I came to write this section I began to speculate on the reasons for this and came up with the following factors: diet, demographics, dental practices, genetics and age.

Firstly, diet. Specifically, my diet as a child. As a little boy I was a funny eater. There was a time when I was vegetarian; for a kid on a council estate in the seventies this was regarded as pretty weird behaviour. The thing was, whilst I was mindful of the

---

[210] Including locating my spectacles which, obviously, can be problematic.

animal cruelty aspect of it the main reason was that I didn't like the taste of meat; eschewing gravy, I would have jam on my Yorkshire pudding! It was all regarded as a bit of a joke by my relatives. I lived exclusively on milk, cheese and tinned peas (See "All-Bran Anyone"). I say exclusively, I should caveat this and add that this was heavily supplemented with vast numbers of sweets; chocolate bars, chews, bubblies, toffees, boiled sweets, and so forth, with triple rations at Easter, Christmas and summer holidays[211]. I think my parents, who had been children during rationing, could never grasp the concept that sweets could ever be a bad thing and would ply my brother and I with the things relentlessly[212]. Naturally, all of this was washed down with gallons of fizzy, sugary pop. Okay, I wasn't going short of calcium but faced with such a relentless sugar onslaught my teeth were always going to have their work cut out.

These days I hardly ever eat sugary foods. Boiled sweets and the like leave me with an unpleasantly acidic after-taste and besides which, I find things like that intolerably sweet anyway. As a child I could sit and eat a whole box of Turkish Delight including all the icing sugar in a single sitting; these days the

---

[211] I had a penchant for cherry nougat which, looking back seems like an odd direction for a kid's tastes to lean.

[212] In the local vernacular sweets were always referred to as spice, as in: *I've got a bag o' spice,* or *gi-us a spice yer mardy get.* Sadly, in latter years the term Spice has come to be associated with a quite different habit.

thought repels me.[213]

However, my sweet abstaining adult diet has not done me any favours. In listing red wine, strong tea, coffee, dark beers and curry, which are all notorious tooth-stainers, I might as well be summarising my diet for the last thirty-five years.

Secondly demographics. The current Mrs Lenity (CM) hails from Richmond in Surrey, I for my part, originate from the Southey Green/Parson Cross area of Sheffield which represents quite a distance on the British social spectrum; I'm Billy Joel to her Uptown Girl[214]. As a child CM had terrible teeth, big, and gappy, they splayed forward from her mouth. If I'd had those teeth as a child I would have continued to have the decayed version of them as an adult. The point is that no one walks about with bad teeth in Richmond whereas there are parts of Southey that are real Duelling Banjos country[215]. Most of my relatives had complete sets of false teeth. It was common practice to have all your (healthy!) teeth removed in order to avoid the inconvenience of dental treatment in the future. When I have told my middle-class friends this, they are shocked, and rightly so.

For many years I had a terror of tooth extraction. This I am sure is a result of my experience of having teeth pulled in the nineteen seventies. When I first told my high-born spouse that

---

[213] Right up until his death (when I was in my late forties) my father sent me a box of Turkish Delight every Christmas. Goodness knows how much I threw away or fed to the dog (that's bad isn't it?) but I never had the heart to tell him I couldn't eat it anymore.

[214] The current Mrs Lenity and I often act out the video for this song when we go to petrol stations.

[215] A reference to John Boorman's film "Deliverance"

little children's teeth were extracted under general anaesthetic at the small dental surgery at the end of our road, she didn't believe me. I have an abiding memory of some hairy-armed old sawbones bearing down on me with a syringe destined to be inserted painfully into the back of my hand. The next thing I know I am coming around in my mother's arms, in a scabby waiting room and crying my eyes out. I am swiftly followed by my little brother who's had the same treatment. I don't know how we both finished up there having teeth pulled at the same time.

In addition to the shock of coming around I have to deal with the void where my tooth once was; I hate its foul, bloody taste, and the sensation as my tongue brushes the limp flaps of gums around the crater. I do think that my early dentist experiences have gone a long way towards developing my fear of extraction/surgery and general anaesthetics.

It is another thirty years before I consent to have tooth removed again. A wisdom tooth on this occasion, my left side at the top. On and off for a few years this had been giving me grief mainly because it is still erupting, which I had assumed would have stopped by this point (mid-forties) but it seems not. The problem is that there is nothing opposing it on the bottom jaw; nothing for it to push against. This also means that insofar as functioning as a tooth was concerned, it doesn't. Think pestle without mortar, or hammer minus anvil. If you are of the Buddhist faith just try to imagine the sound of one-toothed chewing.

The continued progression of this tooth was allowing food to get trapped between it and the adjacent one. It also had a filling which kept falling away and was rather difficult to replace on account of the cramped conditions back there.

"How long have you been having trouble?" Asked my dentist.

"A couple of weeks; I've been on holiday. My teeth troubles always seem to appear on holiday; is that normal?"

"No."

"Does that mean I am special?"

He doesn't say one way or the other. He peers in my mouth and begins poking away with his little tool kit. "You must have been in a hell of a lot of pain!" he remarks.

"Well, a bit." I say, casually, in the way that men who are trained to cope with the extremes of physical endurance do.

"I think it's best if we lose it."

Shit! He's snookered me! How can I purport to laugh off dental agonies one minute and then wimp out of an extraction the next?

"Oh," I say, "er, all right. How does that work then, you just numb me up and yank it out do you?"

He chuckles. This is the only time in a twenty-year association with this man that I have seen him amused. He shares a knowing, professional look with his assistant, a statuesque woman with the shoulders of a javelin thrower. She chuckles too. I am clearly the idiot in the room today.

"I think you'll find," he tells me, "that we are a little more sophisticated than *yank it out.*"

Okay, fair enough, I'm all for that, bring it on. I'm injected with local anaesthetic and the numbing process begins to kick in. In the meantime, he chats with his assistant about last night's *I'm a Celebrity...Get Me Out of Here.* With bated breath I wait to see what twenty first century technology has brought to the process of tooth extraction. Are you ready? Here it is: the pliers come wrapped in a sterile, cellophane packet!

He clamps on and begins with a little wobbling, loosening up.

Every now and again he breaks into a circular motion; I don't know if this is accepted practice or a dash of personal style. The amplitude of the wobbling increases so that he is now swinging on my tooth and I am struggling to keep my head still. I now know why he needs such a burly nurse; it's her job to restrain the patient while he puts his feet on my chest. All right, that's a bit of an exaggeration, but still, I would venture, in the spirit of the occasion. Eventually it pops out and is dropped into a kidney dish. There is a piece of gauze in the bottom of the dish and so I am denied the satisfying ping and rattle as the tooth lands. Disappointing.

"Can I have a look?" I ask, to which he seems a little surprised. "My God, it's huge!" I say; I was not prepared for how much of this thing was concealed in my face. Nasty colour too, though why I was surprised by that I cannot say.

"Can take it home? I want to show the kids."

Apparently not. There's more chance of the Elgin marbles being handed back. It's dangerous it seems, not in the sense that I might bite somebody with it, more from a biohazard angle.

I am sent away with a wad of something in my mouth and a fact sheet on how extractions work. This is basically as follows: a pad goes on the wound to stem the bleeding and to encourage the formation of a clot. It is important not to disturb the clot for a few days as this is the base over which the gums will heal. I hope you've got that as I shall be returning to the process later. The wound heals as it should do, the extraction is a success both medically and psychologically, because, thanks to the breakthrough of cellophane-wrapped pliers, I am now exorcised of my extraction terrors. In fact, I think even as a small child I would have preferred this method to being knocked out.

Dental Practices

Looking back, I don't actually know why I needed teeth removing in the first place. Perhaps they had to come out to let my permanent teeth to come through? Perhaps they had cavities or something? It was never explained to me, I took these things on trust and it is only now, older and wiser, that I have begun to wonder how much of the work I had done as a kid was really necessary.

I am not for a moment suggesting that my sucrose-rich diet in tandem with a lax attitude to oral hygiene isn't the big villain here, it almost certainly is. However, I do question whether this is the whole story. NHS dentists were paid on a per treatment basis, i.e., the more teeth they filled the more cash they got and when the patient is not required to pay anything, as is the case with children under the NHS, then you can see where temptation might lead. I will give you another example. I had a couple of fillings in an incisor. When I was a student a dentist suggested that I might want to have that particular tooth fitted with a crown. "...get it done now whilst it's free," or words to that effect. Of course, I am all for it; he's used the f word. The crown, effectively a copy of the exposed part of my tooth, is fitted into a hole bored into the root, my original tooth having been ground down to gum level. When I say copy, I don't mean *exact* copy. A crown is about twice as thick as a normal tooth and feels cumbersome at the front of my face. Oh, and there is another aspect of it by which a keen-eyed observer might spot the deception; it is a different colour to all my other teeth! For some reason, my shade is not available on the official colour charts[216]. It stands out a mile; especially if I've been

---

[216] Am I special?

drinking red wine because it doesn't colour up like the genuine articles.

It lasts a year or so, right up until I am head-butted in an altercation outside a bar in Scotland. Whilst the adjacent teeth survive unharmed, falsy is loosened so much that before long, it drops out. It is no big deal to have it cemented in again, five minutes work, but what I don't realised is that the root, weakened by boring had split and was therefore not a reliable foundation. This recementing would prove to be the first of many. At one point I have a fatter spigot fitted and this involves the creation of a whole new prosthetic which is a slightly better shade to its predecessor but by no means a seamless match.

Its ultimate demise comes in 2015, on holiday in Majorca, via that great nemesis of dental prosthetics, the baguette. It's the ripping action that does the damage, I know it would be better to break a bit off with my fingers and place it in, but my enthusiasm[217] gets the better of my caution and I chomp on full frontal. I feel it shift, twizzling on its shaft after which the remainder of the holiday is spent eating gingerly and periodically poking my front peg back into its slot when no one is looking. There is always the option of pulling it out of course but apparently a toothless husband in some way reflects badly on his spouse and so that particular avenue is closed off to me. Once more I appear at my dentist's door, prosthetic in hand.

"The root's split right down its length." I am informed, "I think we need to look at alternatives."

He means a bridge. I am so sick of the frailties of the current gap filler that I agree wholeheartedly despite the two-hundred-and-odd pound bill that comes with it. At last I can get back to

---

217 Read *greed* here.

some proper biting.[218]

How naive can you get?

Firstly, a mould of my front teeth is taken from which a denture is constructed. This I will rely upon until my gum heals following the extraction of the bored-out stump. When everything has calmed down the bridge will be fitted. The bridge will consist of a prosthetic tooth glued via metal wings to the back of the two adjacent teeth.

First things first, the stump of the old tooth needs pulling out, or rather, gouging out as there is nothing visible to get a grip on.

"I think we have a bit of infection in there," my dentist notes, "might need some antibiotics."

That would explain the rancid smell as the stump emerges. I wonder how long that infection has been around? I have often noticed a slight off note to the taste of my front teeth.

The bleeding is stanched, and my denture is pushed in place, secured by a plastic plate which is Polygripped to the top of my mouth.

"That might feel a bit uncomfortable at first."

He's not kidding, it's taking up most of my mouth; at least that's what it seems like. Home, and an opportunity to have a good laugh at my attempts to speak; I sound like the Elephant Man. The plate flares away at the back and I catch my tongue on it repeatedly. It also forms a handy shelf on which masticated food builds up and I have no way of removing it without taking out the denture and licking it clean. Once lose the denture is a nightmare, it has a life of its own, shooting forward just when you don't expect it. In the course of

---

[218] By which I mean food; I'm not Hannibal Lecter.

conversation this results in the pointed top of the faux tooth jamming (painfully!) up into the inside of my lip.

It is a real nuisance and if it wasn't for the fact that I was working in a Sainsbury's travel money bureau and required to talk with the customers I would just live with the void. The low point comes one afternoon when, chatting away to a customer the whole thing falls out onto the pile of Polish zloty I am counting. I shove it quickly into my pocket and spend the rest of the shift apologising for looking like Shane MacGowan.

I cannot wait for the salvation of my bridge; I am like a child on the run-up to Christmas, and on the day of fitting I enter the dental surgery with a spring in my step; the end of denture oppression is nigh. The first thing I notice after the bridge is seated is that one of my bottom teeth catches on the metal wing when I close my mouth. This doesn't seem ideal.

"It will take a while for your bite to adjust to it," I am advised, although just for good measure he shaves off a bit of the offending lower tooth. I don't know what he means by *a while,* but the fact is I am still waiting. Every time my teeth come together there is a slight flex across the structure of the bridge; is there any wonder that the bloody thing works loose? And when it does work loose, I have to live with it until it comes out completely; I have to go through a process of gentle wiggling until it gives. On one occasion it comes out with half of the adjacent tooth still attached, so now my denture only covers two thirds of the gap. Not that I wear it much.

Another annoyance, and I think this is a consequence of all the extra hardware glued to the front of my gob, is the way I sometimes *slip* when chewing which causes me to bite my lower lip. Invariably a swollen blister results which just gets further in the way, leading to more biting and more blistering and more foul language at table.

And all this, all this, because I allowed myself to be persuaded back in 1984 that dental crowns were a good idea.

And we come to genetics. I have a small mouth. You might not think so if you had ever seen me in my cups but, in a physical sense it's on the diddy size.[219] Consequently, my teeth are a bit crowded together, particularly at the front. I struggle to get floss in between them. At the back all this jostling for space results in an impacted wisdom tooth from which I have years of trouble.

Impaction of wisdom teeth can occur at a number of angles, the most painful of which is horizontally, which is the card drawn by muggins here. At the point of impact, a void forms which is very difficult to clean with a toothbrush. Food gets caught in there every time I eat and because I can't floss it out, I rely on a series of toothpicks and probes. When they aren't available I resort to anything that is to hand. I remember once eating fish and chips at the seaside and using a bit of nylon thread from an old rope to poke out the debris. This may sound disgusting and dangerously unhygienic, I shan't argue that point, but the presence of food trapped in there can drive a man to anything. At times abscesses form which are very painful and require a dose of antibiotics (metronidazole usually) to put straight. These recourses to antibiotics only happen because my fear of tooth extraction is greater than my fear of a Crohn's flare-up. A number of times I am warned that my wisdom tooth needs to come out and, on every occasion, nod along whilst *fuck off* and *over my dead body* is secretly playing in my inner monologue. Also, it strikes me as a bit perverse to pull out a perfectly healthy

---

[219] I have a small head too, so everything is in proportion.

wisdom tooth on the grounds of impaction when the tooth it is impacting is fifty percent amalgam. If you are going to yank one, surely it's better to lose the one that's at death's door anyway? Eventually, my dentist (Mr K...) suggests this to me but, in the meantime, as long as things didn't get too nasty he will do his damnedest to keep both teeth. And he is good as his word, treating the various broken fillings and abscesses accordingly until late 2017 when, reduced to a slab of grey amalgam lying almost flush to my gumline, my long suffering second molar gives up the ghost; it splits in two down its full length, i.e. right down the root. It needs pulling. Fine, I reason, it's had a good run and tooth extraction holds no fear for me these days.

Numbing up accomplished and the pliers de-cellophaned he sets to work pushing, pulling and wobbling whilst I remain in the vice-like headlock of his strapping sidekick. Because there is very little tooth to grab hold of, other tools are introduced and though I don't see them, from the motion I make a guess at some form of gouge. Eventually something comes out, not the whole tooth but half. I assume that this will free up the other half, but not so; it's not that simple. An x-ray is taken which Mr K... doesn't like the look of and he decides he's not going to risk damaging the nerves and/or the adjacent wisdom tooth and so sends me away with a prescription for antibiotics and a referral to the Charles Clifford Dental hospital.

The appointment (January 2018) turns out to be in a Victorian house some way down the road from the hospital[220] The whole process is remarkably swift. I am ushered into a room by a very friendly nurse who takes down my particulars. The dentist is a

---

[220] I think it serves as the University's student practice

young Egyptian, tall, dark, good looking, and imperious of manner.[221] He asks me why I am there. I tell him and he pulls a face at the thought that anyone would balk at pulling a mere molar.

"Do you still want it removing?"

"Yes."

"Okay. I'll need you to sign this," at which he pulls out a long list of risks associated with the procedure which I read. I try not to dwell on the word *paralysis* as I make my mark.

I am numbed up, which I swear is faster acting than anything I have had in the past and in no time at all he is on the job. Of course, being the patient, I am at something of a disadvantage in terms of observing what is going on, but I think I have a handle on his technique. From observing his movements out of the corner of my eye and from the jolts going through my head I think (layman's terms here) that he just smashed the shit out of what was left of my molar then picked the shards out with tweezers. I might be over simplifying things here but to me it has all the finesse of a builder chiselling out an old window frame.

And that's it, he dusts his hands off and I am kicked out onto the street. Anyway, I don't dwell on it, I have my wad of lint at the back of my gob, and *my what to do after an extraction* crib sheet. Furthermore, I haven't noticed paralysis or any of the other consequences as listed on the sheet of impending doom that I have signed, and this pleases me greatly. *Jobs a good 'un,* as they say in the replacement window game.

However, at some point following the procedure, probably during my sleep, the clot that has formed in the hole where

---

[221] If I was being unkind I would say arrogant

once was my tooth, falls out. I am oblivious to this. I notice a bit of dried blood on my bedding but that doesn't cause me concern; I am an inveterate sleep dribbler and all sorts of flotsam turn up on my pillow in a morning. In the absence of evidence, I assume that I swallowed the clot in my sleep, like some form of somnambulistic, meat-flavoured wine gum. Not that the fate of the clot is relevant, the point is that its absence prevented me from healing in the prescribed manner.

After two days the pain starts in my jaw. I don't pay it much heed, after all I have recently had my head chiselled, but by three days it is quite bad and I am hitting the analgesics. I am curious to know what is going on and by using the bathroom mirror and a torch tiny enough to insert to the back of my cakehole I just about manage to see into the excavation.

My first impulse was that I was developing an infection from bits of food being caught in the hole as I could quite clearly see a piece of potato down there in the depths. Somehow that didn't ring true; apart from anything I hadn't eaten potatoes recently. I gave the vacant lot a gentle suck thinking that I might encourage it to pop out then went in for another gander. It hadn't shifted. With a bit of effort (small mouth issues) I succeeded in angling the torch such that the beam was projecting down into the void. What I had taken to be wedged spud was nothing of the sort, it was part of me. I was looking at my jawbone. Cool stuff in terms of scaring the kids, not so cool in that I was looking at a bit of my own skeleton. I shout down to CM that she needs to see something, taking care not to use the phrase "...my exposed bone..." as I know from bitter experience that this will send her scuttling in the opposite direction.

"Oh Jon..." She sighs, which I take to mean:

*Here we go again, why is nothing ever straight forward with you?*

I have a weekend of face pain, part of which I spend searching the internet for advice. The term *dry socket* keeps popping up and the consensus online is that people with dry sockets need to see people with degrees in dentistry. Monday morning and I phone Charles Clifford Dental Hospital who fit me in first thing Tuesday.

After a brief wait, I am ushered into a large room although *room* is probably a poor choice of word, this is like stepping out onto a factory floor. The space is arranged into a series of individual bays each equipped with the obligatory tilting chair and an array of dental paraphernalia. A nurse shows me to my allotted pen and I am greeted by a child in a white coat who invites me to sit down and tell him all about it.

This is a teaching hospital and the students are allowed first crack at the patients. I'm perfectly happy with this, people have got to learn somewhere. Besides, it's all under supervision so if the kids get into a tizz or the patient looks like they are dying or anything like that, then a grown-up steps in and takes the reins.

Even if he hadn't looked like Doogie Howser MD, it is obvious from the tentative moves of the instruments in my mouth that this is a relative novice. Well, better to have Mr Softly-softly than Mr Poke-around-willy-nilly. I have every confidence in him, not least because I've given him my diagnosis already; all he has to do is fix it. He gets to the stage of flushing me out with a syringe before the Professor is called in. She is excellent, and in contrast to her pupil is very time-efficient. She rattles off an explanation of what they will do; an anaesthetic/antiseptic pad will be left to dissolve over time in my dry socket. This will stand in for the errant clot and allow the gum to close in over it and, as a bonus, it will deal with the nasty infection that is in there. There is a quick warning that the thing tastes nasty[222] and then she legs it leaving Doogie to the spade work. Which he accomplishes admirably, albeit at his own, measured pace. Bless!

Months later, my socket having healed, I begin to notice a sharp, scratchy feeling when I push my tongue around the area of the extraction. Over time it gets more pronounced and so, armed with my little torch I take a look inside. I have a sharp, white, pointy thing sticking out of my gum, directly below the advancing wisdom tooth. A rounder, less white companion can be seen just to the front of it. I assumed these to be bits of debris from the extraction process.

I do an internet search and find that they are called sequestra and are not uncommon following extractions involving a degree of trauma. Over time these things work their way out of their own accord; it's a bit like having a piece of shrapnel in you [223] that's continually moving as your body tries to rid itself of this foreign body.

I have a go at getting it out with a pair of tweezers, but I really struggle to get a grip of it. Also, I am trepidatious as to how big the thing is under the surface. I don't want to create any more wounds to add to hole in my back. (See "Wow that's a big 'un!") Eventually, whilst I am driving on the ring road one morning, absent-mindedly running my tongue over my sequestrum, I feel it move. More tongue work and it comes out completely. Such a disappointment, it is tiny! It felt huge when it was in my

---

[222] Actually, I quite liked it.
[223] Except not nearly as bad.

mouth; here, on the end of my finger, it is miniscule. Because I am driving, I stick it with spittle to the passenger seat of the truck with a view to examining it in detail once I have reached my destination; I am interested to see whether it is bone or tooth.

When I do reach my destination, I completely forget about it and the next time it comes into my head I am driving the girls to piano lessons[224] and the eldest is sitting on it; she isn't very happy when I tell her. It is never found; lost in a jean seam I suspect.

## Test Tube Babies

The world's first test tube baby is born in 1978; her name is Louise. At the time this holds very little interest for me. I am a twelve-year-old boy; why would it? It remains at the very furthest limits of my mind palace[225] until my late thirties when I have to swat-up on the subject pretty sharpish.

The current Mrs Lenity and I begin trying for a baby in 1995; a whole year before we are married which just goes to show you how Bohemian some parts of Yorkshire can get. By 1996, after a quick head count, we are still childless and it is starting to dawn on us that there is something going on here beyond bad luck. We pay a visit to the GP and explain how long we have been going at it (so to speak) without success. Suspecting that this might be an ovulation issue we are issued with a prescription for the fertility drug Clomid[226]. It doesn't make a jot of difference and we know it isn't a dodgy batch because CM

---

[224] I have very middle-class children.

[225] I haven't actually got a mind palace.

[226] I always think it's a very Welsh sounding word: "Look you Gwynneth, triplets is it? That's Clomid see; tidy darts.

gives some to her friend (who has a period approximately once every three years) and she gets preggers at the first shot (literally). Something else must be at fault.

I have a sperm count and it turns out that my semen is packed full of goodness, therefore the problems, likely as not, lay with CM. She is put through a range of tests starting with the basic bloods and progressing to a post coital test whereby her cervical mucus is examined to see if it is impeding my sperm; it isn't. Finally, she is subjected to a laparoscopic examination. This requires a general anaesthetic and involves incisions being made in her abdomen through which a laparoscope (a thin tube with a camera) is inserted allowing the surgeon to take a good look inside the various bits of lady plumbing.

The surgeon seems inordinately pleased with things as he breezes into the post-op debriefing, the reason for which soon becomes apparent.

"I've never seen anything like it before!" He enthuses. "We unearth all sorts of stuff growing in ovaries: fingernails, hair, that sort of thing, but I've never seen anything like this."

"What is it?"

"No idea; nothing to worry about though."

CM has her own theory; it is penis. She has grown a penis in one of her ovaries and that is the reason she has such large hands and unnaturally hairy legs. Keele University gave this woman a 2:1 in biology!

Having discounted her theory, more or less immediately, and still none the wiser as to why we can't make a baby I set about getting my somewhat emotional wife home. She does not respond well to anaesthetic, it has caused her to vomit a couple of times in recovery and it has been decreed by the nursing staff that unless the puking dries up she is staying overnight. This is the last thing she wants. We hang around for another hour during which the tearful CM remains sick free, at which point we were given the green light. I get her dressed and pack up her overnight bag whilst the nurse fetches a wheelchair.

"Ahm gunna bezick!" she mumbles as soon as the nurse is out of the room. I rush forth with a kidney dish in time to catch the spew.

"Ahdonwanna stay. Ahwanagowoamjon. Ahwanagowoam!"

Desperate measures are required. In less enlightened times the drill would have been to deliver a slap and tell her to pull herself together, but those days are gone[227]. Instead I initiate a cover-up. I wipe her face then take the bowl of sick and put it in a paper bag, shoving a few paper towels in to catch any leaks. Then the lot is stashed in CM's case and out of sight; no one's any the wiser.

There is a sense that we have just pulled off a bank heist as I wheel CM down the corridor to the exit; we are lucky that our haste doesn't raise suspicion. That said, the getaway is not without its touch and go moments. Halfway out CM decides she is going to puke again and I am told to about-turn back to the ward. Then:

"No, no, ahwanagowoam" and another about-turn. This happens three times before I manage to get her into the car and back home to Honley.

We now fall within the bracket of *unexplained infertility*, which is a bit of a frustrating category to be in. If you know what a problem is either something can be done about it or,

---

[227] I like Burt Lancaster, Robert Mitchum, James Mason, et al as much as the next man but I have to concede that the demise of the hysterical women slap is probably a good thing.

failing that, you learn to live with it and move on[228]. This is just a sort of limbo state.

In 1997 CM gets a job with the NHS in Sheffield and, as I am already working for the University there, it makes sense for us to relocate. This means swapping hospitals, and because different hospitals have their own way of doing things the initial work seems to be going over old ground. There is the inevitable array of blood tests of course. This time we are also checked out for the clap which includes a swab up the old love pipe; not pleasant but mercifully swift. I also have a repeat of my sperm count which I don't mind because of all the samples one is required to submit for medical analysis that is definitely my favourite. CM's tests, as before, show nothing out of order but my sperm count is, all of a sudden, below the optimum. Which is odd because my previous tally suggested I might be a candidate to help repopulate the earth in the event of Armageddon. Different ways of counting it seems, and whilst, under normal circumstances, my tadpoles ought to be up to the job, when combined with a mysterious *something* being below par on CM's side of the equation, it is leaving us drawing blanks.

Why is my sperm a bit off? Hard to say, I spend a lot of time behind a desk in a warm office and cooler conditions are preferable, I drink beer and coffee with abandon which probably doesn't help. Perhaps I am low on a certain vitamin or mineral? Perhaps it is the Crohn's? In retrospect I think this should have been explored further. If not the disease itself then my medication (mesalazine)? Even now there still remains very little information on the subject so it is hard to say one way or

---

[228] Easier said than done, I grant you.

the other.

If that is a bit of a mystery it is nothing compared to the enigma of what is stifling CM's game. Part of us begins to suspect that the problem is not so much physical as mental. This is a very difficult and emotional time for her. Still in the tumult of grief following the tragic death of her younger brother the further stress of failing to conceive only serves to compound her unhappiness. The more we try and fail the more pessimistic she becomes about things.

I asked her recently what is her abiding memory of that time and she described it as a sense of double mourning; for the loss of her brother and the child she could not have. I recall a lot of sobbing; the slightest pretext would set her off. When something is that all-consuming it is practically impossible to avoid it in normal life. Reminders are everywhere. Approaching pregnant women with; "move along fatty you're upsetting the missus," is not done, apparently.[229]

We embark upon IVF, which was now the only medical course open to us. IVF, in case you are not aware stands for in vitro fertilisation, literally *in the glass* fertilisation. It is commonly referred to as the "test tube baby technique" although as far as I know test tubes are not involved. In essence the process is this:

Eggs are removed from the woman, combined with sperm outside of the body (the in vitro bit) and the resulting embryos are replaced into the uterus in the hope that they develop into babies.

Easy peasy.

---

[229] Well, that was what the police said at any rate...and the magistrate agreed with them

Actually, no. If it was that simple anyone with turkey baster and a basic knowledge of female anatomy would have managed it long before 1978. Firstly, the woman's ovaries require stimulation in order to produce a decent clutch[230] of eggs and this includes drugs to suppress emission via the conventional route. This is not without risks, ovarian hyperstimulation syndrome (OHSS), a complication of the process, can be life threatening.

Next, the eggs need to be extracted and this is performed by inserting a long needle (guided by ultrasound) through the wall of the vagina into each ovary and basically sucking them out.

Selected eggs and washed sperm[231] are brought together, embryos develop and the best of them are transferred via a catheter to the uterus, there to grow into healthy sprog/sprogs. Obviously, it is a highly specialised business and as such is not cheap. At the time IVF was not readily available on the NHS[232] and the debate surrounding whether it should be provided at all was ongoing. We had little choice but to go private and as luck would have it there is a fertility clinic quite close to us, in Nether Edge. If memory serves, I think it costs somewhere in the region of three thousand pounds a shot. If that wasn't bad enough it seems that there are subsequent, ongoing costs which they don't tell you about. Things such as Play Stations, Jack Wills hoodies, Converse trainers, Ed Sheeran tickets, etc., which are staggering. If I had any money left, I would sue.

---

[230] The collective noun for eggs. I don't think this is much used by fertility professionals.

[231] Separated from semen and any dead cells removed

[232] There was a seriously long wait for it. It's better these days but restrictions still apply.

After the initial consultations and basic checks, treatment begins with a series of injections into CM's upper thigh. This is all done at home and at set times of the day. We are fitted out with a spring-loaded injector, a fridge full of drugs and a nice zip-up, lilac carry bag for when we need to do it on the hoof. My job is to deliver the dose, which is surprisingly easy[233].

CM has to go, periodically, to the clinic to have her bloods taken and to have an ultrasound recce of her ovaries. This is not the same as the gentle, gel-smothered belly massage a la ante natal, it is performed trans vaginally. That is to say a full stirrup, legs akimbo job while a medic goes at it with a greasy probe that looks something like a laser blaster from Blake's Seven.[234]

After almost a fortnight of this her follicles[235] have developed nicely and she is in a position to donate her eggs. The same day I am required to fulfil my obligations and *fill-full* a pot.[236] From a personal standpoint this is no problem; the trickiest part for me was washing the old helmet and wotnot, and that's purely down to lack of practice[237].

Not everyone is comfortable with their seed producing duties; the car park is littered with flustered-looking men having a breather before limbering up and trying again. It is strange the effect nerves can have on you. Perhaps if they offered one of

---

[233] Lock and load, point and shoot; it is difficult to get wrong.

[234] That makes me sound like some sort of sci fi ultra-nerd; I promise you I'm not. Look it up, you will see what I mean.

[235] The fluid filled spheroids in the ovary where the eggs are secreted. I think of them as something like the recesses in an egg box, but I don't think anyone else does.

[236] It does not need to be full. The average ejaculation produces less than 10ml so it would take a while even for a small pot.

[237] I joke of course; my glans is as clean as the next man's

those Benny Hill type nurses in stockings and suspenders to chase men around a room waving an empty pot it might move things along a bit? I can't say if anyone else thinks that this would be a good idea as no one in the waiting room says much. Many of the couples here are visibly tense, and it brings it home to you just how important this business is to them. Husband's names are called out and the men shuffle off like they are going to the gallows; mournful look over the shoulder, languid wave as abandoned spouse suppresses a tear.

I'm not getting any of this anxiety. When my name is called I couldn't get to it any quicker if I'd been using starting blocks; I'm grinning as I leave. It's all I can do not to shout "Way-hey!" as I am handed the pot. Why am I the odd one out here? A number of explanations spring to mind:

a. I am so arrogant that I flaunt my ready-for-action stud credentials for all to see.
b. I am quite shallow with a tendency towards the puerile.
c. I have had so much experience of embarrassing medical procedures that a room full of strangers knowing that I have just gone away to *knock-one-out* does not even register on my shame scale.

And the answer is...?[238]

The *private* room is nice; very small, warm and intimate. There is a sink for the aforementioned cleansing of helmets and, presumably, post sample hand washing. There is a comfy sofa, ideally it would have been wipe-clean rather than linen effect because the pot is on the small side and it is difficult to keep a steady aim when one is in the throes of ecstasy, but I am nit-

---

[238] Probably all three.

picking here. There is a mirror for anyone that way inclined and, importantly, there is a lock on the door. All good, but not perfect. Where it falls down is the reading matter. This is very uninspiring. Shut away in a drawer under the sink is a small selection of pornographic magazines. The clinic is on a hiding to nothing here, they dare not risk offending anyone by going too racy, so on the whole, they keep it deliberately tame. Do not draw any conclusions from this. I am not looking for anything specialist, just a little less sanitised; more realistic. Airbrushed models with ginormous fake breasts really don't do it for me and I had to thumb through reams of this sort of stuff until I found something that actually looked like a woman.

It is a strange feeling making a baby whilst a woman other than your partner is on your mind. I'm sure it goes on in the normal sense of things; you hear it spouted in melodramas: "you're making love to me, but I know you are thinking of her". It doesn't normally involve a photograph though. Is it a form of infidelity? I don't know; she means nothing to me now, that skinny, flat-chested reader's wife with her legs in the air. I cannot even tell you her name; I think of her simply as Candy on account of the washing machine she's perched on.

The emphasis switches to egg retrieval, CM is sedated and dosed up on pain killers. Patients are encouraged to bring in a favourite CD; it's played during the process to help them relax. To my mind there is a perfect candidate, the clue is in the title, but CM is not a fan of Frankie goes to Hollywood and so George Michael's "Older" gets the nod. Ordinarily I would argue the point, but I would only get hit by the "you're only here to hold my bloody hand..." argument so I bite my lip. Retrieval goes swimmingly; a good clutch of eggs is harvested and somewhere in the dark recesses of the clinic they are introduced to my sperm.

Embryos are formed and we get regular updates on their progress which is all very encouraging and exciting. I imagine sending your kids to boarding school feels something like this. Finally, the three best looking ones[239] are placed inside mummy and she goes home and puts her feet up. A couple of weeks later we return to clinic for the pregnancy test, a blood sample rather than the pissy-stick affair. CM receives the bad news over the phone the following day. It's upsetting but we are heartened by the thought that we had gotten at least to the implanting stage. Once CM's hormones have levelled off, which takes about six months, we have another go. Our optimism at having gone so far first time out is misplaced, it fails for a second time. At this point we invest in another child substitute and get our third dog; Brenda.

It is a time of reflection and whilst both of us want a child we realise that at some point we have to draw a line in the sand. The whole IVF process is a great strain on the body, let alone what it does to a woman's mental state. We are agreed, one more failed round of IVF and we call it a day and adopt (see "Cricked Neck").

Round three opens and CM engages the services of a hypnotherapist to help her approach things with a more positive frame of mind; we have weekly trips to Tickhill to get her nice and psyched on the run-up. As before, George Michael and of course the ever-alluring Candy get the nod again.

A number of eggs are fertilized but, some are shedding cell matter which is not a good sign. The embryologist is not optimistic; there is a bit head shaking and a lot of sympathetic

---

[239] Presumably the ones that take after their father

looks. Nevertheless, we go through the motions; three "rubbish" embryos are implanted, and we go away and prepare for adoption.

Results day and I come home at dinnertime[240] to make the phone call as CM is too nervous to talk. I know that it bucks convention for a husband to tell his wife she is pregnant rather than the other way around, but nobody cares. It makes me feel like quite the new age man; and CM is the happiest woman on the planet.

Aside from a scare that CM might be developing OHS[241], the pregnancy goes without a hitch, culminating, in 2000, of the birth of our daughter, Bruce. We still make a point of telling her what a rubbish embryo she was.

2002 and we embark on IVF once again. The familiar crew are involved; it was like one of those films where the aging rocker says: "...we're getting the band back together." I was glad to see that Candy was still on the scene but couldn't help wondering what, in the real world, she was draping herself over these days. I would be surprised if the white goods beneath her pert buttocks in the photo have stood the course. We made the mistake of buying that brand once and it was rubbish.

The procedure went well, we even produced half decent embryos this time and on the back of our previous success (a passable child from a dodgy cluster of cells) we had every confidence of a result. To update an old adage; *never count your embryos until they are hatched,* CM bleeds days after the implantation and the subsequent pregnancy test gives a

---

[240] Apparently, according to my middle-class kids, this is called lunchtime.

[241] Ovarian hyperstimulation syndrome.

predictable negative.

Six months later we try again. CM is like an embryo production line, two are implanted with a few spares to put in the freezer.[242] We are quite optimistic to the point where CM admits to feeling different, which is code for feeling pregnant, but experience tells us to temper our enthusiasm. Rightly so, a few days in and CM is spotting blood and we write-off her *feeling different* as imagination; confirmation bias I think the term is. Despite this she still goes through the motions and the morning of the pregnancy test we get a call from the clinic. It's early but CM is showing such a strong positive that the nurse felt compelled to let us know immediately; I still cannot get my head around the logic of that even now.

In clinic it is explained to us that the powerful result on the test could be indicative of a multiple birth, which should be interesting. It is, *doubly* interesting in fact; CM is carrying twins, a boy and a girl, which are delivered by caesarean in 2003. We stopped after that; twins do that to you.

## Tingly Brain

I discover this sensation way back in the eighties, although at the time I tell no one about it as I don't want to be labelled a weirdo. I rediscovered it a couple of years ago after reading a newspaper article about folding towels (bear with me here) and it seems I'm not as peculiar as I thought I was. It even has a (pseudo-scientific) name now, autonomous sensory meridian response or to give it its acronym, ASMR.

ASMR is a strange one to describe; to give it a pocket definition I would say it is a state of intense relaxation which at times can

---

[242] The clinic's freezer, not ours.

include a tingling feeling across my scalp and down my neck. I hesitate to say goose pimples or frisson as these, to me, imply a short-term shiver of excitement whereas ASMR is more of a *deceleration* and the state of relaxation is maintained when the tingling has passed.

ASMR occurs in response to certain triggers and the most common of these seems to be a softly spoken voice or whispering. However, it need not be vocalised sound, light tapping, crinkling of paper, sometimes watching repetitive tasks or movements can do the trick.

Anyway, back to the eighties. Maggie Philbin will always hold a special place in the hearts of red-blooded British males of my vintage. Swap Shop's sweet smiling, girl-next-door antidote to Noel Edmunds, and the sexy face of Tomorrow's World. It may sound bizarre in this day and age where we have a plethora of TV channels to choose from and we can just conjure up a pretty face from the internet as and when required but back then you had to take your chances when they came and on Saturday mornings that meant Maggie Philbin or the slightly more slutty-looking Sally James of Tiswas on ITV. Unless you had one of those new-fangled video recorders then you were going to miss out on one of them.

Speaking of videos, and I am aware that I am drifting away from ASMR here, but this is very important. In researching this book I came across a film of a Blue Peter feature on corsetry. It featured Isla Sinclair, Tina Heath, Sarah Greene and Maggie Philbin all of whom were modelling underwear. Sally James aside, that's like a who's who of 80s teenage fantasies; I can't believe it crept under the radar at the time since I was generally very good at spotting that sort of thing. You can see it on YouTube; just type in Blue Peter Corsets and enjoy.

Back to the script. I think it must have been Maggie's TW incarnation because I remember watching it of an evening, alone on the settee, the only light in the room coming from the screen in the corner. I haven't a clue what the item was about, some giant technological leap, round teabags or something, it's not relevant. The important thing is her delivery; it's doing things to me, but not in the normal way. I have never felt such an overwhelming sense of contentment without actually going to sleep and, icing on the cake, it is coupled with a strange tingly feeling in my scalp. I don't know whether the ambience of the room contributes (it can't have hurt) but when the item ends the sensation ceases. Clearly Maggie Philbin, or her voice, or round teabags, or some combination therein is the motive force here.

It is years before it happens again, this time while I am incarcerated in Lodge Moor Hospital in Sheffield. I have been placed under the care of a dietician who is charged with assessing what I have been getting in the way of nutrition and, because the answer is very little, what can be done about it. Our conversations, she sitting on the edge of my bed speaking in her soft, measured, professional tone, the light scratching of pen on clip-boarded paper are, for me, bordering on ecstasy. My contribution is quite limited of course, I just lay back, answer her questions as best I can and try to stop my eyes from rolling back into my skull. This is the perfect antidote to *overfriendly* nurses, needles, tubes in various orifices and commodes. (See "Bovine TB")

Onward to the internet age and, my interest piqued by the towel folding article, I go on-line and take a look for myself. It certainly strikes a chord with me. Obviously, things have moved on a bit since my first Philbin tingle. These days everyone is using binaural microphones and you need to listen through headphones in order to take full advantage, but at its core this is pure Mags.

There is no end of ASMR practitioners to choose from too, my personal favourites are Maria (the towel lady), Darya (the Russian lady) and Latte (doll-like Korean lady). You may see a pattern emerging here, particularly if you take a look at those three. Most ASMR practitioners appear to be attractive young women, many of whom indulge in what may seem like *kinky* roll play for the benefit of the viewer. I understand, therefore, why friends and family have accused me of trying to legitimise internet porn. After all, if you are a middle-aged man who has just been caught with a laptop watching a beautiful Russian woman who dresses up in the uniform of a ticket inspector on the Trans-Siberian Railway, then it's very difficult to mount a credible defence. These accusers all have one thing in common, ASMR doesn't work for them! It's like being able to roll your tongue or taste the nastier aspects of Brussels sprouts; there's them as can and there's them who can't. If there is a sexual element to it then it's way out on the periphery of the experience. I have seen some ASMR sites which have clearly set out to provide a sexualised form and for me they just don't work; the sensations are all wrong.

My son D..., it seems, may have the gift, his favourite port of call being the softly spoken painting tutorials of the late Bob Ross. I've tried Bob myself and whilst it predates the use of binaural microphones and can get a bit repetitive (it's always about bloody painting) you do get the same sort of ASMR feeling. If you aren't familiar with Bob, look him up and I am certain you'll agree there is no finer argument for ASMR being non-sexual. I rest my case m'lud.

214

## Trapped Nerve
See "Cricked Neck"

# U is for...
## Ubermucus

This is not an *established term* as far as I know, even in Germany, though            I suspect it is only a matter of time before it's splashed across the Lancet. At the moment I am the only person (to my knowledge) to have suffered from it and I have been struck down on no less than two occasions.

My first encounter happens in Ecclesall Woods back in 2008. As a stay at home dad[243], one of my jobs is to take the kids to school which is very pleasant because I get to walk through some pretty scenery. It is even better on the return journey because I get to walk through some pretty scenery without kids. It is often a rush to get them to school (for one reason or another) and this occasion is no exception. In addition to the general kerfuffle I am feeling lousy, I've had a virus of some sort which has lasted for weeks it seems, exacerbated no doubt by the long hours spent making pies and working on chilly market stalls.

Halfway to school I stop to blow my nose and find that I can't make anything come out; there is no flow. I do what anyone would do in that position, snort inwards whilst at the same time tightening my throat in the way one does in order to dig out a phlegm ball. Nothing comes up. Instead, I feel a strange, elastic, pulling sensation in my sinuses.

I have another go, retching and rasping loudly. All this, remember, is in the middle of the woods with my children and

---

[243] Or sponger as my mother-in-law terms it.

dog watching-on innocently, and a stream of Goretex-clad, pram-pushing mums going past trying not to catch my eye. After a good minute of me bent double, hacking away, I feel movement; there is something rubbery in the back of my throat. Thankfully CM is not around so there is nothing to stop me from going in. More mums pass. There will probably be a discussion when they meet up at school:

"Hacking up phlegm you say? When I saw him he had his fingers down his throat gagging."

"Must be the same bloke."

"Yeah, the weird one; doesn't wear Goretex?"

I didn't care. As Oscar Wilde said:

> "there is only one thing in the world worse than being talked about, and that is not being talked about."[244]

I have a grip of my quarry and I am determined to bring it out into the light of day irrespective of the social consequence. I pull. It stretches but doesn't give, it just pulls back. I use a different technique, a slower, more gradual force, which is an improvement as I can now feel some motion deep in my cheek. I carry on, my eyeballs dragging slightly into my skull at which point I lose my grip and everything twangs back.

I don't give up, apart from anything I am thoroughly enjoying myself. I hook it again and drag, this time I feel my left knee rising. I joke of course, but there is a definite lifting in my throat. Teasing the elastomer slowly forward I supplement the movement with a rasp of my throat at which point everything shifts forward. Nose, throat, ears, sinuses empty until I have the amorphous beast in my mouth. It is like chewing on a huge

---

[244] Uttered prior to his experience of serving two years hard labour for gross indecency.

toffee, a similar colour too. This is no ordinary flob, this is the next level in greeny evolution; it is like coughing up Stretch Armstrong. I christen it Ubermucus.[245]  I try to hang on to it, retain it in my mouth but because of its size it is affecting my speech and so I am forced to spit it out and watch it scuttle into the bushes[246]. A bit of a shame really.

## UTI
See "Prostate"

## Under the Knife
I sit on a stinking toilet clutching my bloated body feeling like I might be dying[247]. Evelyn Waugh, Catherine the Great, Elvis; I wouldn't be the first. Sweat bursts from what must be every pore of my skin's surface. The spontaneity is alarming; it feels as if someone has just thrown a bucket of water over me. The pain in my innards surges further and, as my head begins to swim, I look at the orange emergency cord dangling before me. Perhaps I should grab it now? If I do faint, then chances are I'll be pitched forward onto the floor and the cord will be out of reach. Another nauseating surge and I look at the floor between my knees; yellow and drying it looks like someone has spilled pot of cheap varnish over it. It reeks of ammonia and I feel its tackiness through the soles of my Crocs; I tug at my pyjama shorts lest they drag through it. Do I really want to collapse onto that? Absolutely not! It occurs to me that if I really am dying then I probably needn't worry too much about the substrate on which I do it. Who knows?

---

[245] Nothing to do with taxis
[246] No scuttling actually.
[247] See "Death"

My left arm is attached, via three canula, to an array of bags and drug pumps clamped to a wheeled stand; if I go over that's going with me. I prop an elbow onto an adjacent low shelf to brace myself for the wobble. My elbow is resting in a trickle of brownish liquid; my eyes follow it along the shelf to the source. Missing of a cradle, someone has decided that this is a reasonable place to store the toilet brush; the brush is plastic, white and innocent, but like a bottle-blonde its dark roots give away the truth.

After much concentration I pass a little urine, but it brings no relief, rather it seems to prompt further contortions. Something will give; it can't not. I'd like to force the issue, but the effort is beyond me.

A little over a week ago I shifted five tonne of hardcore in an afternoon and thought nothing of it. Not to be confused with nicely rounded gravel, this was twenty mil, Derbyshire limestone, angular and not the kind of stuff a shovel slides into readily. I don't cite this as evidence of my physical prowess, rather I offer it up as an example of the complacency with which most of us go about our everyday business. Which is natural, I suspect. We don't tell ourselves how fragile this existence is, or how the health we enjoy so blithely relies on a rope of sand for its retention. We don't tell ourselves because it's not natural to tell ourselves; only weirdos and sick people think like that.

The reason for my sudden change in fortunes? Surgery, the bullet I've been dodging for all these years has finally found its mark. I'd had my routine colonoscopy at the start of the year (2018) which had gone very much to form. Better in fact, since I managed to persuade the nurse charged with distracting me from the general unpleasantness of the process to buy one of my books.[248]

With his usual aplomb Dr J... had negotiated a route through the crazy golf course that constitutes my colon, saying lots of positive things along the way and chomping off little lumps of tissue to fill the array of plastic pots before him. I, for my part, downed as many gas and air cocktails as I could reasonable get away with and slurred out responses as and when required. Retaining the crazy golf theme, this was all par for the course.

Except, three weeks later, a letter arrives. In fact, two letters arrive. The first is from the Charles Clifford dental hospital informing me that I was now on a waiting list for the removal of the same tooth stump they had yanked out a month earlier; very thorough you see! The second is from Dr J... The word *surgery* leaps out at me; also *Dysplasia* (isn't that something Alsatians get in their back legs?) and MDT catch my attention. I get on Google and discover that Dysplasia is *the presence of cells of an abnormal type within a tissue.* That is to say, not cancer but getting that way. MDT is multi-disciplinary team which no doubt scuppers my chances of playing the *I demand a second opinion* card. To be on the safe side I read the letter a further time, just in case I missed the postscript that reads: "Oh, hang on a minute, forget all that, I'm thinking of somebody else. What am I like!"

There is no postscript.

Thanks to a cancellation I get a consultation with Dr J... in a matter of days. CM tells me later that I spend the whole session with a visibly clenched jaw; I never realised I did that but apparently it's a sure sign of Lenity tension.

---

[248] Wife-swapping Nazis of the Inner Hebrides. Have you read it? You should, it's very good.

"Complete surprise!" He says, "Nobody is more shocked than me," he adds. Dr J... is his usual affable (and of course handsome) self, if a little tired looking. I'm the last patient of his shift and it can't be easy breaking bad news to people all day. "Everything looked fine. It was one of the random samples that came back dysplastic."

DALM is the key point here apparently. Another acronym you'll note, in this case standing for dysplasia associated lesion or mass.

"Is that bad?" I ask. Not good. It indicates that I have had some quite severe episodes of inflammation in the past. I know this, I was there. DALMs alone are bad enough, I learn, but combined with my age, the two strictures, the array of polyps and the duration of my illness, etc., etc., the prospects of colorectal cancer at some point soon are, more-or-less, nailed-on.

"Remarkable really," he adds "I don't think I've encountered anyone who ticked quite so many boxes."

"Does that mean I'm special?" He doesn't answer; I assume that I am. Something is bothering me. Until this point I have told myself that surgery in this case would mean something along the lines of CM's hemicolectomy (see "Mrs Lenity as Proxy"). That is to say, taking out a section, albeit a significant section, then joining up the ends; this scenario seems to sit uneasily alongside all the enthusiasm surrounding boxes ticked.

"How much of the colon are we talking about?" I ask, already knowing the answer.

"All of it."

"You mean a bag?"

"Yes. Or we can leave a small section at the end and join the small bowel to that. The choice is yours."

"If I had the bag would it mean I would have my bum-hole stitched up?"

"You'll need to discuss that with the surgeon. That's the next stage; see what they can offer you."

"Right..." I say hesitantly, my mind trying to conjure up the sensation of being arsehole-less.

"We have some excellent surgeons." He adds.

That's encouraging; he wouldn't say that if it wasn't true, would he? He wouldn't say: *we have a couple of run-of-the-mill sawbones who can probably muddle through a giblet job,* would he? Of course not, this is a teaching hospital, it's rammed full of expertise.

"I'll refer you to the IBD nurse too. She will be able to talk you through aftercare and so on." He means slopping out the belly bag, "help you come to a decision."

I'm struggling to find words, CM picks up the baton and runs through what is left of our list of prepared questions. I think of one more:

"What would you do? Would you go for the bag?" I ask. Dr J...'s countenance suddenly changes. Has no one posed that question to him before now? His vacillation is more telling than his ultimate answer, which is (eventually) the ileostomy[249] option with removal of the whole colon.

I dig around the internet trying to get a feel for what it's like to have no colon. There is a hell of a lot of stuff on ileostomies, from message boards to YouTube videos and everything in between. Many of the videos are made by young people (teens, twenties) which must be so much harder to come to terms with

---

[249] Ileostomy involves the diversion of the small intestine out through an opening in the abdomen.

at an age (it strikes me) that is more insecure and image conscious than it has ever been. And let's be honest, even the most enlightened of suitors will have a degree of unease about the set up. At the risk of marginalising colossal perverts (apologies if you fall into that bracket) there is really nothing sexy about a stoma. Yet for the most part, the message they impart is a positive one; there is life after colectomy.

The optimism of the videos is in contrast to the message boards which are pretty much chock-full of woe. Leaking bags, farting bags, blockages, pain, skin irritation, general misery. This is understandable, the youngsters of YouTube are optimists with stories to tell, they are evangelists. Many of the message-boarders are strugglers; they are looking for answers and support. Here too the story is: *there is life after colectomy*, however, it's not a terribly pleasant one.

Important, then, not to be swayed towards one camp rather than the other. Balance is required. One boarder I noticed had clearly had enough of all the negativity and after being sympathetic for the majority of the thread, was tipped over the edge and finished with:

"Jesus, you've had your ass moved a few inches higher, it's still your ass!"

Ass is American for bottom I believe. It's true of course, but at least the old-fashioned anus has the good grace to pucker up and shrink away between a pair of conveniently placed slabs of meat; it doesn't poke out like an angry little sewage outfall pipe.[250]

---

[250] Why do we have such an arrangement? Is there an evolutionary advantage to having this built-in clag trap? Other than the

What of the alternative? The joiny-up option. Instinct tells me that this is the lesser of the two evils if only on the basis that it allows for the fall-back position of an ileostomy. The other way around, bag reverting to joiny-up (one would think) is less achievable; once you bumhole's gone it's gone for good.

First things first, I need a name; even with the most accommodating of search engines *joiny-up option* doesn't get you very far. I need a bona fide term. I find it in *anastomosis*. It means, according to Wikipedia: *a connection between two normally divergent structures*, in my case the end my ileum and the last bit of my colon. It will be an ileo-something anastomosis, depending on where the chop is made.

I commit the term anastomosis to memory. AN-ASS-TOE-MOSIS. Straight forward enough? Apparently not. I seem to have a mental block with the word and every time I try to recall it my brain serves up ANAMASTOSIS instead, which, unless you are interested in Greek singers from the 1970s, is not much use at all.

Initial searches yield less than I had hoped. It bothers me that there is such a dearth of information on anastomoses, particularly in comparison to ileostomies. Search for Greek singers of the 1970s and there is tonnes of stuff; kaftans and trademark specs abound.

Surgical fashions bother me. One thinks of all the perfectly good tonsils that have been binned, the popularity of mastectomies on the strength of Betty Ford's experiences, the rush to replace healthy teeth with dentures before they get chance to rot. My own mother always maintained that she was

---

preservation of modesty I cannot think of one. Point scored for the creationists I think.

forced into a hysterectomy she didn't need.[251]   I find a few research papers covering bowel related anastomosis but most of them seem quite dated. Besides, I need something more for the layman; there is an inherent danger in me putting too much emphasis on knowledge that I'm not equipped to understand. There is no merit in me reading beyond the abstracts and even some of these are beyond my ken. That said, I'm getting positive vibes from the limited material I have to work with. I must be careful here; there is a temptation to grasp with both hands any kind word that supports the cause. It's a trait known as confirmation bias and we are all prone to it.

What I am really missing are first-hand accounts, the equivalents of the videos and message boards of the ostomy camp. These, as far as they relate to my situation as I see it, are very few and far between.

I get a call from the IBD nurse and arrange to meet that day. Quite by chance I am temping at the hospital where my surgery will take place, which is great in terms of convenience, not so good for taking my mind off the subject. And my mind is on the subject, permanently. The uncertainty surrounding surgical options, quality of life, timescales, etc. is wrapped up with my long-standing terrors; it clouds everything I do. I feel like I am conducting my life through a net curtain.

Nurse B... is very nice and talks very positively about ostomies;

---

[251] I have only her word for this. It may be true but bear in mind that she also maintained that I was the rightful heir to Wentworth Woodhouse, Britain's largest stately home. In 1994 she claimed to have identified Yorkshire's first wild pelican which had ditched the fish-heavy diet of the tropics in favour of a string of skanky peanuts in the back garden of a Sheffield council house.

technical advancements, carbon filters, home delivery. I was hoping she would have a couple of sample bags to let be play with (you know, try on for size, blow up, that sort of thing) but she doesn't; she's not strictly a stoma nurse you see. I mention ileo-rectal anastomosis, but she's had no first-hand experience of one, which mirrors my search efforts. The subject of Greek singers isn't mentioned so I must have got it right on this occasion. She is familiar with the ileo-anal pouch[252] and I learn that this is generally undertaken as a two-stage procedure, a few months with the bag and then a join-up. I digest this information.

On the subject of surgery, she confesses to sharing my terror of the knife, more specifically, the panic over loss of control when falling under. I'm totally with her on this one. Even after her first surgery the terror remained and for her next op. she was offered a sedative to get her in the mood, so to speak. It only served to exacerbate the panic. This information I digest also. She mentions a rectal stump[253]. Often, the last bit of the gastrointestinal tract is closed off at the cut and left in place. The blood supply remains and in its own truncated and isolated fashion Old Stumpy functions as he did before. The benefit here being that the bum area feels relatively normal. It even needs wiping from time to time since it still produces a bit of gunk.

I finally get a date to see the surgeon, and it looks like it will be Mr A..., he of the Stalinist moustache. I am pleased with this;

---

[252] A joining of the ileum to the anus whereby a pouch is surgically constructed as a "reservoir" for poo thus avoiding faecal incontinence. A stand-in for the rectum, if you like.

[253] A good name for a punk band, don't you think?

not only has he a terrific reputation but we also have a personal understanding (see "Mrs Lenity as Proxy"). Unfortunately, the appointment is weeks off. Of course, I'm no sort of emergency and I've no reason to expect an expedited service but it doesn't help with the sense of uncertainty. That said, it gives me a chance to do a bit more digging into anamastosis. Sorry, anastomosis.

The issue, as I see it, is one of control. In basic terms, removal of my colon will make me poo a lot more frequently. Because the colon is responsible for removing water its absence is likely to produce watery poo. With an ostomy, you can monitor this, you can see when the bag is getting full and plan accordingly. Could the same be said for the anastomosis? I've every confidence in my sphincter, it's served me faithfully over the years despite some very challenging situations. Battle hardened and grizzled, it remains an indefatigable sentinel; it is the Chuck Norris of ring pieces. But there are limits, even Chuck can only hold back a gravy tsunami for so long. Add to that the complication of whether to gamble with the occasional fart and it begins to feel like life in the danger zone. In contrast, ostomy bags these days are fitted with fart release valves and carbon filters to take the flavour out.

Days before my appointment with Mr A..., I finally find a bit of first-hand knowledge. I say "I", strictly speaking it's the Current Mrs Lenity who should get the credit as it comes via a work colleague. After a few missed calls I finally connect with P... who, in his broad Lancashire tones, proceeds to relate his tale. It is a catalogue of woe and misfortune and he could be forgiven for allowing himself the odd whimper or gripe at the fickle nature of fate, but he doesn't. Quite the opposite in fact, he is remarkably positive considering the list includes: a stroke (a real one, not just dodgy specs, see "Stroke"), perforated bowel, various episodes of surgery, and, wait for it... gangrene. Bloody gangrene! I thought that sort of thing went out with Scutari, but apparently, it's still available for selected patients. The upshot of all this is the removal of his colon, a year or so of an ostomy bag, then reconnection with the leftovers.

"Would that be an ileo-rectal anastomosis?" I ask.

"That's the one."

Bingo! Not only is P... a good fit for my preference but he can also provide an authentic comparison with the alternative.

"So, how's it been?" I ask, which, I know, is a very broad question considering the various stages that P... must have gone through.

"I'll be honest with you," he confides, "for a long time it was bloody terrible. I'd say it took about a year after the op before I started feeling well again."

"But you function now?"

"Yeah, I'm fine. I'm on my way to the pub as we speak."

"To drink beer?"

"Yeah."

This is sweet, sweet music to my ears.

"How often do you poo? If you don't mind me asking." I'm certain he doesn't. In this game any pretence at modesty goes out of the window when the first probe breaks through the cat-flap.

"Twice a day."

"Twice! I was expecting double figures."

"Loperamide mate. As long as I dose up on loperamide I'm fine. Unless I eat prawns; don't know why, but prawns go through me."

I am decided; anastomosis is the way forward and if I never eat another prawn, well, who gives a toss?

CM and I are ushered into a cubicle and await the consultation with Mr A... After five minutes or so a young surgeon arrives and introduces himself as Mr W...
"I work under Mr A..." He explains.
This throws me. It shouldn't really, but these days it takes very little to knock me out of kilter. On the back of my chat with Lancashire P... I now know what I want. Mr W... however, seems to be telling me that I can't have it. He's a terribly earnest young man and he explains to me, in his terribly earnest style, how the only way to be certain of avoiding bowel cancer would be to remove the lot; a protocolectomy, i.e. the full bag-&-bumhole job; though he didn't use that term exactly. This, he stresses, would be their recommendation. I tell him that I don't much care for his recommendation and please can I have different one. He offers two more, colectomy with ileostomy (bag) and rectal stump, and an anastomosis of some sort, emphasising the shortcomings of each in terms of residual risk of cancer. The ileoanal pouch, it seems, is not an option for Crohn's patients. I suspect he thinks I am a little bit slow on the uptake which I don't blame him for since I've lost the ability to form coherent sentences. I want to tell him that I know the protocolectomy cuts a very close path to the nerves around the prostate and after a year of hell from that department I'm loath to mess around there if I can avoid it. It doesn't come out like that, sadly. Neither does my question about risk which should have been: *Does reduction in risk correlate to the proportion of bowel removed?* Whatever it was I said in this regard it presumably wasn't as clear as that. He looks at me like I'm talking Esperanto and continues to make the case for B & B.

I feel like a child whose parent is trying to persuade it to accept the blue dress, which just happens to be in the sale, over the pink one that the kid actually wants. "It will go with your shoes,… it won't show the dirt as much,… there's a risk of peritonitis."

It's not quiet coercion and it's a long way from bullying but there is certainly a sense of being corralled somewhere. Despite what Mr W… thinks I do understand where he's coming from; he wants to save me from a nasty disease in the most effective way he can. Laudable, but it takes no account of quality of life as I define it. And so, in our little room, we sit at something of an impasse. One of us steadfast and earnest, the other two struggling to make a contrary case but refusing to give up in the face of medical authority. It takes an act of God to break the stalemate; Mr A… breezes in.

In case you missed the reference, I am saying that consultant surgeons are like gods. I don't throw that in as a criticism, merely as a statement of fact. In some ways they have every right to their apotheosis. Perhaps, because they inhabit a higher astral plane to the rest of us, we find it easier to come to terms with letting them cut into our bodies whilst we sleep.

In ancient Rome, so I am told, when a general was awarded a triumph a slave was employed to whisper reminders of mortality into the great man's ear. I am happy to say that Mr A… has not lost touch with the earthly realm because I once bumped into him in Tesco's; he was being dragged around various aisles by a young woman whom I assumed to be his daughter. Our household, too, is forced to live, on a periodic basis, under the jackboot of female teenage oppression. I have often threatened my eldest daughter with a hysterectomy, though to little effect. Perhaps with Mr A…'s scalpel wielding pedigree the ultimatum would carry more weight[254].

As I was saying, Mr A... breezes in and I am mighty glad to see him. He greets me warmly.

"It's been a long time." I say.

"Yes, ten years is it?"

Longer than that, over fifteen I would suggest. I notice that he is a little greyer and the Stalinist moustache is barely visible, lost in a short beard. I worry that he might be turning hipster. I discount the thought; a hipster could never remove a colon, it's an original feature. It would be like ripping out an art deco fireplace.

Mr W... summarizes.

"And how do you feel about surgery," A... asks, "in the past you've avoided it, I know."

"I don't think I have much of an option this time; I just need to make a choice of what's on offer."

Mr W... once more makes the B&B case. I state my preference for a bag-free life.

"Oh," says A... casually, "he's got a good section in the sigmoid; we'll just join up there."

"Suits me." I enthuse, suddenly having rescued a little bit more bowel.

"Well, that's what I'd do if I had to choose." Adds A... "I'm looking forward to operating on you."

Mr W... says nothing. He looks slightly crestfallen and I feel a little sorry for him. It's not easy when the gaffer strolls in and contradicts everything you've just said.

CM asks:

---

[254] He's probably prohibited from that kind of thing; Hippocratic oath and all that

"After all the hundreds and hundreds of bowels you've seen, how can you remember his?"

"Oh, it's much talked about."

"Does that mean I'm special?" I ask.

"If you like."

I always knew I was.

There is an important point here, not about my uniqueness, though it is noteworthy, more about choice. Single decisions can have a profound effect on the direction our lives will take. In days gone by being told by a medic that B&B was the option to take would (probably) have been the end of it. No second opinion needed, bish-bosh goodbye arsehole. This is no longer the case, emergencies aside, informed decision making is available to almost everyone and we are selling ourselves short by not availing of it. We would do well to be a bit more Socratic here[255] and remember that medical opinions are still *opinions* when all is said and done.

We need to sort a date. Although I would prefer not to have the spectre of impending surgery dominating my life, I realise that, not being an emergency, I am unlikely to get a slot any day soon. I've just bought a fishing licence convinced that I will get some use out of it this summer.

"I can fit you in three weeks today, that's the twenty third of May?" Suggests Mr A....

---

[255] After the Greek philosopher Socrates. The Socratic method posits that questioning and dialogue lead to the development of critical thinking. He is famous for the quote *The only thing I know is that I know nothing.* Not to be confused with Brazilian midfield maestro Socrates, famous quote being: *I smoke, I drink, I think*; he died quite young.

Shit! So soon. I know, I know it's what I wanted, and it gives me the summer to recover, and the hospital won't be full of winter flu victims and the like, but shit! All of a sudden it seems distressingly real.

I am booked in for a pre-op check. It's Friday afternoon. The previous Friday I'd managed to do the splits (unintentionally) whilst playing squash; I sprain the ankle of one leg and take the skin off the knee of the other. Ordinarily this would have been a minor inconvenience but poring over spreadsheets in a sweaty office for a week has done my graze no favours at all. The only pair of office trousers I possess are heavy cords which stick to the scab as I work. The moment I stand up the scab is ripped off, the wound opens up, and the process starts over again.

I know from experience that sticking plaster would be a waste of time, so I set upon the idea of coating my knee in grease and wrapping it in clingfilm. A minor addition to my morning routine which, I have to say, seems to work rather well. Occasionally, I disappear to the toilet, jar of lubricant in hand, to top things up and allow a bit more blood to flow to my foot as the clingfilm can be a bit constricting after a while. Nobody questions what I am doing; by now they are used to me sloping off every twenty minutes to have a fart; not that I advertise it as such.

At the pre-op check I am ushered into a cubicle by a sweet little nurse wearing bright red epaulettes on her uniform. I am intrigued and about to quiz her on why she alone is afforded the honour when she asks:

"Do you have any open wounds or sores?"

"Just my knee."

"Can I see?"

"Promise you won't laugh," I say, dropping my trousers. Seasoned pro that she is she keeps a straight face. She's on the lookout for germs, particularly MRSA, and my weepy knee is swabbed. A swab from around the wedding tackle is also required and it crosses my mind that the red epaulettes are for me to grab hold of whilst she kneels to do the necessary. Unfortunately (or *fortunately* depending on your attitude to such things) I am handed a long cotton bud and instructed to go self-service.

Next up, a different nurse. She has no epaulettes and I am set wondering why; I have an image of them being ripped off on the parade ground like Chuck Connors in "Branded". Thrown out of the hospital gates after a stern-faced matron symbolically snaps a thermometer over a knee.[256] I am ushered into a small room and invited to sit down. She asks me various questions related to my health and lifestyle; the usual stuff. Every time I answer a question she responds with: *Ah, bless you!* It's quite a popular way of speaking at the moment, along with *Oh my days!* to express surprise and the use of *So* at the beginning of every sentence. It could be regarded as tiresome but remember, it's not that long ago that *Far out!* and *Groovy!* were common parlance, so we should count our blessings.

Bloods are taken.

"You OK with needles?"

"Should be, I've seen enough."

---

[256] "BRANDED, scorned as the one who ran. What do you do when you're branded and you know you're a man?" Episodes of this (including the title sequence) can be found on YouTube. See also *The Rifleman* and *Tin Can Alley* for more of Chuck.

"Ah, bless you."

Next, an ECG is run.

"Do you mind taking your top off?" She asks.

"No problem."

"Ah, bless you!"

"You're very hairy, they might shave you for the operation."

"I don't mind; it grows back."

"Ah, bless you! You're very cold."

"I always am. Don't know why."

"Ah bless you! Hm, has anyone ever mentioned you have a quiet heart."

"No."

"You have."

"Is that bad?"

"No, it just means it's hard to hear."

Good, at the moment I haven't got the mental space to process a dicky ticker alongside everything else. Ten minutes and several benedictions later I leave with a bag of pre-op energy-boosting drinks, a sheet of instructions, and a brace of Capri Sun style enemas. My scabby knee feels wet and is sticking to my trousers; I sigh at the thought of three days of successful cling-filming gone to waste.

A week before my op I receive a letter of postponement; annoying but at the same time feeding my natural procrastinating tendencies. I am in for the following week (30th May) so it's not much of an inconvenience/let-off.

The night before the big day I warm up the Capri Sun and administer. Surprisingly enough this is my first proper enema (See "All-Bran Anyone?"). It is a very straightforward process as everything is pre-lubed and nicely streamlined. The instructions talk about the need to try and keep it all in for five to seven minutes; I'm at about half an hour with no trouble at all and I have to go and dance around a bit before we see any action. This cannot be just down to my Chuck Norris sphincter; I seek clarification via the internet. Plenty of enema related stuff on there, it turns out, including videos. Most of these involve women in stockings and suspenders being administered to by other women in stockings and suspenders. Perhaps if they had paid more attention to dietary fibre and less time choosing lingerie then all that business with the funnels and rubber tubing could have been avoided.

The other thing I discover (I have gone off on a tangent by this point) is the popularity of coffee enemas. Plenty of theories and a heap of what seems to be pseudo-science behind it. Not for me, I think. I don't have a problem with the coffee it's the sugar cubes and the custard creams that worry me.

I pack a valise[257]: toothbrush, books, phone, couple of quid in change, that sort of thing. I don't have pyjamas; I go to bed to sleep not to have my codlings strangled. To the amusement of anyone with the misfortune to see me in it, I favour a traditional nightshirt. Think Wee Willy Winky but without the hat.[258] A public display of hubby in a nightie is too much for CM and a prohibition is announced. I refuse to buy pyjamas for the sake of a single week so instead I dig around for a couple of pairs of shorts and vests; it's not going to be sartorially pleasing but she accepts the compromise.

---

[257] Great word *valise*

[258] I did have a nightcap, it came as part of a set. However, it was painfully tight, which, when you consider how small my head is makes you wonder if the manufacturers ever expected anyone to try to wear it.

Five o'clock the next morning I have my second Capri Sun and my last two sickly high carb drinks; they are meant to aid recovery I am told. As per instructions I take a shower because nobody enjoys chopping into smelly patients. Drying off I notice my groin, it looks like W.G.Grace. Seeing as it's going to be on display (albeit to a select audience) I give it a trim. Then I have another shower; Mr A... wouldn't thank me for shedding all over his best table.

CM looks rough, she is holding it together, but I can tell she is a bag of nerves. She's had a restless night. I on the other hand, have slept like a baby, which is a surprise; perhaps another example of how regular enemas can benefit a person's well-being. I don't suggest it to her, I've used my Capri Sun quota and they look tricky to refill.

I don't know what I expected from Theatre Admissions Unit; it certainly wasn't the seething mass of humanity that we encounter. All right, *seething mass of humanity* is probably an exaggeration and not everyone is a patient but still, it does seem ever so busy. We all stand in line, approaching a desk individually; it's like passing through Customs. A couple of checks to make sure we are who we are supposed to be, then we are shown to a bed in what appears to be the colorectal section. We wait.

There is a fat old bombast in the opposite bed forcing his bonhomie on anyone with the misfortune to come within hailing distance. He is the proud owner of a stoma, a necessity since his arse is used exclusively for talking out of. It's his type that give Yorkshiremen a bad name; loud, opinionated, self-important, arrogant, did I mention loud? A great toad of a man; propped up with pillows that he may dominate the ward from a comfortable and elevated position. Stomatoad is having his workings replumbed because (according to him) the surgeon at Barnsley cocked up. Oh, the misery he has endured, well you couldn't describe...except that he does, at full volume. But, he announces, his situation will soon be resolved, Mr B... here is the *Main Man, the Top Banana* when it comes to this sort of thing. How does Stomatoad know this? Stomatoad knows everything of course because at the very first consultation he will have appointed himself as the surgeon's best pal. Now we, the lowly, the unworthy, the unenlightened can benefit from his association. He is the conduit of all medical wisdom.

The subject matter in some ways is irrelevant: in another situation he would be speechifying about football or Strictly Come Dancing or immigration; few subjects are outside of his area of expertise. I cannot say he bothers me unduly; he is a nobhead and, not surprisingly, he exhibits nobhead traits. That is his nature. CM, however, is seething; she sees things from a healthcare perspective.

"Somebody could be really upset by him going on. A nervous young kid or something. I'm going to tell the bastard to shut his gob!"

She has a point. If he was your sole source of information you would think that 99% of surgeons were cack-handed and all you could look forward to is years of post-operative misery and endless chop, chop, chop.

Stomatoad has managed to introduce another old man to the debate. For *debate* read *quest for ward domination*. He's in for something similar to Stomatoad and of course keen to tell his own tale so naively engages, little knowing that he is but a stooge. He has been set up to fail. In comparison to the master he has nothing.

"Flop your stomata on the table boys, see who's got the biggest."

The poor sap doesn't stand a chance.

A terrible thought occurs to me as I recount the tale of Stomatoad. Am I, with these scribblings, doing the same as him? There must be parallels; the urge to tell one's story for instance. No, we're not the same, he's ramming it down people's throats at least with me you get a choice.[259]

Respite comes in the form of a nurse who examines my midriff and, using a marker pen, inks on two optimum positions for locating stomata in the event that things go belly up in theatre.[260] One is lower tummy left, the other lower tummy right. Fucking Brussels telling us where to put our stomas; after Brexit it will be right hand drive only. British stomata for British stools that's what I say. The good news is I get to keep the marker pen; they never use them twice because of the risk of belly contamination.

She leaves me with a couple of the familiar barearse smocks and a pair of TED socks. More of a stocking than a sock these will prevent blood clots gathering in my legs. They are bloody difficult to put on. Rising to just over the knee they are a bit too Britney Spears for my liking. And they are white; they couldn't be any tartier.[261]

Next to poke their head around the curtain is the anaesthetist. She is charming, engaging and attractive. Her traditional white coat compliments her neat figure and her lustrous, flowing auburn hair makes the perfect frame for her face, the

---

[259] Unless this gets adopted as a GCSE set text of course. Not especially likely to happen.

[260] Poor choice of words.

[261] Unless they were fishnet. Or involved suspenders. Or garters. Or any number of accessories actually.

crowning glory of which is a pair of dark, deep, sensual eyes. There is just a hint of the young Maggie Philbin in there somewhere (see ASMR). In short, she is everything you could possible wish for in an anaesthetist.[262] I now feel vindicated in having my trim this morning; I know she'll be concentrating on heart rates and breathing and wotnot but if she does pop down the other end at any point I want to look my best.

She explains how the anaesthetic will be allowed to flow into me via a canula and that I may, in addition, be given an epidural but this had yet to be decided.

"Anything you want to ask me?" She offers. I explain my history of sleepwalking and sleep paralysis. Does this matter?

"No one has ever asked me that." She says laughing.

"Does that make me special?" I get no answer. She hasn't answered my first question either, but it doesn't really matter. She could have said: *Oh, if you try to walk off, me and theatre nurses just punch and kick you into submission...* and I wouldn't have responded. If you are confident and attractive you can get away with pretty much anything.

Events suddenly accelerate as I am promoted to first slot of the day; Mr A... it seems cannot wait to get to grips with my entrails. I am walked to a small room, where my Philbinesque anaesthetist awaits. I lie on a table and a canula is fitted. She and the theatre nurses engage me in idle chit-chat. I recognise the practice from my many colonoscopies; it's designed to put the patient at ease and distract them from what is happening. It's the usual thing: *do you watch so-and-so on telly? You got children? What do you do for a living?*

I almost let slip that I have been working here for the last three

---

[262] Knowing about anaesthetics is also useful.

months but I check myself just in time. Such is the rancour surrounding Lorenzo (the new patient administration system) that I deem it wiser to keep schtum; I can't risk one of them doing a Shipman on me.

"I write." I say.

"Oh, what sort of thing?"

"Books. Wife-swapping Nazis of the Inner Hebrides."

That's usually a conversation stopper.

"I'm reading a good book at the moment," announces my anaesthetist, "Don't laugh but it's about economics,"

I wouldn't laugh. I've read the odd book like that myself. It's good to have diverse interests. Did not the divine Philbin herself co-host both Tomorrow's World and Multicoloured Swapshop?

"It's called Doughnut Economics," she continues "and it's about why growth is not necessarily a good thing and how we are working to outdated models."

"Really?" My interest is piqued. This could be an opportunity for me to look smart and well-read. "I've often wondered what the big thing about growth is." This is true by the way; I struggle with the whole consumption aspect of it. I want to ask her if she is familiar with the *Positive Money* campaign and if she has read Ha-Joon Chang's *23 things they don't tell you about capitalism,* but I don't. I can't remember the words for any of that and it comes out as: "there's this book by a Korean bloke in Cambridge that's..." She's hooking up the drugs now, warning me that I'm about to go under and then, before I have time to properly register the words, I am gone. No panic, no hairy handed dentists, none of that *count to ten* palaver, just bang! Nothing.

## Unruly Patient

This next bit is a little blurry around the edges so forgive me if the account is less than precise. It relies heavily on the eyewitness accounts of wife, little brother and daughters because I, fully awake at last, am trollied in both senses of the word. I am completely off of my tits *and* I am on a trolley. There are various tubes going into my arm, one clipped to my nose and another (of which I am blissfully ignorant) coming out of my John Thomas.

The combination of relief that the chopping is done with, and the opiates being pumped into me by a mechanically operated syringe and the remnants of anaesthetic (including a dash of horse tranquilizer[263]) is a heady one. I get to operate the opiate pump myself, via a little red button. I give it several rapid presses before I realise that the thing is limited to one shot every five minutes. This is stifling my creativity, I could have been the next Thomas De Quincey.[264] Despite this disappointment I am quite the *happy bunny*, no, better than that, I am quite the *euphoric bunny* and am letting the whole ward know about it. I am ebullient, witty, erudite, charming and (at times) humorously ribald. In fact, I carry all the standard misconceptions that make those under the influence so irritating to those who aren't. It's not my first peccadillo today it seems. Apparently, during the first stages of consciousness I was throwing punches left right and centre. Thankfully I was incoherent.

---

[263] Ketamine, street name Special K

[264] The 18th Century writer, not the crime fighting pathologist portrayed by the late Jack Klugman. See *Confessions of an English Opium Eater;* but only if you are desperate for reading matter.

There is no real pain around my midriff, just a sort of ache; the kind you get the day after attempting sit-ups. I have a quick look. Whoa, baldy belly! I haven't seen that since the early eighties. After the initial shock of my shearing I examine my wounds; there is no dressing you will note. They consist of a 5cm horizontal cut to my lower left abdomen and five small, *satellite* cuts (puncture wounds) circling it across my tum. Presumably, the little ones are where the instruments went in and the larger one is where the gut was dragged out. It is amazing that such a large organ can be fished out with such economy. It's all so neat; the stitching is immaculate. I want to show everyone, and CM has to be on hand to stop me exposing myself too much, such is the enthusiasm with which I whip up my gown for all and sundry.

There seems to be an issue with my breathing. The staff nurse is concerned that I have sleep apnoea. This is a condition whereby the sufferer stops breathing during sleep. Because of this I am moved to HDU, the high dependency unit, rather than to the surgical ward where I am expected. It makes no difference to me because, at the moment, I am away with the fairies.

HDU is nice; own room, quiet, nurses at my beck and call and all willing to listen to the inane chat of middle-aged space cadets. I spend a very comfortable night there. Next morning (Thursday) I am woken by those insidious bedfellows, pain and sobriety. Not surprising really considering what has been done to me. My belly might be a picture of suturing minimalism, but it belies what has gone on inside. The colon is a big old thing with various blood vessels and other connections. It's not just swimming around in there like some giant, shit-filled worm; it has to be cut away and all the loose ends dealt with. To the naked eye it might look like minor works but below the surface I have been sliced up a treat.

I restart my opiates after a night of abstinence; push happy button, wait five minutes... push happy button, wait five minutes...push happy button, wait five minutes... It doesn't take too long before I start to feel the benefits, but something is wrong, I sense a little frostiness from the nursing staff. They keep asking me questions about why I'm here, and when I mention suspected sleep apnoea they nod and give me *that* look. They think I'm a fraud; it couldn't be more obvious if they rubbed their chins and shouted: "Oh Jimmy Hill!" [265]

This is hardly my fault; I never said I was. They do various tests on me, one of which involves shaving patches of my chest hair and attaching sticky pads of some sort. According to some scoring system they operate, I barely get off the mark.

Mr A... arrives with his nice Spanish colleague in tow.

"You took some finding," he says, "why are you here?"

"I think there were concerns about my breathing."

"Really? How are you?"

"Not so bad. Nice stitching by the way."

"Thank you." With which he is gone. As they move off, I hear him say to his colleague "Might as well throw a thousand quid in the bin!"

It's nice to feel valued.

My anaesthetist pops by.

"Doughnut economics," I say.

"You remembered."

I have; Ha-Joon Chang still eludes me though.

---

[265] The host of Match of the Day known for his prominent chin; his name became a synonymous with the expression of disbelief.

After cadging a toothbrush (my valise hasn't found me yet) and a squeeze of paste I get myself cleaned up and I am encouraged to have a good cough. One of the complications of surgery can be a build-up of mucus in the lungs which can lead to pneumonia; a few robust coughs are supposed to shift it. It's not the most comfortable of remedies after a disembowelling. I give my happy button a press and take solace in the new toothbrush to go alongside yesterday's free marker pen.

Operation "shift out the malingerer" begins as a porter arrives to wheel me to the ward. All my accoutrements are stacked atop the bed and I am whisked out. Presumably this is the way I arrived in HDU last night, but I have absolutely no recollection of that particular journey.

The bustling ward is very different to HDU, it smells worse too. It is designed around a central nurse station with different sections spurring off. My bed is manoeuvred into a vacant lot one bed from the end of the *Old Buggers Wing.* I am easily the youngest there and by the look of things the only one without a stoma which might explain the general fug of the place.

Nobody seems to know where my valise is. Everyone is very busy and it doesn't seem right for me push the point. No doubt it will turn up at some juncture. I need to eat; this is stressed on me. What remains of my digestive tract needs reminding that it still has a function. Ileus, a condition whereby the small intestine effectively goes to sleep is a common complication following bowel surgery. I am recommended a little soup when the time comes.

The food here exhibits an interesting phenomenon, it has its own early warning system, the scent of soup. It runs a good fifteen minutes ahead of the trolley screaming: "for God's sake save yourself while there's still time!" Strangely enough the same scent still proclaims the arrival of breakfast which is odd since soup is not on the menu at that time of day.

How to describe it? Imagine the compost pot in your kitchen, the thing all the peelings and cabbage trimmings go into prior to being taken up the garden. Further imagine that left for a week; the stage where things start to get nice and buzzy. Then, take a stick blender, insert and blitz to a pulp. Thin out with the urine of an asparagus eating woman, season and serve.

You may be thinking, *here we go, old chestnut, easy target,* etc., etc. but that is far from the case. Whilst I was working here I made use of the cafeteria on numerous occasions and the food was excellent. Either there has been a rapid downturn in standards in the last week or something is done differently for patients. And, I would add, the current fare bears little relation to the stuff that was served up on my previous hospital stays in the eighties and nineties. Something has changed; perhaps it is the way food is *delivered* to the ward and the risk aversion associated with hot holding. There may be an over reliance on microwaving because of this. And of course, there are always the constraints of ever tightening budgets. Whatever the reason, the result is piss and compost soup. It must be frustrating for trained medical staff who, dedicated to healing the sick, are required to serve the same patients with a bowl of liquid relapse three times a day.

The soup for me is a struggle, it would have been a struggle even if it had been palatable. My appetite is non-existent, tea and especially coffee have little appeal and I struggle to sip water. This is very common and to prevent dehydration I remain connected to my fluids bag. On the subject of bags, the one below my bed continues to fill which I am told is a good sign. Mindful of all the UTI problems I have had in the past I am keen to clear my urethra of foreign bodies, but no one seems in a rush to whip this catheter out of me.

My first evening on the ward and I am starting to get more pain; in view of this I am prescribed tramadol to get me through the night. Sleeping is difficult, I am near the toilet, which is well used, and there's generally a fair bit of noise, which is something one can get used to, the real problem is comfort. It is increasingly difficult to find a position that suits. On my back with knees up works for a while but I soon need to swap; I attempt other attitudes, involving a variety of leg and arm positions, pillow supports and bed angles. The food might have gone to the dogs, but the beds have improved since the last time I was here. They are electrically operated these days; and the mattresses have a different type of rubberised cladding. The ward is very hot and I still sweat heavily but this is as nothing compared with my earlier stays which was like going to bed in a gimp suit.[266]

Friday morning and I persuade nurse P... to remove my catheter. Nurse P... looks and sounds a lot like the late Les Dawson. I should point out here that Nurse P... is a man in case you were wondering. He has been in the job since the eighties and is every inch the grizzled old veteran; all he's missing is a bandolier and a well chewed cigar stump. He is quite vocal insofar as he moans a lot; salary, unsocial hours, workload, crap managers, Lorenzo, all the usual stuff. The career he embarked upon thirty years previously has not panned out the way it was supposed to, but despite this he maintains his professionalism; and is a dab hand at the painless removal of

---

[266] I imagine.

willy tubes.

I am mobile again. If shuffling around with various intravenous accoutrements can be classed as mobility. If you need a comparison, then tape a couple of small electrical appliances and a hot water bottle (filled) to a standard lamp, link your left arm to it in some way and then try steering it around the house.

The mantra now is *eat and move*, my system requires a little encouragement to get going again. The abdominal muscles, Nurse P... tells me, have a big part to play in peristalsis and I need to get them on the case. Opiates, whilst their benefits are obvious, also have their drawbacks; they slow the gut down as I know to my cost (see "Lumbar") so I am encouraged to manage without those, which is disappointing though by now I can probably get a bit of Pavlovian relief simply by looking at the red button.

I am getting no sensation of motion, in many respects the odd bit of pain is the only sign that anything exists in there. It seems devoid of feeling. Nurse O... is now on the case. A big woman of Nigerian extraction, she has only recently moved to the city and chose a locale based upon bus services to and from the hospital. She is less than enamoured with her choice. It is where I grew up, a working class area dominated by vast, labyrinthine council estates it resides amongst the worst 2% for deprivation in the country.

"I don't think they have ever come across a chocolate coloured woman before," she states without going into the details of the abuse she has received. I empathise, we once had SWFC sprayed across the bonnet of our car. It was a targeted attack I am sure.

Nurse O... (and I mean this in the nicest of ways) is quite bossy.

She uses the phrase *tough love* a few times in her efforts to get me moving and eating. I am starting to feel poorly by this point, I have no energy, all I want to do is sleep. I try to read but struggle, I cannot concentrate enough to hold the thread of a story in my brain. My efforts at taking nourishment, once token at best, are now even less than that. Zero appetite! I cannot even generate saliva. I have only to pick a fork up and my mouth goes all Atacama on me.

Despite my anti-emetic medicine I feel nauseated and when the scent of P&C soup wafts in, all I can do is lie down. I begin to notice feelings of tightness developing in my belly; this, I hope, is a pre-curser to peristalsis. Still Nurse O... is on my case; she is as tenacious as I am implacable and as long as we restrict this to a battle of wills, I am content. If it comes to a grapple I'm buggered; even if I wasn't in a physically weakened state, she would have on the canvas "crying uncle" before you could blink.[267] In an attempt to show willing I take a trip to the loo. I wish I hadn't! There is stale piss on the floor, shit on the seat, shit on the floor, shit smeared all over the bin used for disposal of non-flushables. I guide myself and my standard lamp through the brown maze, pull my shorts down just enough to allow me to hover over the bowl. It is quite an effort for such meagre micturition. On the way out I pick up a smear on my toe, luckily missing the edge of my Britney Spears stockings. Moving about is difficult enough without having old man's cack on your foot.[268] I find Nurse O... and mention that the loo is a bit of a mess. She takes a look.

---

[267] Do people still use that idiom? It's many years since I have been involved in a decent pinning-down. Sadly

[268] Or *any* cack, for that matter.

"I see what you mean." She says, pulling a face. I wonder if she realises that I am only the discoverer; I wouldn't want her to think this was some kind of dirty protest against her tough love policies. I point to my toe.

"This is why you need to wear slippers," she chides.

"Call me fussy but I don't particularly want shite on my slippers either."

"No, I suppose not," she agrees, getting to work with a wipe.

I am definitely getting bigger; I can see my abdomen growing by the hour. I am feeling more and more bloated with it. Discomfort and pain are building. It is a truly strange feeling, like the heavy bloating one experiences after an eating binge but more so and without the prospect of any trumping solace. There are no rumblings, no spasms, no gurgles; it feels quite dead save for the ever-mounting pressure.

Change of shift and Nurse A.., the blonde and beautiful English rose. She has a dramatic effect on the ward; all the old men are fawning over her like she was the original angel of mercy. I find it a little sickening actually and feel a quite sorry for the other nurses who cannot quite cut it in the looks stakes. Should I feel sorry for them? Would anyone aim to be the recipient of all that quasi-sexual sycophancy. Nurse A... takes it in her stride. The night shift is, as usual, busy and she is being pulled from pillow to post. This only adds to her appeal, her labours bring a blush to her cheek and a sheen of sweat to her brow. This sends the Nurse A... Appreciation Society into meltdown:

"Oh, you're ever so good..., if anyone deserves a holiday it's you..., it's a bloody disgrace how nurses are treated..., they should get rid of some of them bean counters, give you a pay rise,...wait till Brexit then we'll see some changes..."

It annoys the shit out of me[269], how is it possible to spend so long on earth and still be so ill informed and naive. And who do they mean by *the bean counters* anyway? Presumably anyone who's not a clinician. This is how they view the NHS, a few stethoscope-wielding young men in white coats supported by ranks of attractive, hard-working, oppressed young women, of which Nurse A... fits the profile perfectly; attractive, kindly spoken, Anglo Saxon and wearing a nice lilac frock. Somewhere in the mix there is probably a Hattie Jacques, no doubt a James Robertson Justice lurks in the wings scowling at the capers of cowering young doctors. And that's all you need really isn't it? Everyone else is a "bean counter"; sinister, corporate-suited, Janus-faced executives with Peter Lorre sidekicks, miserly accountants, lazy middle-managers, bleeding heart social workers.

It riles me because I witness the hours that CM works and they are ridiculous! And, during my few months employed by the NHS, I have seen the way non-medical staff (for want of a better description) go about their work and it is with the same reverence for patient welfare that I see on the wards. The NHS needs a lot of managing, it's bloody enormous! The system would not run without non-medical staff and yet overt cuts here are tolerated for some reason.

I am having a rotten night and it is nothing to do with the aged fools in the other beds. I am sweating heavily, and the sheet and counterpane are clinging to me and hindering my every attempt at negotiating a comfortable position. The hydraulics of my electrically operated bed are having a busy shift. The paltry amount of sleep I manage is interspersed with regular

---

[269] I wish it would.

manoeuvrings in the search for comfort.

I haven't touched the happy pump in ages; I am doing my bit in the interests of encouraging peristalsis. Instead my pain relief comes from Tramadol[270], Paracetamol and Ibuprofen.[271] Tramadol, whilst being an opioid, is thought to have a negligible impact as far as my lazy intestines are concerned. It does, however, give me strange dreams. I've had a lot of weird ones in the past (see "Audi Coupe") and as far as dream narratives are concerned these are nothing to write home about. Where they distinguish themselves (for me at any rate) is the range and vividness of colour; gold with bright pinks and turquoise specifically.

At some point in my technicolour journey I remember feeling a movement in the pipes. It's nothing much, a faint gurgle, but in my vague lucidity it seems highly significant and I think I remember encouraging it with a little squeeze or two. Sleep improves after that point, I have obviously relieved a little of the pressure because when morning comes, I realise what I had assumed to be my sweat-sodden sheets are nothing of the kind. I beckon a nurse and a Code Brown is called.

In the toilet I strip out of my soiled shorts and shirt with a view to cleaning myself up at the sink. What a way to spend your Saturday morning. The image facing me in the mirror shocks me. The bloating across my middle is stark and seems to be extending up to my chest. Worse still, it has moved south, my knackers are gigantic and a very unappetising shade of grey. It is difficult to see them without the mirror on account of my huge gut so I sit on the edge of the toilet, thrust my hips

---

[270] Street name "trammy"

[271] Street names "paracetamol and ibuprofen"

forward as best I can and get a hold of them. My penis has no obvious aperture to it; I don't know where it ends. I try examining the various folds to no avail; it's like peeling back the creases on a Sha Pei's face.

I return to my newly changed bed and lie down, exhausted. The scent of P&C wafts through the ward presaging breakfast. I manage a cup of tea but even that is a struggle.

There is a new face on the ward, he has the look of a man in his fifties but there is every chance I could be ten years out. He has the sunken-cheeked, broken-nosed, haggard look of a smack head, which may account for his infected leg. This probably explains why the young nurse is struggling to get a canula into him, the more obvious veins having, effectively, worn out. He calls her a "stupid bitch" for her efforts.

There isn't an ounce of fat on him and his musculature (visible because he wears only a pair of shorts) stands out in stark relief from the frame of his skeleton. He reminds me of Golum from Lord of the Rings. Except that Golum has a nicer tone to his voice and a politer turn of phrase. Everyone has him marked down as a scumbag lowlife and you can taste the air of disdain in the ward.

Golum, we discover, though it shatters no one's illusions, has spent time in prison. We know this because he lets everyone on the ward know in no uncertain terms how much better the food is there.

I have finally got Spotify to work and I am listening via my son's spare headphones to Wayne Shorter whilst staring apologetically at the bottle of vanilla flavoured Fortisip that I know is destined for the bin. I hate the thought of unnecessary waste, but I can barely manage a glass of water so a sickly brew like that has no chance. CM arrives.

"Hey," she says, nodding in the direction of Golum, "there's a new patient down on the end; he looks like you!"

It's time I dragged myself out of the nineties and ditched the heroin chic look.

I tell her about my massive genitalia. She responds with the same disinterest she has for my standard sized ones. She has brought me a couple of books, but I cannot generate any interest.

"Why don't you put the telly on?" She suggests. Above every bed a dedicated TV and integrated phone is attached to a long, Anglepoise-type arm, ready to be swung into action.

"I don't want to."

"Is it because you have to pay?"

"No."

"It is isn't it?"

"Well, yes, partly. What would I watch anyway? The old fella next door pays eight quid a day for an hour of Murder She Wrote. Eight quid for an hour of Angela Lansbury! How can you say capitalism isn't evil?"

"Stingy bastard!" She replies, evading the question. I must have touched a nerve. Strange, it's not as if I'd dissed Homes under the Hammer.

Chronologically speaking, we are back to where the account of my surgical odyssey began. Remember? Me sitting on the loo feeling like I'm dying? A bit of a low point. The bloating had continued all day and into the night. A difficult, uncomfortably hot night full of shouting, swearing and hacking coughs as Golum makes his presence known. Every now and again someone will remark in frustration: "bleeding shut up!" or "for God's sake!" but it is always in a fairly hushed tone and always safely anonymous.

Another newbie is K..., a stroke victim I believe and very frail. He looks as if he is on the way to a hundred, but I find out later that he is barely into his seventies. K...'s trips to the toilet are a cause of some consternation. It is quite a physical effort for him to get there and he moves at the pace of a glacier. There are no doubt other people wanting to use the facility and there is plenty of time for a few of them to get in and out before K... gets to the threshold, but out of politeness nobody does. Not even Golum, and he's in and out of the bog all night. The other thing about K...'s visits is that they invariably end in him falling off the seat and all the disturbance that entails as alarms are raised and staff rush in. On the occasions that he does make it back to bed without the flashing lights and sirens, the next visitor is usually faced with a mess because K..., not surprisingly, is a rotten shot.

Back to my nadir. Weak and sick of the discomfort of trying to lie down, I take myself to the toilet on the strength of what may or may not have been some movement in the pipes. This is my first attempt at a proper push. After cleaning the seat, I get in position and start proceedings with a widdle. A feeble yellow stream dribbles out of the Sha Pei's face and down my yak-sized testicles. I try to squeeze out something more substantial, but nothing's doing. My chopped-up abdomen seems to prevent it, as if there is no purchase, nothing to grab. I try to sit more upright, I am told it aids the passage of stool, but the only way I can do that is by grabbing both knees and rocking backwards on the seat. I dread to think what sort of filth I am leaning onto. I doesn't work anyway, and I flop forward, supported by the bogbrush shelf; I am edging towards unconsciousness.

Then it happens, spontaneously, like a sudden gust of wind

blowing a door in, a squirt of brown liquid emits from my posterior. It doesn't matter that this is just a token evacuation or that my yak balls are caught in the crossfire, the relief is profound. I take a minute to compose myself; I am still horribly weak. I clean up, prise my feet from the sticky-piss floor and go back to bed. This feels like a small victory.

Sunday morning and despite having slept I feel terrible; weak, unable to eat and as bloated as ever. I am lying on my back atop the sheets of my newly made bed. My shirt has been dispensed with, I am hot, and I find it uncomfortable on my torso which is now more bloated than ever. The left portion of my chest as far as the armpit is swollen and my shaven belly towers over the rest of me, taught and engraved with the signs of surgery. Beyond that, my legs and arms are getting skinnier by the day; the muscle (I haven't any fat to lose) is dropping away. Lying there immobile I must look like an alien autopsy.[272]

Doctors' rounds and I watch as a couple of new faces show up. One is a very tall Indian chap who concentrates on the patient opposite me. I am fascinated by the distinct Dicky Davies flash of silver amid his otherwise raven hair. More doctors are arriving, a senior surgeon by the look of the retinue he has in tow. He's another Indian, a very small man this time but he is sporting the same DD flash as his lanky compatriot. I imagine a scene of them painting a sloping ceiling together; one at the high end, the other where it gets more cramped.

Although I am not on his list, the smaller of the two emulsioners pulls up sharply as he enters Roswell and spots my limp, prostrate form.

"And who is this fellow?"

---

[272] Discounting my tiny head of course.

I am introduced. He questions me with concern, I clearly look like shit. I am worried about the shape my body is adopting.

"I don't like the way it's extending upwards into my chest," I say. "I was looking at myself in the mirror and…"

"Oh, that is not a very good idea," he clearly enjoys a little joke, "I wouldn't advise looking in mirrors. No good comes of it."

Easier said than done matey. I challenge anyone with an undercarriage as big as mine to resist the urge to admire it. He examines me, looks concerned and orders further blood tests and a CT scan.

It is Sunday and the CT scan doesn't happen for hours. CM phones in that evening and is told by a junior nurse that Diagnostic Imaging won't make an assessment until the morning. CM, who knows how the place is run, recognises when she is being told a porky; he is just trying to get shot of her. She is hopping mad when I talk to her. That nurse doesn't know what he is messing with. CM knows a lot of important people at the hospital; a word in the appropriate ear and he might find himself garrotted.

Interpretation does come through from the experts and it appears that I have a *collection* and *infection,* but the good news is this is not due to leakage from the anastomosis. I start on antibiotics straight away.

I let CM know and she calls off her plans for the extraordinary rendition and water boarding of the fibbing nurse.

"An infection collection?" She says.

"Yes. It sounds a bit Dr Seuss when you say it like that."

"What are you on about?"

"You know, Cat in the Hat."

"Just tell me what else they said."

"An infection collection it is, can't you see?

We'll fix it with this Anti-B, Intra-V."
"You're an idiot!"

Monday morning and I am already feeling perkier off the back of my antibiotic cocktail. I have a go at an omelette this morning; given a bit more flavour it could pass as a Vileda sponge-wipe; I manage a mouthful. Still Atacama in there.

Little brother appears, he always turns up when he is on shift. He is in constant communication with CM and knows the score. What he doesn't know about are my unfeasibly large genitals. I tell him the news.

"You should take a selfie," he says.

My phone isn't very good, I don't think the camera would do them justice. Is that what you are supposed to do in this situation? It seems to be the case because later in the day, squash buddy S... pays a visit and he says exactly the same. There is a whole world of big knacker photography out there that I never knew existed.

Tuesday and my ginger cordial arrives. Nurse P... recommended this to me a couple of days ago and CM has tracked a bottle down. He's right, it does help and I suddenly get an urge to eat a packet of crisps. CM encourages me to walk with her to the shop; not a great distance but it is something. Why is it so difficult to buy a simple packet of cheese and onion potato crisps? There are dozens of flavours except cheese and onion, which every right-minded person knows is the best. I settle for Dorritos and hope that they are salty and greasy enough to satisfy my needs.

As we walk out of the shop I bump into two of my workmates. I say hello but it is obvious they have no idea who has just accosted them. It has only been three weeks since we last shared an office and now I have to tell them who I am.

The rest of the week sees steady progress, and there is now talk of going home at last. The only real impediment is my lack of appetite but that too shows positive signs. The swelling has receded including my codlings (to a degree) which is probably a good thing otherwise I would not be able to squeeze them into my new nappy. I have to say I am not crazy about wearing one. It is quite a large accoutrement; even allowing for the meat that I'm packing in it the thing extends from just above the base of my spine down between my legs and up to my belt line at the front. It is held in place by a pair of pants made entirely of elasticated netting. Trying to get nappy and net pants to work in concert is less straightforward than you might imagine. No doubt there is a knack to it. Trying on the pants without the pad takes me to realms of eroticism not previously explored; they are the kind of garment that Iggy Pop[273] might wear. With the pad inserted they are somewhat less racy. Warm though! Warmer still once they are full.

There is a new patient opposite me; quite young, early thirties I should say. From what I gather he has been through the mill with his condition, whatever that is. Various episodes of stoma construction and repositioning, anastomoses, and bowel adhesions have left him an old hand at the colorectal game. That said he still manages to pull out an arterial cannula in the middle of the night. The toilet looks like a murder scene.

Golum is still causing waves of an evening. He's constantly in the loo which always involves a dramatic coughing fit. The middle of Thursday night sees it reach new heights and Nurse O... trots along to check if he is all right.

---

[273] An inveterate nob flaunter.

"A...!" She calls. "Are you okay in there A...?"

"I'm having a shit!"

Nurse O... must have caught a whiff of something other than shit[274] creeping under the door.

"Are you smoking in there A...?"

"No! Fuck off will yer, I'm having a shit!"

"I'm coming in A..."   Assistance arrives in the form another nurse from the other end of the ward. I cannot give a description of her as the ward is very dark, but she sounds like the resident tough guy. The one they keep in reserve for when things kick off. Tasty with her fists and always up for a scrap.

The toilet door is unlocked and even the barrage of Lynx Africa body spray cannot quite mask the lingering smoke. Nurse O... delivers a brief lecture on the dangers of smoking in hospital, that is to say, the immediate ones relating to fire and oxygen cylinders. The one regarding long term conditions such as heart disease and lung cancer she saves for another date. She sounds disappointed rather than cross. Still Golum fights his corner.

"I wasn't smoking! You can't come in here accusing me of smoking when I'm having a shit."

"There's a cigarette butt there." Adds Tough Nurse

"S'not mine. You can't say that's mine."

"Give me the lighter A..."

"No."

"Give me the lighter!"

"Get your hands off me you fuckin' lesbian. You can't touch me. I've had enough. I'm leaving."

He stomps back to his bed and starts pushing things into a

---

[274] Makes a change!

holdall. Nurse O... is amazing, she tries to calm him down, pointing out that it is two in the morning and not the best time to discharge yourself. I don't know whether she has been trained for this sort of thing or whether she is naturally calm and measured but not once does she raise her voice. I couldn't have done it. It would have come to blows long before now if I was on the case. The scene is resolved when, without warning Golum vomits. There must be gallons of it as the sound of spattering chime seems to go on for minutes. His puking is in the same style as his coughing, loud and dramatic, like Al Pacino in Scent of a Woman. Ooh-aah!

Friday morning and Mr A...'s nice Spanish colleague finds me first thing; I am to be discharged today. I celebrate with bacon and toast for breakfast. It's peculiar stuff, the rashers are stiff and folded over as if they have been cooked on an ironing board. They don't even taste of bacon.

Golum is also being discharged today and there is much joy amongst the residents at the prospect. Even though I would have gladly punched him last night, this morning I can't help feeling a little sorry for him; the lot of a pariah cannot be an easy one. And when your life is dictated by the poor decisions you have made in the past it makes it so much harder to make better decisions in the future. The elevated ground from which we judge Golums is piled high with our own good fortune; *there but for the grace of God* and so on. That said, would I want the scumbag coming around my house? No I bloody wouldn't!

Golum is out by midday, I am left waiting. I don't think this is a coincidence. Much as I have lauded all here for their compassion you can see why they wouldn't want to hang on to him for longer than they necessarily had to. Lenity on the other hand, they are loath to part with and I don't get out until 9 o'clock at night, and even then it's a convoluted process as I am talked through my drugs and shown how to inject myself.

I think their reluctance to part with me is down to a combination of factors. Firstly, Pharmacy is slow, they are notorious for it, secondly the ward staff are simply too busy to process me, and thirdly, it turns out I'm a bit of a draw for the student nurses. I shall explain this in the next but one section.

# V is for...

## V.D.

Isn't it a shame, don't you think, that venereal disease has been eradicated and replaced by sexually transmitted diseases? Veedee had such a ring to it, especially in conjunction with the word *clinic*. A chap knew where he stood with V.D., it sounded nasty and dirty and definitely to be avoided. S.T.D. sounds like something you would plug into your computer. Compared to V.D., S.T.D. is a crap acronym.

I have had neither, by the way.

## Veins

I am something of a vascular man. This may or may not be a bona fide term; either way I wouldn't waste time looking it up. What I mean by this is that I have very prominent veins. I cannot explain why this is, no one else in my family is blessed in this fashion. I am a phlebotomist's dream. As a consequence, whilst I am hospitalised I am marked down as a teaching aid and student nurses are brought by to have a go at fitting cannulas into me. They have to learn somewhere and old *road atlas arms* here is a nice, gentle introduction to the art. I remember one girl being particularly nervous.

"Ever done this before?" I asked.

She shakes her head, biting her bottom lip pensively.

"You always remember your first you know," I tell her, roguishly. It was an attempt to put her at ease, but it came out a little bit more predatory than I'd intended and I don't think it helped her nerves a bit.

## Verruca
See "Feet"

# W is for...
## Warts

I have a couple of seborrheic keratoses aka seborrheic warts, aka senile warts. These are common in people over fifty although I have had mine since my teens and as far as I can tell I am not senile. My long-standing ones are on my belly and look like dark brown paint-splats. They have a slightly raised surface and sometimes yield a nice crop of dead skin from scraping, although I am sure this is not advised.

I had a very dark one on my temple and my GP went at it with what looked like a blow torch but was in fact a kind of freezing gun; cryotherapy. It worked, up to a point; about three quarters of the wart disappeared. It stung for hours!

## Water on the Knee

I confess that this is a somewhat misleading title. I do not have, I have never had, water on the knee, which is a swelling of the joint due to an excess of synovial fluid. *My* water on the knee is more of an intermittent sensation of wetness on my right leg and not nearly as nasty as the real thing[275]; in fact there is no pain at all.

It started some time in my forties and continued on and off for about a year. Despite the regularity and consistency of the sensation I always feel compelled to roll up a trouser and check; there is never any physical wetness. I have no explanation for it, hence my erroneous w-on-the-k designation. A search on the internet offered a few suggestions (Lupus, sciatica, MS) but I never pursue any thread; you can scare yourself sick playing that game. It doesn't cause me a problem and goes away as discretely as it had arrived. It remains a mystery.[276]

## What it's like to have no colon.

All right let's get this one out of the way, the title is not strictly correct. I am not absolutely colon-less, I do retain a few centimetres but the vast bulk of it has gone in the offal bucket[277]. That little bit of sigmoid, Mr A... tells me, will give a better function over an ileo-rectal anastomosis. That's caveated though, bowel movements, he warns, will be more frequent; *significantly* more frequent.

I am determined not to drag my recuperation out longer than is absolutely necessary. The sooner I can get back to some form of normality the better. CM takes the opposite view. This difference in opinion has been running since the surgery bombshell was dropped on me weeks ago. To be fair, she is

---

[275] Meaning water on the knee or knee effusion, not the *The Real Thing*, British soul band of the nineteen seventies.

[276] Update: I had it again recently and it was like bumping into an old friend.

[277] It was actually sent to a pathologist and given a good checking over. By all accounts I definitely needed to get shot of it.

speaking from experience having been in this position a few years earlier (see "Mrs Lenity as Proxy") whereas I am basing my predictions purely on *man knows better* bravado.

Whilst I have been in hospital, she and my father-in-law have brought the heavy IKEA bed-settee downstairs and set it up in the back room. My father-in-law is seventy-five; it's a wonder she didn't have two invalids on her hands! I have absolutely no intention of sleeping downstairs, even if I wanted to. Neither do I require the car to be brought to the door of the hospital, which is another service being heavily pushed. I walk there, and just in case there is any doubt as to how I want to play this, I take the grass bank rather than the steps down into the car park.

I am not a good passenger and CM (so she says) struggles under my scrutiny. All the near misses and jumped lights and hogged bus lanes are completely my fault. When I'm not watching her, she is a brilliant driver.

I must learn to handle my fear and to keep my mouth shut. There is going to be a lot of this; received wisdom says that you can't drive for weeks after major surgery. However, no one seems to be able to put a figure on precisely how long you should abstain.

"You need to be able to make an emergency stop," someone told me which is ironic since as a passenger with CM at the wheel I make no end of them. I'm pumping that imaginary brake pedal like billio.

It is a fine, fine feeling to come home after a hospital stay. The dog greets me feverishly at the threshold then spends the rest of the evening pinned to my side on the sofa. Even my son, heir to the Lenity millions, lifts his head up from his console and nods in recognition.

At eleven o'clock I take myself upstairs to bed, pop my Tramadol, drop a pint of diarrhoea into my own toilet, clean up and don my nappy/Britney stocking combo. I am up once in the night to empty my bowels; that brief splat-fest aside, my night remains deliciously uninterrupted.

Next morning, Saturday, I have a proper perusal of my drugs. They consist:

Mesalazine, aka Pentasa: the horse pill sized tablets which I have been taking for some time. This is the standard drug used in maintaining remission of Crohn's disease. It is also regarded as a preventative in relation to bowel cancer. The little piece of colon I have left will be the focus of interest from now on;

Pain killers: paracetamol, ibuprofen and tramadol;

Antacid and anti-sickness: lansoprazole and ordansetron;

DVT prevention: dalteparin;

Antibiotics: cefurixime and metronidazole.

I work down the list, envisaging how it will shrink over the coming weeks. My infection collection is well under control, so the antibiotic will be out of the picture fairly soon; I have less than a week of pills left. Tramadol I still need for the time being, I shall play that one by ear. Pleasant though it is, I intend to dispense with it at the first opportunity, my thinking being that even if the pain is only barely manageable, I will manage it and in that way I can monitor my situation more accurately. I want things to be undiluted, so to speak.

Paracetamol and 'brufen are neither here nor there.

Sexy stockings and the associated dalteparin I am unclear on and I'm struggling to get a definitive answer. I have a month's supply of dalteparin so I shall worry about that later. Dalteparin comes in one-shot disposable syringes and I have to inject myself with it of an evening. It's easily done, just grab an inch of flesh around the midriff and whack it in but it's not much fun and I shan't be sorry to see the back of it. And the bright yellow sharps bucket clashes with the duvet cover.

I don't feel sick at all, so I make a decision, there and then, to drop lansoprazole and ordansetron; it feels like a big step towards normality.

Steps towards normality are coming thick and fast on my first full day back; after a little persuasion CM agrees to take me shopping. When I have managed that I propose to cook a meal. First things first though, CM and the kids head out to pick up four rescue rats[278] that are joining the throng. We've had rats before, and guinea pigs and a rabbit (in fact we are beginning to run out of lawn under which to bury them) so it's nothing new in that respect. However, our previous rats had all been ladies, these four are most definitely not. Perhaps you are familiar with rat gonads? No? Neither was I; they're huge! They drag on the floor! I am having flashbacks to my recent swelling episode in hospital.

Aldi's car park and my first steps towards the trolleys reveal to me the limitations of slow-release Tramadol. I have a powerful stitch-like pain in the right side of my abdomen; round about where the appendix is, sorry, *was*. Instinctively I press my hand to it and the pressure seems to help. As soon as I release the pressure, the pain returns and so I spend the next thirty minutes wandering around the aisles, hand to appendix, elbow cocked like I am auditioning for a slo-mo version of Come Dancing.

---

[278] Rescue rats as in previously abandoned rats rather than rats trained to climb into burning buildings or dangle from helicopters to save stricken yachtsmen.

The pain is with me all the way home and beyond, into the chicken with cream, mushroom and tarragon. I pop a couple of 'brufen, neck half a bottle of Rioja and begin to feel better. I've slightly overcooked the pasta, but nobody seems to mind. My appetite has returned with a vengeance and I stuff my face. Under the circumstances it feels a little reckless and I will probably pay for it later but it's so good to eat real food without the stench of piss-and-compost soup polluting the atmosphere that I throw caution to the wind.

I do pay for it. Indigestion initially, followed by a nip into the en-suite in the wee small hours. We sleep in the attic which is sort of open plan, in that there is no bog door and everything that goes on in there is fully audible. I cannot avoid waking CM who blinks at me in the glare of her bedside lamp.

"Did you shit the bed?" she asks.

"No."

"Are you sure?"

"I think I'd know; besides I have a nappy on."

"Did you shit in that?"

"No."

"Oh." She replies disappointedly. CM, you see, has a secret wish, although in truth it's not all that secret especially now I'm putting it in print. She would love me to let one slip out under the covers. This all goes back to her hemicolectomy and a period of violent diarrhoea she suffered some months later. She had a couple of accidents and now is desperate for me to follow suit, which is a weird wish when you consider whom I share a bed with.

This first week home I am beginning to see a pattern emerging, a poo pattern that is. Early mornings I get the urge. It's not a sudden thing, I can feel it building as I lie in bed but when it gets to a critical mass there is no denying it its freedom. Despite having Crohn's for over thirty years this sense of urgency every time I need the lavvy is a new one on me. I know for many others this is the norm; I've just been very fortunate in this respect.

Emptying my bowels seems to drain the energy from me and it takes a good half an hour's lying on the bed before I feel like the system has reset. Often, I fall straight to sleep. Almost everything I have read about the aftermath of colectomies mentioned the tiredness and urge to sleep. It's not surprising really, my body has had quite a kicking, it needs all its resources for fixing the damage. I had imagined something along the lines of the fatigue I have associated with a Crohn's flare-up but it is anything but; in a way it's rather pleasurable. The summer is a hot one, ridiculously hot by Yorkshire standards and the attic, with all Veluxes agape, is a perfect place to secrete oneself and nod off. I sleep like a dead man, a deep sleep, what they call fast-on around these parts[279] and it can last for hours. After that I am charged with energy for a period, run flat and have to lie down again. I am living my life as a puppy.

Occasionally, I will take a few rays on the balcony or in the back yard. I don't know whether it's wise to expose stitches to sunlight, but it feels nice; at least for a while. My middle is still a little distended and lop-sided but improving all the time. The stiches are receding too, leaving a thin, flaky residue that looks like dead skin but might be some form of dressing on the wounds that I am not familiar with.

Dog walking returns to the agenda. We are well served for dog walking in our neck of the woods precisely because it is that; a

---

[279] Sometimes "hard-on". Care needed with that one.

neck of the woods. Although our house stands on a fairly significant thoroughfare, beyond that is mature woodland with miles of easy-going paths and bridleways; once I have negotiated the traffic I can go at my own pace and let the dog get on with her thing. She seems to know that I'm not firing on all cylinders and takes the opportunity of consuming every piece of nastiness she can get her paws on whilst I hobble after her shouting weak threats. Mouldering carrion is good, as is ordure of any description. Pay dirt (by her estimation) is fox poo which, joy of joys, can be worn as well as munched. What would she do if worst came to the worst and I was caught short? I dismiss the thought; if I don't ponder it, it won't happen. I take precautions and try to empty out before I set off for anywhere. I'm not even sure I could do it anyway, it's so alien to me. I recall the struggle I had on a camping holiday in France when I was forced to use one of those barbaric hole-in-the-floor jobs they have over there. It was awful! It went everywhere. And that was me in my era of solidity. God knows what it would be like now, the stuff comes out like bomb blast. I have a vision of me slinking into the bushes, there's a loud report and the next thing you see are dozens of dazed woodland creatures coughing and retching as they stagger out of the undergrowth dripping in liquid shit.

Within a hundred yards of entering the woods I am in pain, the now familiar stabbing stitch on my right side. I engage Come Dancing mode which works for a while until we hit a steep descent at which point no amount of pressing has any effect. By the time I reach the valley bottom I am walking almost doubled over and have a pained expression on my face. I must look like I've just been knifed. Thankfully I don't meet many people and the ones that I do avoid my gaze. But then I am no stranger to that. It seems that I missed my vocation in life I should have been a dangerous and/or unhinged criminal, I just have that look; it's the eyes I think, dark and malevolent. Bravado has got the better of me; I have overestimated my strength and underestimated the distance. Were I well, this would be no sort of length at all, a mere stroll but at the moment it feels like a marathon. And not one of these modern marathons that it seems anyone and everyone can do but the old type, where the runners all looked like they were dropping dead on the finish line.

Thankfully there are a number of benches throughout the woods; many are memorials to dead loved ones. I find one and sit hunched over until the pain eases and strength returns. I am there for so long that even the dog gets bored of thrusting her drool covered tennis ball at me and takes herself off for a sit in the stream. I don't blame her, I am poor company. When I finally kick the bucket I shall make it a stipulation that any bench erected in my memory comes with an integral magazine rack. And cushions!

Home, and I am attic bound, intent on one of my Worsley afternoon naps[280] but first I must deal with the outstanding issues of the walk. I sit on the step in the porch brushing the dog's teeth. She hasn't got many on account of her penchant for chewing stones but what she does have are caked in something horrid, the provenance of which I dread to think. I use a standard human toothbrush as I find this is best for poking out the deep, interdental filth pockets, but the toothpaste is a specialist, enzymatic concoction designed for dogs. It is poultry flavoured and looks and smells worse than the poo it is

---

[280] For *afternoon nap* read *afternoon coma*

supposed to be eradicating.

I fancy a beer. This is quite a relief as I was wondering if I had lost the taste for it; I can do without mulling on *life not worth living* scenarios like that thank you kindly. There are a couple of bottles of Hoegaarden, those dinky ones, left over from a trip to Belgium the previous autumn. That seems like a good place to start. My passion is home brew and I have plenty of bottles of that in the cupboard, but it seems a little risky going on what the stuff does to you even *with* a colon. The Hoegaarden slips down a treat. So well in fact that I go for the second bottle. No indigestion, no gassy bloating; the portents are good. The only adverse effect, and it's one that might equally be construed as a positive one is that I feel a little bit pissed; more than you'd expect from two diddy bottles. Clearly, further investigation is warranted.

I am dispensing with the nappies, leastways for a trial run; they will stay in the cupboard until I am happy that the level of control I'm enjoying is no false dawn. I still experience bloating at night which makes for an uncomfortable sleeping experience. It is particularly bad after a meal of spaghetti bolognaise in which the meat had been replaced with brown lentils[281]. It has long been my philosophy to eat anything and everything I want and bugger the consequences, but I might have to temper that approach, at least in the short term. I try lentils again, tarka dhal this time and I have another horrible night although it's probably unfair to lay the blame solely on lentils when you consider the great raft of pilau, naan, bhajis, chicken tikka and saag madras that they are floating on. I bloody love food!

---

[281] Vegetarianism and teenage daughters go hand in hand.

By the end of my second week at home the first-thing-in-the-morning poo seems to have established itself. It still leaves me tender and knackered from the effort of it but I'm sure that will go with time. Despite my voracious eating sessions, I am still only emptying my bowels at most three times a day. More often than not it is just a single visit, which is as it was when I had a colon.

One thing that has changed markedly is consistency. It's just water these days and it comes out at a rate of knots. Imagine a brown geyser. This has its repercussions and dealing with the splashback is now and I suspect will continue to be, my standard routine. Wiping is no longer restricted to the Lenity cleft; it includes the wider buttock area, genitals and the underside of the toilet seat. On some occasions the blast is so strong that it flies out of the bowl altogether.

Which brings me around to the issue of farting. I still do! And, much to CM's chagrin, they still stink. This is counter to what we were led to believe. That is to say, farts are generated by the bacteria of the colon, so no colon, no trumpin'. It may seem perverse, but I am rather glad. They may not be up to my pre-op standards, but they can still turn a stomach or two on a good day. It's a good feeling to know you've still got it.

It is my fourth week at home and I am still struggling with pain in my lower right abdomen. It seems to be, for the most part, associated with being upright although there are occasionally times when it occurs when sitting or lying. When this happens no amount of pressure eases it and since I vowed to dispense with pain killers I have to grit my teeth and hope it passes. It always does.

We don't have a set of bathroom scales, so it takes until this point and a visit to parents-in-law before I weigh myself. I am sixty-four kilos which is just over ten stone; my normal weight is eleven. I cannot say I'm surprised; despite all my eating I still look painfully thin. It will come back, I have no doubt, I've been here a few times before, and I'm hitting the fried breakfasts like they are going out of fashion. Perhaps if I had a haircut and a shave it might improve my appearance. I haven't done either since before I went into hospital and combined with my now poorly fitting clothes I am beginning to look like I've been shipwrecked.

I examine my skinny frame in the mirror; most of the bloating has gone which has served to expose the toll that all this has taken on my physical shape. The muscle has dropped away; mainly from my legs but also from my arms and upper body. I attempt a few press-ups and manage twenty. I am pleased but it very nearly kills me. I make a point of not mentioning this to CM as she would very definitely kill me. Sit-ups are another matter, I can't manage one of those. In view of my wounds and a lingering thought of something twanging apart inside of me, I give up.

Week six and I have an appointment to see Mr A... He seems pretty pleased with my progress and a little shocked to hear that I'm still a one poo a day man.

I mention the pain I have been getting.

"Nothing in life is without pain," he tells me, shrugging.

That's either sage-like wisdom or the Northern General is trying to cut back on analgesics.


My eighth week at home and I have to put an end to the horror of life as CM's passenger. It's not just the travelling, our shopping trips are a trial too. This and all kitchen related activity, I like to think, are my domains. I am very careful what I buy and prefer to build meals around what is in season or on offer. CM on the other hand is drawn to anything shiny. I've only to turn my back for a second and another item of pointless shit hits the trolley. Aldi and Lidl have a deliberate policy of loading the central aisles with tempting, non-food items, each one designed to tempt impressionable spouses in new and exciting ways. I need to drive myself; any more of this and I can see our marriage crumbling.

I phone the insurance people knowing that they can be a bit precious about these things. As it turns out the young man on the end of the phone couldn't have cared less, which surprised me. I had imagined they would have all sorts of fancy formulae and algorithms, but he just said do it when you feel up to it. Very laid back. He reminded me of Dylan from the Magic Roundabout.

First trip out and I am charged with taking Bruce, my eldest daughter (the one with the abnormally small toes) to Sainsbury's to stock up on Beanfeast and noodles for her upcoming Duke of Edinburgh trip[282]. You know how peculiar it feels to get back behind the wheel after you've been on holiday for a week or two? After nine weeks of abstinence I was expecting that feeling in spades but actually I'm fine with it and bounce the pick-up down our tight and precipitous drive like I'd never been away. On the strength of this I volunteer to do the driving this weekend when CM and I are having a night on the Lancashire coast.

We are staying in Heysham, I'm not yet ready for the

---

[282] Our kids are horribly middle class. I blame CM; there's never been any of that sort of thing on my side of the family.

excitement of the full Morecambe experience. The drive is a piece of cake, although there is one moment of consternation when I think I have soiled myself. A quick check at Lancaster Services Northbound reveals this to be just a sweaty arse and CM breathes again; she's very precious about her car's leather seats.

Fish and chips and then a stroll to the pub. I munch my way through a *Moby Dick* which is the local jumbo version. This is a mistake, as I then struggle with my first pint and am forced to abandon the second barely two sips in. This is not something that I make a habit of, but I just feel so full. Not bloated in a gassy sense but just devoid of space; as if something needed to drop away at the bottom before I could put anything else in at the top. Nauseated, I struggle back to the house intent on making a bit of room. I sit on the loo for a good ten minutes, but nothing materialises. This is interesting; more proof (alongside being able to fart with impunity) that there is not necessarily a standing body of liquid in there. There must be some part of my system taking up the slack, so to speak. Encouraging, I think.

We are back to Yorkshire the next day and I am now certain that my driving is back to normal because I take us home via the M62 by mistake. I am notorious for this kind of thing; my mind (and occasionally my vehicle) has a tendency to drift.

The next week I mow the lawn, move the IKEA bed-settee back upstairs and perform various other feats of physical dexterity. Things are starting to feel quite normal again. The caveat to that being that normality only begins once I have opened my bowels for the morning; until then and for an hour or two immediately after, I am still quite the sickly specimen. It will be some months and another interlude with the Northern before that improves.

## Wind

I cannot remember the first time I farted. When I say *farted*, I mean consciously farted; I'm sure I released a few nappy flappers as a baby, but they don't count. As a young boy I suffered from constipation and I can honestly say I do not remember ever letting one go (a fart that is) during my entire retentive period. I was always envious of my grandfather who seemed to have an endless supply; it was just a case of pulling his little finger. It didn't seem as if I had inherited his gift.
Little did I know.

I cannot say whether my emergence as an accomplished gasificator[283] grew from my transition to a comparatively normal diet or whether it was linked to some precursor of Crohn's disease but by my mid-teens I was farting with aplomb. A couple of years later I discovered beer and moved up another gear which was impressive enough, but when I hit my late teens and the onset of IBD, few could match my prowess.

> 'My name is Ozymandias, king of kings;
> Sniff upon my works, ye Mighty, and
> despair!'

I was doubly gifted you see, not only did my farts attack the nostrils, they were also loud and booming. If I so chose. Yes, I had great control and was able to manipulate their release as I deemed appropriate. I have cleared pubs, gassed relatives in cars, and caused innocent dogs to be kicked by their owners. I have delighted and disgusted in equal measure[284] and I even

---

[283] A made-up word. I'm quite pleased with it.
[284] Actually, not true; mainly just disgusted.

have the dubious accolade of ruining a sofa. The latter I cannot take full credit for since my little brother, who has an irritable bowel, was equally involved. My parents had a newly upholstered suite, it was covered in a pale grey, almost tweedy fabric which when wrapped around a foam cushion acted in the capacity of a battery. Over a series of weeks, the pair of us would sit watching telly of an evening, carelessly pumping gases into the unfortunate piece of furniture. It wasn't until my mother was plumping up the cushions one day and happened to remark (in a slightly choking tone):

"Ooh, what's that smell?",

did we realise just what we had created. No amount of hoovering or air freshener could deplete it; Shake 'n' Vac in this case most definitely did not put the freshness back. We had unearthed an inexhaustible supply of stale farts, accessed simply through bashing a cushion. It was quite a discovery, but as far as practical applications were concerned, quite limited.

After more than two decades of being on the receiving end, CM could not hide her delight when Dr J... informed her that the removal of my colon would probably put an end to all the farting. I don't condemn her for this, it cannot have been easy for all those years. Unfortunately, for CM at any rate, Dr J... was somewhat wide of the mark. I still fart. Admittedly, not nearly to the same extent as I did con-colon but when I do, I am still a force to be reckoned with.

In a way I am rather glad. One of the things I miss sin-colon is having a solid poo; it's one of life's little pleasures, a relaxing moment of privacy, cup of tea and crossword in hand. That is lost to me now in the ochrous maelstrom that is my morning routine. But there is life in the old dog yet and I take solace in the knowledge that I can still let rip when I get the urge.

I am a burper! I don't know why that should be the case, but it is. Perhaps it is a function of Crohn's disease, I don't know, I have never really had any trouble in that neck of the woods save for a bit of gastric reflux. It may be that I just take in a lot of air when I eat and drink. That is just on a day-to-day, tea and coffee basis, if I consume anything gassy, pop or lager for instance, I can really croak one out. I had fancied that I might be a little gifted in that area until I compared myself to some of the burping stars on You Tube[285]. I now realise my limitations; I am a mere dilettante. Ah, well, another dream shattered.

## Wining and Dining

In the period immediately following the initial diagnosis of Crohn's (1985) I was very restrictive with my diet (see "Crohn's Disease"). Such was the medical advice. I also undertook an elimination diet to establish if any particular foodstuff exacerbated the condition. All this seemed perfectly reasonable. Even though I didn't have a particularly adventurous palate at the time this was still something of a pain in the arse and not a little frustrating in that it failed to unmask any food culprits.

By the time I had finished my first year at university all circumspection in relation to what I shoved down my gullet went out of the window. I ate what I wanted when I wanted and if it didn't agree with me then I would face the consequences; shit it out and move on. It took all the anxiety out of food and allowed me to live a normal life, at least between flare-ups.

Despite having now had significant surgery I am still holding on to this approach. Pulses can have me up in the middle of the

---

[285] I urge you to check them out.

night, but I choose that over ditching tarka dhal. Likewise salads. Stouts and porters rumble through noisily and make an awful black, splattery mess when they emerge [286] but I know what is coming and I wipe clean and carry on.

It might not suit everyone; I'm just lucky that it works for me.

## Witchcraft
See "Bacon"

## Worms
See "Parasites"

## "Wow! That's a big 'un!"

It is 2018 so that's eight? nine? years since the last eruption of my shoulder volcano (see "Cysts") but according to my instruments[287] there has been a surge in seismic activity in the left shoulder region; my cyst has returned! Well it never actually went away, it just stayed quiet and inconspicuous on the corner of my scapula.

It had become more prominent in the aftermath of my bowel surgery due, I assumed, to all the weight I had shed. When the weight returned however, the cyst remained standing proud and indomitable. It was filling again and if it was to follow form, then I was due for an infection. Sure enough, in due course the tenderness developed and was soon followed by the angry redness, the heat and the swelling. I began to feel "rough" with it too. Remembering my previous lancings, I hold on until it is looking ripe before seeing my GP. This time I intend to have drugs; considering all the antibiotics I have consumed in

---

[286] On account of the high muzzle velocity.
[287] I have no instruments.

the last couple of years it seems a bit pointless to get all precious about them now.

The GP is a locum, I've never seen him before but then that's nothing new. I am registered with a big practice these days and I seem to see a different face every time I turn up.

It's a double appointment which I am sharing with my teenage daughter Bruce, who is struggling with bowel problems[288]. Ordinarily, sitting in a room with her father and a complete stranger talking about her medical issues would have sent her into a dicky fit but not today. The prospect of seeing the lancing swings it; the lure of the yellow is strong.

If I didn't know our locum was a doctor and was asked to guess a profession, I would plump for children's TV presenter. He has a permanent smile on his face which and a patronising sibilance to his voice. Father and daughter are propped side by side.

*Are we all sitting comfortably? Then I'll begin.*

The sense of kindergarten continues. I reveal my cyst.

"Wow! That's a big one!"

So big in fact, and so hot and such a smashing bright red colour, that I received a gold star and a course of flucloxacillin. What I don't get is a lancing, much to mine and my daughter's dismay. I don't think the policy is to stab them these days, unless they really have to.

"It will probably burst of its own accord." I am told.

In continuance of the children theme we walk out of the attached pharmacy holding identical, sealed parcels like two kiddies leaving Santa's grotto.

Flucloxocillin comes in inch long capsules, presumably to spare

---

[288] There's a surprise!

the patient from the foul-tasting drug itself. I don't know what substance the capsules are made of but it's hard to imagine the drug being any worse. The smell when I pop one out of the blister pack is enough to make me gag.

My abscess doesn't burst of its own accord. Contrary bastard that it is, it just gets bigger. And angrier. And hotter. It is so tender now that I can barely touch it and it makes any physical activity that involves the left shoulder (such as reaching up to a shelf or sitting on a chair with a back) quite painful.

It is conical with a distinct glowing top. It looks even more like a volcano and I should know I have a geology degree.[289] It even has a parasitic cone just to the south east of the main vent. I try giving it a squeeze, but this is extremely painful and fails to produce any rupture although the surface bubbles up with cheesy promise. Surely one little nick of the skin and it will all be out.

I have a hot bath to get things moving inside the cone, sterilise a new razor blade with surgical spirit and give Vesuvius a similar going over. CM is recruited as all the kids have chickened out, including Bruce who has aspirations to be a doctor. So that bodes well for her patients doesn't it![290]

CM is keen though.

---

[289] NB having a geology degree is not necessarily a guarantee of proficiency. See "Wife-swapping Nazis of the Inner Hebrides" by J.F.Lenity

[290] If her bedroom is anything to go by, any ward she works on will be knee deep in bedding, tampons, mucky knickers, plates and teacups. She'll be lucky to find her patients and even if she does the chances are the insanitary conditions will probably do for them anyway.

"Let's do it in the shower."[291] She says, "That way we can wash off all the splats."[292]

I point out that the shower has no mirror and seeing that the abscess is on my back a mirror is integral to me wielding the blade.

"Do you want me to do the cutting then?" she proposes nervously.

It's no small thing to offer and I don't want to come across as ungrateful so, mindful of her feelings, I reply:

"Never in a million years!"

She looks a little crest fallen but at the same time slightly relieved. I've allowed her to pop inaccessible spots before and the pain associated with it is totally out of proportion to the size of the pimple. It is a mystery to me how she can extract such misery from such small areas. Abnormally large hands I think.

"Anyway," I add, "you faint when I bleed."

This is true. She had an attack of the vapours on the occasion of my ear piercing. Psychologically she has an issue here; bad things happening to those she regards as her protectors or something along those lines. CM maintains that her wilting had more to do with the atmosphere and that only a true tight wad would have his ear pierced on a stall in the fish market.

She fires up her phone camera as I wait, blade poised over the central cone. I make a small nick with the corner of the blade, my body tensing at the sting of the cut and in expectation of erupting custard. A small bead of blood emerges, a precursor of the yellow tide; surgeon and camera crew hold their breaths and...nothing happens! I try again, this time on the secondary

---

[291] Long time since I heard that one.
[292] Ditto

vent. Same result. I try a bit of a squeeze; it hurts like hell and I stop immediately. I half expected this, previous lancings had involved cuts deep into the magma chamber. All I have succeeded in doing is nicking the skin which produces nothing beyond a little superficial bleeding. Enough to send CM into a swoon though, and she sits on the edge of the bed, head between her knees.

The flucloxacillin seems to be having an effect; I don't feel quite so unwell although this upturn is countered by the increased pain of the further enlarged abscess. By Thursday (two days into the course) it is half as big again. By Friday night it has almost doubled. It looks angrier than ever and weeps constantly but not sufficiently to relieve the pressure. I haven't slept properly for days and Friday night despite (or possibly because of) being dosed up on alcohol and 'brufen I barely sleep at all.

The redness is spreading, and CM is worried about sepsis. "I'm taking you to the minor injuries unit!" she announces, and I cannot think of a reasonable counter argument.

"Where is it?"

"My left shoulder."

The receptionist draws a long breath through her clenched teeth.

"That's torso, that is. We don't touch torsos. You need to go to A&E."

Forty minutes later we arrive in A&E, make our introductions and await triage. Whilst CM is off sourcing coffees my name is called and I am shown into a room to explain myself to a nurse. As I pull my shirt over my head I hear an excited squeal behind me and turn to find the poor woman staring at pus dripping off of her chest and onto the floor. The action of flexing my shoulder must have been enough to burst the thing.

At that point CM (carrying latte and flat white) enters to find a young woman wiping my bodily fluids off her bosom. To make matters worse (or *better*, depending on your point of view) it is quite a large bosom. The Carry On scene over, my defiled angel of mercy takes a proper look.

"Wow! It's a big one!"

"Yep."

"It needs a doctor to take a look at that. Wait outside and someone will call you."

We do wait outside. CM, prepared for the long haul, has brought her laptop and starts working. I pick up where I left off with the Boris Akunin paperback in my pocket. A&E seems quiet, so I am optimistic. A door opens and a name is called.

"James Brown!"

No one owns up to it and the door closes again. Five minutes later the caller tries again.

"James Brown? Do we have a James Brown?"

Again, no response. He probably couldn't face the prospect of being asked:

"...and how do you feel Mr Brown?"

CM has arrived at the same point and makes a similar witticism. It's not unheard of for the Current Mrs Lenity to make jokes, but funny ones are rarer than hen's teeth.

"Wow! That's a big one!" Says the young doctor as I take off my shirt. I never tire of hearing that phrase[293].

"Yeah. I'm afraid it soiled one of your nurses earlier."

---

[293] Never have, never will.

"Don't worry, we've got loads of them. Look, can you hold on there a minute, I need to measure it."

She comes back with a tape and makes her calculations.

"I want a surgeon to take a look at it," she tells me. "I'll take you down to the clinical decisions unit."

The CDU. I recognise this from my time working on A&E waiting time breaches[294]; as soon as a patient enters CDU the clock stops. We are another couple of hours in CDU before being seen but we both get a free cup of tea and I get an egg sandwich, so it's *swings and roundabouts* really.

Eventually we are ushered through and meet a couple of the surgeons. The senior of the two has a passing resemblance to Omar Sharif. I explain the situation and take off my top. Omar takes one look at Uncle Carbuncle and says:

"It needs the knife!"

Nice one Zhivago; there's nothing like breaking it to your patients gently. I don't mind actually, I'm rather fond of a decent turn of phrase. While I'm topless he takes the opportunity to have a gander at my colectomy wounds.

"Nice job!" he says. We could have been discussing a newly resprayed off-side wing. "Who did it?"

"Mr A..."

"He's good."

Well, I'm happy with it and it's always nice to know one hasn't been sold a pup, so to speak. No one is very optimistic about getting me *knifed* today so I am told to turn up at SAC (surgical assessment centre) for seven thirty tomorrow (Sunday)

---

[294] The operational standard (at the time of writing) is to process ninety-five per cent of patients within four hours or face the consequences.

morning.

"Fine," I say, since I splattered the nurse much of the pressure and therefore pain has eased. "And this will be quick will it? Just a local anaesthetic I assume"

"General."

"Oh."

I wasn't expecting that. I'm shocked and probably look a little scared, though in truth I'm not. Four months ago I would have been shitting bricks but I think I've put my fear of anaesthesia to bed. My only worry is that I'll come out of it like Scrappy Doo with his dukes up again.

We arrive on time at SAC and I get to sit in a lovely orange reclining chair while I wait. A sign informs us that these chairs are for patients only. Beside me CM is consigned to an altogether inferior, brown piece of furniture and there's nothing she can do about it; the sign couldn't be clearer.

By eightish we are ushered into a private room and I am given the familiar bare arse gown and measured up for the sexy stockings.

"Should I wear anything underneath?" I ask

"Yeah, you can keep your boxers on."

How did he know I was wearing boxers? Nurses are probably trained to spot the signs and can recognise a boxer or a thonger or a y-fronter just from their demeanour. All this bodes well, we must be well up on the list; with a bit of luck we shall be on our way home by midday.

The room is quite cold and I'm feeling it. One of the side effects of not eating or drinking I suspect. Plus, I have hardly any clothes on. I get into bed to warm up and within minutes I am asleep. It's gone eleven when I wake and other than repeated obs, there is no sign of any action.

Midday and someone appears:

"We need the bed, I'm afraid. We shall have to move you to TAU[295]. Do you mind?"

I do not, I'm bloody freezing in here. They can keep their privacy if it's going to be this cold. Give me crowded and warm any day of the week.

My section of TAU is populated with A&E'rs from Friday and Saturday. Opposite me is a chap with a broken arm sustained after falling over outside the pub. Next to him is a fell runner with a gashed knee. The poor chap had lugged a barrel of beer over Kinder Scout without so much as a scratch then promptly slipped on a paving stone yards from the finish line. No broken bones but the wound needs cleaning and stitching under general anaesthetic and so he's been sat here, nil by mouth for twenty-four hours. He's from Penrith and only came to Sheffield because he didn't fancy chancing it with the Cumberland Infirmary.[296]

Sometime after four a nurse arrives and informs Broken Arm and Wounded Knee that they won't be operated on today. Both are offered a place tomorrow (in theory) and Wounded Knee, on account of being from out of town, is offered a bed. Unfortunately, he and his chauffeur are due at work tomorrow. He's a farrier, interestingly enough, and the only farrier I have ever met[297]. I have a vision of horses sat around in Cumbria, looking at their watches and muttering: *where the bloody hell is he? Look at the state of that hoof; I can't go out with it like that!*

---

[295] Theatre admissions unit

[296] His assessment not mine

[297] Or ever likely to meet.

No one tells me I have to vacate, so either I've been forgotten or I'm still on the list; there has been no sign of my Britney Spears socks though, which may be a bad sign. Word on the street (ward?) is that a couple of urgent cases have sent the schedules into chaos. If I take anything from this escapade it will be: "don't get sick or have an accident at the weekend."

Six o clock and an anaesthetist turns up. Sadly, not the lovely, dark eyed, economics-curious lady from my previous op. I suppose it was asking a lot to expect her twice on the trot. The new guy confirms the dire state of play; however, if they possibly can, they will fit me in.

Seven-thirty and a pair a heavily built men arrive looking for me; theatre nurses. I am taken aback because they are wearing the bright green scrubs (including the hats) over which are draped bright blue polythene overalls of some kind which are billowing out at the side and look for all the world like the national dress of a West African country. Think Eddy Murphy in Coming to America; all it needs is one of those horse-tail fly swatters.

I am whipped through to the anaesthetic room where the introductions are made. The anaesthetist (a different chap to my earlier interlocutor) goes through his checks:

"Do you know why you're here?....Where is your abscess?...Wow that's a big one!...

Canula in-worst part, big dose painkiller, might sting...here we go...."

Goodnight Vienna.

I cannot remember anything much about being in Recovery. I know I asked whether I had punched anyone, I hadn't, and I know I asked someone the name of the painkiller I had been given which I promptly forgot.[298]

Back in TAU I am wheeled back into my previous slot just in time for the evening's tea round. It's nine o'clock now and all I've had to drink in the last twenty-one hours is a brief sip of water.

"Can I have two cups please?"

"Yeah, what do you want?"

"A tea and a coffee please."

I know it's a crime these days to drink instant coffee, but I don't care. I won't live under this hipster hegemony any longer. I neck them so swiftly that there is time for a third before the trolley of desire fades into the misty realms of hospital catering.

As the residual effects of the anaesthetic wear off, I am filled with a surge of well-being. The very same feeling I had when the cyst was drained for the first time years ago. Although my shoulder is painful the physical relief of having had all the infection cut away is staggering. Poison removal.

There is an episode of Steptoe and Son where a crippled Albert suddenly realises he is cured and jumps out of the bed in his nightshirt and performs a joyous little dance.[299] That's how I feel at this point, though I curb the urge to cut a rug.

The pain is pretty short-lived too, and apart from all the obs every couple of hours (my blood pressure is a bit low) I have a good night. Next morning (Monday) I am ravenous, I haven't had a crumb since Saturday teatime and I am looking forward to breakfast. Since this isn't a proper ward, breakfast is a bit on the spare side (toast and bran flakes) which is disappointing,

---

[298] It began with a "W" I think.

[299] "Upstairs Downstairs"; it's on You Tube

but at least the bran flakes will be put to good use; I haven't had a dump in forty-eight hours which for a man with no colon I think is unusual.

Home, and I am now left with the issue of a significant hole in my back. The wound is not stitched up, rather it is left open and packed with a dressing of some sort and allowed to drain naturally; it will close up in its own sweet time. I get an appointment with the nurse at my GP practice for two days' time.

I arrive with a ream of dressings courtesy of the hospital and a desire to see what is going on back there as, so far, things have remained concealed beneath a pad.

"Oh, we don't use that type in primary care." the Nurse J..., tells me, looking at my dressings. "The hospital keep sending them[300] but we prefer the Aquacel. I'll see if we have any in the practice and I'll get a doctor to give you a prescription for a few weeks supply."

I disrobe and present my back. I am sitting, topless, the wrong way around on a chair. Think Christine Keeler but with specs and less hair. Nurse J..., peels off the protective dressing.

"Wow it's a big one isn't it!" she exclaims as it is revealed. I'm still not tired of hearing it. She takes a photo of it for my benefit; it looks like a bright red sinkhole has opened up on me. "It's going to want dressing every day; you'll need to make appointments for the next fortnight at least. Have you taken any pain relief?" she asks probing inside.

"No, should I?"

"People normally do."

---

[300]Just a thought, but perhaps if someone let the hospital know maybe they would stop?

I know it sounds like I'm *proper nails* here, but the truth is it just doesn't hurt all that much. Obviously, a sinkhole in the back is a sinkhole in the back and it isn't going to be without some sensation, but it really isn't as painful as you would suspect from looking at it.

Dressed to the nines I make my way to reception to book in for the next couple of weeks. Easier said than done. There are only a handful of nurse slots to be had and only then by running into extra time. The receptionist accesses the hub of shared facilities from other city practices; there's nothing much to be had there either and she is toing and froing at her keyboard for an eternity. It takes longer to make my bookings than it took to perform the actual surgical procedure[301] and even then there are some significant gaps in my schedule. These I shall have to fill by going into Town and queueing up at the walk-in centre. This is operated by a private health firm subcontracted to the NHS and to all intents and purposed serves as primary care for Sheffield's student population. Not something I'm looking forward to; I never particularly warmed to students even when I was one. I shall make a point of going before midday; they should all still be in bed then.[302]

I don't mind driving to these different localities, my GP is a drive away anyway, but it would be nice to have a bit of continuity. You know? This sentiment is echoed by Nurse J... the next time I see her, which is almost a week after the first visit. She is happy with the state of my wound but just to be

---

[301] If you discount the preceding eleven hour wait that is.

[302] I don't think that is the case anymore; not since they were made to pay.

certain she takes a swab for analysis.

"Sorry if this hurts," she says poking around in my hole.

It doesn't, but it's a question I keep getting asked so I am beginning to wonder if it should. A few days later and the swab result comes back; I am infection free.

Two weeks after the procedure and from all accounts I am progressing nicely; or rather my open wound is, I am still trudging the interminably bleak domestic rut I have been travelling these many years.[303] My sinkhole is filling with new tissue and is only half as deep as it once was.

Three weeks and there is even talk of leaving out the Aquacel packing; it is there to soak up the gunk that oozes out, but a side effect is that it can limit new tissue growth. We try it and it leaks down my back, so as a compromise a single layer is applied.

"Have you taken any pain killers?" asks the latest nurse, whose name I forgot almost immediately. By this stage I have stopped committing them to memory. Just another faceless female to add to my collection. This whole episode has been a succession of one-morning stands.[304]

"Let's do it by the mirror baby, I wanna watch you dress!"

A month on and I am itching.

"It's looking a bit red around the edges says the latest mystery woman, I'll take a swab. Have you had any pain killers?

Two days later (early evening) I get a call from one of the GP's telling me that my swab results show that I have an infection and a prescription for another round of flucloxacillin is waiting

---

[303] I josh. That is just the public perception of me. I'm actually quite a jolly fellow; just cursed with a naturally miserable face.

[304] Actually, for the most part I am seated.

for me in reception. I am mightily impressed with the efficiency of the service and arrange to pick it up first thing. Unfortunately, it's not there but I am in Saturday for my flu jab so decide to run the risk of gangrene and get it then.

"We don't do prescriptions on Saturdays," I am told at reception. This is just a flu vaccination clinic. I don't need telling, the place is swarming with old women; it's like being at a Daniel O'Donnell concert.[305] After a bit of persuading the receptionist checks her computer.

"Apparently it was done on Thursday!" she says and disappears into the back of the practice and five minutes later emerges with the familiar green sheet. It's a good job I'm not on methadone, I'd be ready to take hostages by this stage.

# X is for...
## X-rays
See "Diagnostic Imaging"

# Y is for...
## Yoghurt, Fasting and Staying Well
"Oh yes I'm the Great Fermenter!" sang Freddie Mercury; or at least he would do if he were interested in the subject. And he wasn't dead. In short, if he was me. My love of fermenting goes back yonks, as far as my school years, when I began brewing beer from Boots kits. I still make beer; more than I ever did in fact, but in recent years I have broadened my cultural horizons[306].

In the early 2000s probiotic yoghurts appeared on the scene.

---

[305] I imagine.

[306] Did you see what I did there? Culture?

Neatly packaged in little plastic churns they offered a modern take on traditional live yoghurts which had always been regarded as a bit hippyish and as such deserved to be scorned. Up until that stage in my Crohnie career there had been little emphasis on the role that gut flora might play in alleviating symptoms and potentially preventing flare-ups of the disease. I decided to give these probiotics a go but found them a bit sweet and a bit on the small side. Instead I used them as a starter culture and produced pints of the stuff on a weekly basis.

Some time later I began to hear about a substance called kefir (pronounced keff-ear) which is like the big daddy of natural probiotics. If yoghurt has goodness in it then kefir has the same and then some; bacteria, yeasts, a little bit of alcohol and fizz. It originated (allegedly) in the Caucasus and they have been swilling it down out East for centuries because, you know, what is there not to like about fizzy milk?

Well, the taste for a start. It is super sour[307] and I am the only person in the family that can tolerate it; even the dog turns her nose up. And it whiffs a bit too, but those points aside, it's yummy.

Kefir is made by inoculating milk with kefir grains (little agglomerations of yeast and bacteria that look like mini cauliflower florets) and allowing it to ferment. Traditionally, this is achieved inside the skin of a goat, but I use a plastic jug with cling film over the top as it works better in the dishwasher. I used to have kefir with oats for breakfast, but I was advised that it is more beneficial on an empty stomach, so these days I

---

[307] I can only speak for my efforts; I have tried one of the supermarket varieties and found it very benign in comparison.

have a glass first thing, along with a cup of tar-like coffee. I think that's fine because the coffee is not a million miles off body temperature by the time it hits my stomach and so unlikely to kill the kefir. I would like to find some definitive guidance here but unfortunately there is such a lot of mumbo jumbo surrounding the subject that it is hard to know which is credible and which is nonsense. Nevertheless, there does seem logic in helping it through the acidic environment of the stomach as quickly as possible, so I am sticking to the regime until I am told otherwise. By the way, it is quite a hangover tonic; assuming you can keep it down after a night on the pop.

My next foray into the world of fermentation is sauerkraut which is a little more difficult to make as it involves massaging salt into thinly sliced cabbage. This really upsets clan Lenity, bringing on the gag reflex in a couple of them. Strangely the dog loves it. You can get sauerkraut in supermarkets, but this is not the same stuff; it has been pasteurised and as such (in theory) should be devoid of any live bacteria. A word of warning: live or pasteurised, expect fart production to ramp up if you consume it to any degree.

A second, more serious word of warning; make sure you know what you are doing before you attempt fermenting food as there are risks (notably botulism) associated with it.

I have recently tried my hand at sourdough bread having developed a starter by mixing flour with water and allowing it to sit for days. A decent sourdough starter is quite a prized asset amongst the artisanal bread-making types around here which just goes to show how perceptions can change; when I was a kid flour and water was glue!

One fermented food I've not tried is kimchi which is a sort of Korean sauerkraut. Also, kombucha which is a kind of fermented tea, again from the mystic East. They are on my list. The subject of mumbo jumbo is an interesting one. Fifty years ago if you are a vegetarian yoghurt swiller who spends an hour a day at the downward dog then you are the height of weirdness. Fast forward a bit and I would say that that this is a fair description of half the people I meet. The point being that yesterday's m-j is today's mainstream[308] and for that reason I try to make sure at least some part of my mind is kept open.

For instance, back in the mid-1990s CM and I were living in Honley, a village on the outskirts of Huddersfield in West Yorkshire. Among the facilities that Honley offered (and for its size it was surprisingly well served amenity-wise) was a beauty therapist by the name of R... R... is a lovely little woman in (I guess) her sixties, and as well as being a dab-hand at nail painting and moisturising and whatever else beauty therapists do, she is also fully immersed in the world of the aforementioned mumbo jumbo. At the instigation of CM, I book myself in for session of reflexology.

Reflexology, in case you do not know, relies on the manipulation of reflex points or zones in the hands and feet in order to treat other parts of the body. This is not just a random foot rub, the reflexologist will work to specific areas as defined on a series of detailed maps. The theory is that gentle massage can unblock the channels down which the body's energy qi (ch'i or often chi) flows. By freeing up qi our body can rebalance itself.

Okay, this is pseudo-science, let us not fool ourselves here, there is no scientific evidence (as far as I know) for the presence

---

[308] Especially if it is marketable. Right comrade?

of qi[309], but does that make reflexology a waste of time? I would say not, mainly because it is such a damned pleasant experience. You lie in a darkened room, the air smells of essential oils (there is an aromatherapy aspect to it), whale music is playing in the background and a softly-spoken lady sits at your feet and gently caresses them. Frankly, once R... gets to work I don't give a shit if the qi is flowing or not; by about the half-way point I am asleep anyway. It is ridiculously relaxing! R... wakes me at the end of the session, my feet wrapped in soft towels, then sets about cleaning my aura. This involves physically scooping handfuls of something (aura dirt?) and flinging it onto the floor. It goes on for a couple of minutes and given the size of the therapy room she must be knee deep in the stuff by the end. This is the point where we go beyond the boundaries of pseudo-science and enter the realm of pure bollocks, but even that is not without its merits. Despite the surreality of it, aura cleansing is a strangely relaxing experience; slightly tingly in an ASMR sense (see earlier) and indeed a number of ASMR practitioners do the whole Reiki/aura thing too.

I suppose the point is that you don't have to subscribe to a "philosophy" to gain benefit from it. Relaxation, physical and mental, is important to our well-being; without it we invite ill health. That is not me getting all *new age*, the science behind it is robust. And is reflexology the best way to relax? I don't know. The way we go about relaxing is rather irrelevant; if you choose to lie on a table whilst a former Inca princess (R... had a previous life apparently!) rubs away at your pods then good for

---

[309] Acupuncture is based on the concept of qi and there is plenty of evidence that it works for certain conditions.

you.

Of course, there are other ways. It could be mindfulness, yoga, fishing, rambling, bird watching, the list is long. On a personal level I would say that my Crohn's has been on its best behaviour when my state of mind has been buoyant. In practice this has coincided with my carousing years and much as I would like to espouse the efficacy of heavy drinking, late nights and the spliff & Balti diet, I know I am on shaky ground. There is such a thing as balance you see. Nevertheless, I stick by the premise, a happy head makes for a happy gut.

How much of an influence does our mind have on our physical health? The answer is probably more than we realise. And it is more than just the brain telling the bowel what to do.

When I was first diagnosed with Crohn's disease in the mid-1980s I remember watching a short television item of one family's experience of what was then a little discussed disease. The parents of the lad with Crohn's were sat opposite the consultant explaining to him how they believed that stress was contributing to their son's condition. Not to put too fine a point on it, the consultant laughed them off. Things have changed; though not well understood the interaction between head and guts is recognised to be a complex relationship with the latter now known to have much more autonomy than once thought. You may hear the term *second brain* bandied about in relation to the bowel? It is a slightly misleading term as this is not the thinking organ we associate with the term *brain*, and in evolutionary terms it is probably older than the standard grey matter so *second* is debatable too, but it gets the point across. It seems that the enteric nervous system is quite a big deal. For a start it has more neurons than the spinal column and, here is the funky bit, there is growing evidence that as well as communicating with the brain it also communicates with our biome. That is to say, it chats with the bugs in our guts; of which there are shit loads. It is all very interesting and has spawned a whole new branch of science, neurogastroenterology.[310] However, all that is beyond both the scope of this book and my intellect; I am but a simple fellow from the city of spoons. However, I know this much, in 1991 my state of mind caused a flare-up of Crohn's sufficient to hospitalise me. I don't know what was going through my head, maybe a sympathy thing? God knows, but the fact is I thought myself ill. See "Growing (further) Up".

Jobless, I had sat around the house maudlin, feeling sorry for myself, getting no exercise. I spent much of my time drinking and smoking the odd Barlinnie[311] as well. Smoking, it is now believed can make Crohn's worse and can initiate a flare-up though at the time (1991) there was little empirical evidence for this.[312]

It is important then to look after your state of mind not just in the interests of avoiding a flare-up but also in terms of managing one. I don't think anyone will gainsay that suffering a chronic illness messes with your noggin; well, it's bound to isn't it? One needs to be mentally tough then? Easy to say, less easy to affect. And what exactly does *being mentally tough* mean anyway? There are other coping strategies out there, it's

---

[310] Strangely enough the basis for this and the idea that guts could work independently of the brain dates back over a hundred years but was somehow *forgotten* as other theories prevailed.

[311] A thin roll-up; named after Barlinnie prison in Glasgow.

[312] Interestingly there is some evidence that smoking can be beneficial to sufferers of ulcerative colitis.

just a case of finding one that suits. The key, I believe is openness. If the stigma of the physical elements of these diseases can be exorcised in this way (see "Arse"), then surely the same applies to the mental dimension. In short, talk to someone.

Since around 2012, if memory serves, CM and I have fasted for two days out of every seven; what is popularly called the five-two diet. Neither of us needs to lose any weight, our motivation is the improvement in our health and longevity for which there seems to be some compelling evidence. Specifically, the claims that it can reduce the risk of developing cancer since both of us are at statistically higher risk than average.

I struggle with it more than CM, perhaps this is a testosterone thing because, despite the conflicting evidence (my slender ankles, her big hands and the penis she grew on her ovary-see "Test Tube Babies")I still maintain I have more of the stuff than her. By tea time, having had only a few cups of black coffee and some or other infusion that tastes nothing like as appealing as it smells, I am quite prepared to kill someone. In fact, I could probably do it by breath alone; by mid-afternoon it stinks, and my teeth feel as cacky as anything. Some days my wee has a peculiar whiff to it as well although that might be down in part to dehydration; I am not very good at keeping up my fluids when milky brews are off the menu. As if that was not enough to put you off, I suffer from the cold too, especially during the winter months. It's surprising how much we rely on the burning of food calories to maintain a reasonably comfortable body temperature.

Have there been benefits? Difficult to say; the trouble with evaluating longevity is that it takes a long time, so the jury is out on that one. As for general health, since taking up fasting I have had my colon removed, a chronically infected prostate, a badly infected cyst which also required surgery, a bad back and half my teeth have fallen out. Imagine, then, the state I would be in if had just eaten normally.

The day following a fast day (we rarely do two days on the trot; blood would be shed) I always feel quite cleansed and, of course, ravenous. If nothing else, it certainly makes you appreciate the pleasure of food.

Exercise has a big effect on me. Simply put, I feel better when I do it. There is nothing new in this, most people have heard of *runner's high* and the role of endorphins, the happy chemicals that are released in the brain in response to certain stimuli, including exercise. This is not my point. I am not talking about instant chemical gratification but rather my broader well-being and specifically the functioning of my digestive system.[313] I don't know why this should be.

Exercise is known to reduce stress and help with anxiety and depression so perhaps the knock on from that is better gut function? Or perhaps there is a direct chemical effect? There is some thinking that exercise may have a role in the reduction of inflammation though I would question how that could be used in the event of a flare-up as the last thing you feel like doing is going for a jog around the park.

## Youth Hostel
See "Audi Coupe"

---

[313] This is still the case despite having my colon removed.

# Z is for...

## Zoster

See "Shingles"

# A Postscript

It is now one whole year since dysplastic cells were discovered in my ascending colon; nine months since my colectomy, and I have to say that things are functioning way beyond my expectations. For the most part I open my bowels once a day (in the morning) occasionally twice but very rarely more than three and usually I can assign that to my overindulging in something or other.

Pain is rare and limited to bloating or the strain of retaining the contents of my rectum on those occasions when it all gets a bit urgent. For the most part it is all perfectly under control.[314]

My stools are always liquid and remain as splattery as ever. I don't know whether they are more acidic than they once were or whether the extra wiping is taking its toll, but I do seem to have resurrected my sore arse problems of the mid-eighties (see "Arse" and "Growing Up"). To this end I have invested in a portable bidet. This sounds a good deal flasher than it actually is and consists of a plastic squeezy bottle with an angled spout and spray attachment.[315] That said it works a treat, allowing me to wash my nethers to my heart's content, and without resorting to the shower. This is an abhorrence as far as CM is concerned and I am obliged to hide it in the sink cupboard, behind the bleach. Irrespective of efficacy I think the obviously e-bay, made-in-China cheapness of it offends her more than

---

[314] Hardly a *wet fart* since leaving hospital!
[315] What do you want for four quid?

anything. Perhaps if John Lewis made one?

Continence, under the circumstances, is pretty good. I must own to a few soilings since the op but on the positive side these have all been down to poor judgement on my part rather than chronic leakage. To elaborate; what I thought were trumps, were altogether more substantial and to the detriment of my underpants.

On the subject of underpants, these make quite a difference to my soreness. It seems that airier is better as far as my tradesman's entrance is concerned. Baggier is better. I have recently taken delivery of two pairs of cellular trunks (see earlier reference to Iggy Pop in "Unruly Patient") but these are still being put through their paces and I will reserve judgement until the appraisal is complete. I am hoping to go backpacking in the summer and I have a feeling that adequate ventilation will be critical. I am also investing in a lightweight backpacker's trowel in case I am caught short on the moors. This may be optimistic on my part in light of the issues associated with my aforementioned "muzzle velocity".[316]

Time for my check-up with Dr J... This time it will be a flexible sigmoidoscopy rather than the full colonoscopy and I am furnished with Picolax rather than Klean Prep in order to flush the pipes out. It is the lesser of the two evils.

No canula is fitted as there will be no need for Buscopan and I am wondering whether this is going to put my Entonox (gas and air) fix in jeopardy. Thankfully this is not the case but I am mindful that this might be a quick affair so I am sucking on the

---

[316] Also, I'm not the world's greatest squatter. Some preparatory work on the abs, quads, glutes and hams needed.

gas spout the second I hit the table. I am fuzzy-headed and talking in an overly loud voice within seconds.

"How are your movements? Asks Dr J... handsomely.

"Once a day usually, sometimes more." I slur.

"Wow! Really?"

"Is that unusual."

"Yes."

"Does that make me special?"

Once more he evades that particular question and gets down to lubing up the kit.

"This looks really good," he comments as my insides appear on the screen. The Picolax has made a poor job of cleaning me out; there is a good bit of debris around. "Can't see any sign of inflammation," he adds, "Oh, there's the anastomosis."

For my benefit he goes back and points it out again. There is a very clean, pinkish seam on the screen. Aside from all the residual shit hanging about it looks very neat.

"There's not much colon there," he adds, "I think next time we'll go for an enema."

Which suits me, I'm good at those. "...and we'll see you again in three years' time."

That's a long time to wait for a bit of gas and air.


With a couple of caveats (sore arse, indigestion, occasionally breaking mud, urgency when the time is nigh) I would say that all is well on the bowel front, but what about the other stuff?

The hole in my back, where once was a cyst, has healed over completely leaving me with an interesting (read ugly) circular scar from which I get the occasional itch but nothing more.

My prostate seems to be behaving itself too and ASMR still makes my brain tingle so tickety-boo there.

My sleep is not as good as it once was (sometimes my guts wake me) but I haven't had any duvet moments, and as far as I know, not sleepwalked.

Joints and back are ok and I am playing a little squash without issue though I still can't be arsed to do my stretches so no doubt back trouble will rear its head at some point.

My teeth continue to disintegrate; the bridged incisor is very wobbly again and I spit out amalgam-encrusted tooth pieces[317] on a regular basis.

My syncope has improved since I upped my salt intake (I have rediscovered bread and dripping) so presumably my blood pressure is back in a normal sort of range.

The trumping continues unabated.

My pre-diabetes has been left up in the air, although I have done a bit of background reading and am shocked by some of the things that are levelled at sugar's door. I now make a conscious effort to limit the volume of sugar crossing the Lenity threshold. Bloody difficult actually, it's in everything!

I still fast two days out of seven and I don't think anything has changed since surgery to affect that. Fermented food is still on the menu, as are cold showers, although I rarely have more than one full body wash a week. The pocket bidet is proving an inspired purchase.

Winter was as bad as ever as far as my extremities were concerned; blue fingers and the like and I really ought to go and see the GP about it.

I still worry about Alzheimer's every time I forget a fact. CM and the kids, with obvious frustration, are forever telling me I

---

[317] Perhaps this should read tooth-encrusted amalgam pieces considering the dearth of genuine material in my cakehole.

have forgotten something or other that they have told me. This is not a concern; they are confusing *forgetting* with *not bothering to listen in the first place* which are quite different things...and on that pearl of wisdom I shall call it a day.
JFL

## Acknowledgements

Many thanks to everyone who took the time to read and comment on the various drafts of this work; you know who you are. And special praise to all my family members and those health professionals who have had to put up with me over the years.

Printed in Great Britain
by Amazon

30198813R00180